# Your daily Kingdom Guide

365 devotions
that will impact your life
with love, hope, & truth

*Dawn René McCann*

© 2011 - Liberty Life Center; Pastor Dawn Rene´ McCann

All rights reserved. This book is protected by the copyright laws of the United States of America. This book may not be copied or reprinted for commercial gain or profit. The use of short quotations or occasional page copying for personal use or group study is permitted and encouraged. Permission will be granted upon request. Unless otherwise identified, Scripture quotations are from the New King James Version (NKJV) of the Bible. Scripture quotations marked KJV are taken from the King James Version of the Holy Bible. Scripture quotations marked NIV are taken from the New International Version of the Holy Bible. Scripture quotations marked AMP are taken from the Amplefied version of the Holy Bible. Scripture quotations marked MSG are taken from the Message version of the Holy Bible.

Compiled by Travis Stealy

Published as

ISBN 9780615578866

A product of

Liberty Life Center

(954) 583-8350

www.LibertyLifeCenter.org

Printed in the United States of America

First Edition 2011


Cover Images (front and back) credits and interesting information:

Credit and special thanks to ESO, European Southern Observatory (www.eso.org)

for allowing us the usage of their images

Front Image:   This photo shows a three colour composite of the well-known Crab Nebula (also known as Messier 1), as observed with the FORS2 instrument in imaging mode in the morning of November 10, 1999. It is the remnant of a supernova explosion at a distance of about 6,000 light-years, observed almost 1,000 years ago, in the year 1054. It contains a neutron star near its center that spins 30 times per second around its axis. In this picture, the green light is predominantly produced by hydrogen emission from material ejected by the star that exploded. The blue light is predominantly emitted by very high-energy ("relativistic") electrons that spiral in a large-scale magnetic field (so-called syncrotron emission). It is believed that these electrons are continuously accelerated and ejected by the rapidly spinning neutron star at the centre of the nebula and which is the remnant core of the exploded star.

Back Image (upper-right):   This colour-composite image of the Helix Nebula (NGC 7293) was created from images obtained using the the Wide Field Imager (WFI), an astronomical camera attached to the 2.2-metre Max-Planck Society/ESO telescope at the La Silla observatory in Chile. The blue-green glow in the centre of the Helix comes from oxygen atoms shining under effects of the intense ultraviolet radiation of the 120 000 degree Celsius central star and the hot gas. Further out from the star and beyond the ring of knots, the red colour from hydrogen and nitrogen is more prominent. A careful look at the central part of this object reveals not only the knots, but also many remote galaxies seen right through the thinly spread glowing gas.

"It seemed good to me to show the signs and wonders that the Most High God has performed toward me. How great are His signs! And how mighty His wonders! His kingdom is an everlasting kingdom, and His dominion is from generation to generation"

(Daniel 4:2-3 AMP)

WWW.LibertyLifeCenter.org

# "I AM"

**Day 1**

The following 4 Kingdom Guides "I Am" are directly from a prophetic word that the Lord gave me for the church of today...

The Lord says:

Don't you know that I've always wanted to, I've always been able to, but you see, it takes praise, it takes you knowing Me, honoring Me, wanting Me in your life, for the fullness of who I am to begin to occur for you individually, corporately, even in this city, even in this county, even in this state, even in this nation, even in the world. Until My name is of utmost importance to you, I will not be able to be the utmost High God in your arena. But when you understand who I am, and that I am yours, and that you are Mine, when you are truly abiding on the inside of Me, when there are no walls of separation - I broke down the partition and made it available, and yet many have not walked through. They have not come into the place of My presence, because they have held on to the past. They've held on to doing it their way, of trying to understand it with their minds, when in fact you cannot understand Me with your mind.

You will understand Me by abandonment. You will understand Me by surrender. You will understand Me by seeking for Me with all of your heart, and then I will be found of you. Then you will begin to understand that I revealed Myself to Abraham, to Moses, to Noah, to John, to Peter, to those that are called by My name – revelation after revelation – authority given after authority given – because they were depending no longer on the arm of the flesh, but on their God, the God that they knew – the God that they had relationship with - the God that was no longer a God that they talked about, but a God they walked with – a God that had taken on their personalities, a God that had changed them from the inside out, a God that had defined them, refined them, and released them into who they were always meant to be.

*You will understand Me by seeking for Me with all of your heart, and then I will be found of you.*

# "I AM"

## Day 2

As you come to Me, as you lay everything else down, as you cry out for all of Me, all of Me shall be found of you. Then the earth will shake again. Then the world will begin to come into the light, they will begin to see the focus that I have seen from the beginning of the ages. You will begin to see with the eyes of the spirit what I have seen all along – that there will be a day of reckoning. But for My people, there would be a day of glory and it is now. Now is the time for you to walk in the fullness of who I Am and the authority that I have given you by My name and that which I have already decreed and put into place for right now, not for later, but now.

As you get a revelation of who I Am to you, you will cause those things to shake. – You will cause the atmosphere to change; you will cause things to come into order. For don't you see that is exactly the testimonies that were given today – as they placed Me first, as they sought Me, as they praised My name, as they allowed Me to shift things in their heart and shift things in their life and shift things in their thinking, that they became a walking billboard to My glory on the earth right now.

Do you not know that this is the time, this is the season, this is the place that I have called you to be on the earth? My ambassadors, My priests, My kings, the ones who walk in authority because they understand My authority, because they've had a revelation, because they've had a revolution, because now they are one with Me. Do you understand? Can you comprehend? That becoming one with Me unleashes all that I am.

When you are one with Me, who can separate you out from My power, from My ability, from My wisdom, from My strength, from My knowledge, from My favor?

*Now is the time for you to walk in the fullness of who I Am and the authority that I have given you.*

# "I AM"

## Day 3

For you are sons and daughters of the Most High God - the One you have praised today – the One you have declared about, the One who is now present in your midst to answer the cries of your heart, to answer your needs, to turn situations around. If you will just believe, if you will just believe in who I am, if you will just believe that I am who I said I am, if you will just declare that you are one with Me, you will begin to see and feel and know that you are more than able to take this mountain! You are more than able to take the country! You are more than able to storm the gates of hell! My church will prevail! My church will prevail! My church will prevail! The gates of hell have no power against My church when My church rises in the knowledge of Me, when My church acknowledges My name and who I am and every facet of My character, every facet, everything I have released to you.

You will come into new awareness, new understanding, new ability. You will see that the things that were hard are now easy because you're so aware of My presence with you, in you, and moving through you. Today – your God is available to you. The Most High God, the Creator of the universe is your God!

Will you give Me permission to take every part of you?
Will you abandon every piece to Me?
Will you walk away from the things I ask you to walk away from?
Will you speak those things that aren't as though they are?
Will you take authority on the earth and make declarations with power and authority by My name?
Will you reach out and touch those who have needs and believe that I will reach them where they are?
Will you lay hands on the sick?
Will you declare their recovery and believe it with your heart?
Will you allow Me to be the God who is available right now?
Will you give Me permission to be the utmost High God to you, and to them?

*Today – your God is available to you.*

# "I AM"

## Day 4

I am the God of the mountain. I stand at the top of every mountain in the world. I am higher than the hardest places. I am higher than any resistance. I am higher than any problem.

I am El-Shaddai.
I Am.
Let go...
Let go. Let go of unbelief.
Let go of doubt.
Let go today of fear.
Let go of lack.
Let go of people that hold you back.
Let go of your way of thinking.
Let go of your insistence.
Let go of your pride.

And come to Me. Become one with Me today. See if I will not prove My character, My love, My ability. There is no one like Me. There is no one like Me. I am forever. It has been forever settled. And I am forever available to those who seek Me. If you cry out to Me with a whole heart, if you come to Me, the Great I Am will be for you.

Pray: Lord, I thank You that this is a time of the Fatherhood of God being released on this earth. We will not know about You anymore, we will know You as our Father, our Provider in every way. I thank You that You are wrapping Your arms around every individual in this place today, You are showing them Your fatherhood, You are showing them that You care, You are loving on them and releasing them to higher places in You. Lord, we choose to abide in You. We abide in Your words, they abide in us. There is nothing that will be impossible for us. Lord, it's your Word.

*If you cry out to Me with a whole heart, if you come to Me, the Great I Am will be for you.*

# GOD WANTS TO HAVE A RELATIONSHIP WITH YOU

**Day 5**

Our God is a personal God who created you for fellowship and wants to share a love relationship with you. When sin entered the world, it dulled mankind's ability to hear God's voice and desensitized our spiritual senses so that the human race as a whole does not respond to God's voice.

*Then the Lord God called to Adam and said to him, "Where are you?" So he said, "I heard your voice in the garden, and I was afraid because I was naked; and I hid myself." Genesis 3:9-10*

After Adam and Eve sinned, they still had the ability to hear God. Cain heard God's voice clearly after murdering his brother. God was eager to speak to the rebellious people of Israel through Jeremiah, even when they didn't want to hear God's voice.

God has not limited Himself to a distant relationship with the human race. He so desires intimacy with us that He has broken down every barrier so that He can commune with us. In this Kingdom Guide Series, we will investigate why and how our God communicates with us.

I. Why God Wants to Communicate

I John 4:8- tells us that "God is love." Mankind was birthed out of God's great love. Every move of God is motivated by love.

God wants to communicate with us because He loves us. Intimate communication is not just a good idea; it is a part of who He is. Communication is a part of His very nature and being.

God is, was, and always will be speaking to us.

It is up to us to hear Him.

Can you think of any hindrances in your life that might keep you from hearing God's voice?

*God is, was, and always will be speaking to us.*

# GOD WANTS TO HAVE A RELATIONSHIP WITH YOU

## Day 6

Is there scriptural evidence that proves that God desires to communicate to us personally?

Yes, throughout the Bible we see God communicating to His creation in a very personal way. We are designed to hear His voice!

1. As we have already identified, God spoke to Adam and Eve in the garden because of His desire to fellowship. He spent time with them. It is recorded that He walked with them in the cool of the day.

*And they heard the voice of the LORD God walking in the garden in the cool of the day: and Adam and his wife hid themselves from the presence of the LORD God amongst the trees of the garden.*
Genesis 3:8 KJV

2. God spoke to Noah to give him specific instructions.

*And God said unto Noah, "The end of all flesh is come before me; for the earth is filled with violence through them; and, behold, I will destroy them with the earth. Make thee an ark of gopher wood; rooms shalt thou make in the ark, and shalt pitch it within and without with pitch. And this is the fashion which thou shalt make it of: The length of the ark shall be three hundred cubits, the breadth of it fifty cubits, and the height of it thirty cubits." Genesis 6:13-15 KJV*

3. God spoke to Abraham and revealed Himself as a God of covenant who desired relationship.

*Now the LORD had said unto Abram, Get thee out of thy country, and from thy kindred, and from thy father's house, unto a land that I will shew thee: And I will make of thee a great nation, and I will bless thee, and make thy name great; and thou shalt be a blessing: And I will bless them that bless thee, and curse him that curseth thee: and in thee shall all families of the earth be blessed. Genesis 12:1-3 KJV*

**We are designed to hear His voice!**

# GOD WANTS TO HAVE A RELATIONSHIP WITH YOU

**Day 7**

Scriptural evidence that God interacted with His chosen people:

1. God and Moses

Here we find Moses speaking to God.

*And Moses said unto God, "Behold, when I come unto the children of Israel, and shall say unto them, 'The God of your fathers hath sent me unto you;' and they shall say to me, 'What is his name?' What shall I say unto them?" Exodus 3:13 KJV*

Then we find God answering Moses. That is pure communication.

*And God said unto Moses, "I AM THAT I AM:" and he said, "Thus shalt thou say unto the children of Israel, I AM hath sent me unto you." Exodus 3:14 KJV*

2. God always has a plan and He will speak to those who will be obedient to carry out His plan.

*And he said, "I have been very jealous for the LORD God of hosts: because the children of Israel have forsaken thy covenant, thrown down thine altars, and slain thy prophets with the sword; and I, even I only, am left; and they seek my life, to take it away." And the LORD said unto him, "Go, return on thy way to the wilderness of Damascus: and when thou comest, anoint Hazael to be king over Syria..." 1 Kings 19:14-15 KJV*

Is prophecy limited to Old Testament?
Nope!

*He saw in a vision evidently about the ninth hour of the day an angel of God coming in to him, and saying unto him, "Cornelius." And when he looked on him, he was afraid, and said, "What is it, Lord?" And he said unto him, "Thy prayers and thine alms are come up for a memorial before God." Acts 10:3-4 KJV*

Today, as followers of Jesus Christ we are His "chosen people" and as Spirit filled beleivers with the Holy Spirit living within us how much more should we be able to hear from God?

*God always has a plan and He will speak to those who will be obedient to carry out His plan.*

# GOD WANTS TO HAVE A RELATIONSHIP WITH YOU

## Day 8

God created us to hear His voice!

*The hearing ear, and the seeing eye, the Lord hath made them both. Proverbs 20:12*

It's Easy and Normal.
Most people today feel that hearing the voice of God is unusual and difficult. But the Word of God teaches us that hearing His voice should be easy and frequent, since God made our ears to hear.

*I am the good shepherd; and I know my sheep, and am known by My own. And other sheep I have which are not of this fold; them also I must bring, and they will hear my voice; and there will be one flock and one shepherd. John 10:14, 16 NKJV*

Thank God... It's Not By Being Righteous

Our ability to hear God is not based on our righteousness. If it were, it would be works and not a gift. We do not have to strain to hear the voice of God, because we were designed by God to hear Him. Hearing His voice is available to all of God's children.

*My sheep hear My voice, and I know them, and they follow Me. John 10:27*

As a people who love God, we can relax in the knowledge that He designed us with the ability to hear His voice and that He is continually communicating with us. It is not a mysterious process, but a normal activity for a believer.

We should receive it as normal and natural, and encourage ourselves to tune in to the Holy Spirit continually.

Today, take time to purposely tune-in and listen to the Holy Spirit. It may not be easy, but through practice it becomes natural... Remember, you were created capable of communication, not only with people on earth, but also your Heavenly Father!

*We do not have to strain to hear the voice of God, because we were designed by God to hear Him.*

# GOD WANTS TO HAVE A RELATIONSHIP WITH YOU

**Day 9**

So why does it seem difficult?

The effects of sin, such as doubt, unworthiness, fear, guilt, hardness of heart, bitterness, unforgiveness, and condemnation, can hinder us from opening our spiritual ears.

What is the first step to better communication with God? Desire!

If you desire to hear His voice, you can hear His voice. Sin may hinder, but it can't stop you. Your desire for God releases your ability to hear.

What prerequisites are there to hear from God?

1. You have to know Him.

*My sheep hear my voice, and I know them, and they follow me John 10:27 KJV*
Who hears Him? His SHEEP

2. You need to be filled with the Spirit of God.

*Pursue love, and desire spiritual gifts, but especially that you may prophesy. For he who speaks in a tongue does not speak to men but to God, for no one understands him; however, in the spirit he speaks mysteries. But he who prophesies speaks edification and exhortation and comfort to men. 1 Corinthians 14:1-3*

Want to be utilized to help others to the fullest extent? Simply ask God to cleanse you of any sin and make you pure from your inside out. Ask Him to rid you of any pre-conceived notions of what He has to say or how He will do it. Forgiveness doesn't have to be earned no matter who you are or what you have done. God's purifying forgiveness is a gift of grace, all you have to do is ask. You can be cleansed, set free, and hear from God all in a moment!

**If you desire to hear His voice, you can hear His voice.**

# GOD WANTS TO HAVE A RELATIONSHIP WITH YOU

## Day 10

*And there he went into a cave, and spent the night in that place; and behold, the word of the Lord came to him, and He said to him, "What are you doing here, Elijah?" So he said, "I have been very zealous for the Lord God of hosts..." Then God said, "Go out, and stand on the mountain before the Lord." And behold, the Lord passed by, and a great and strong wind tore into the mountains and broke the rocks in pieces before the Lord, but the Lord was not in the wind; and after the wind an earthquake, but the Lord was not in the earthquake; and after the earthquake a fire, but the Lord was not in the fire; and after the fire a still small voice. So it was, when Elijah heard it, that he wrapped his face in his mantle and went out and stood in the entrance of the cave. Suddenly a voice came to him... 1 Kings 19:9, 11-13*

God heard Elijah's desire, sought him out, and spoke to him. But Elijah did his part...

He desired, he waited patiently, he exercised discernment by filtering through all the noises and distractions around him, and he humbled himself as signified by the covering of his face When we talk about prophetic, our natural mind imagines some loud thundering voice from heaven as the skies open. But the reality is, that is hardly the case.

Experts say that 90% of all our communication human to human is non-verbal. It's just how we were created. We have senses that enable us to communicate a clear message without ever speaking a single word. It is as easy as this: Have you ever hugged someone who was going through something and though never saying a single word to them, you were able to convey comfort to them?

It's the same way with God. You don't have to necessarily hear words to sense what God wants to convey to you. And when you want to communicate with God it can be in a variety of ways and it's usually not in the same way that it was the last time.

You simply have to desire to know, be patient in waiting, discern distractions from God, and stay humble through the process.

*Experts say that 90% of all our communication is non-verbal.*

# GOD WANTS TO HAVE A RELATIONSHIP WITH YOU

## Day 11

Now it's time to be activated!

Over the past few days we have proven throughout scripture that it is God's desire to speak to us, it's easy, and it's possible today!

Take time after reading through today's Kingdom Guide and close your eyes. Imagine you are in the place of the prophet Elijah. Put yourself in his shoes (or sandals in this case). Imagine that you are all alone in a cave, no one else around. Your desire is not what you are missing on TV, not what you are going to eat, but your sole desire is to hear from God, whatever it takes, and however it comes. You are desperate to hear from your Father in Heaven. You are in need of hope, comfort, and direction.

Know that you are His child and His greatest desire is to communicate with you. Ask Him to speak to you on a personal level like never before. This is not about anyone else, it's about you and God.

Now wait…

Listen with all of your senses to what God is conveying to you personally. Stay humble; He is God…

Now write down (either to the right or on a separate sheet of paper) what you feel He is speaking to you, whether it be verbally or through your senses. It could be a single word, a picture, an emotion, a story. Just write down anything that comes to you. It will be your first thought, your first impression, your first picture.

Begin like this...

*Dear (Son or Daughter),*

*…*

**Ask Him to speak to you on a personal level like never before.**

# God's Methods of Communicating

## Day 12

God's desire is to fellowship with mankind freely as He did in the garden with Adam and Eve. Because of the effects of sin, not everyone has been open to hearing Him. But Jesus, the second Adam, reversed what sin had done and made a way for God to freely express Himself to man.

God has set in place several methods of communication to reveal Himself and His plan to mankind. Where does Jesus dwell now? Inside of us! So when we are aware of Him, and we are in fellowship with Him, we will be able to tap into expressions of God that flow through Him. In the fullness of time, God spoke to mankind through the person of Jesus Christ, who is God in the flesh and is the full, complete expression of God.

*God, who at various times and in various ways spoke in time past to the fathers by the prophets, has in these last days spoken to us by His Son, whom He has appointed heir of all things, through whom also He made the worlds; who being the brightness of His glory and the express image of His person, and upholding all things by the word of His power... Hebrews 1:1-3*

In His earthly ministry, Jesus fully revealed God the Father to mankind. He was a complete representation of God's thoughts, words, and love toward us. Jesus was more than a prophet; He fully understood His heavenly Father and expressed His Father's words and actions.

*Do you not believe that I am in the Father, and the Father in Me? The words that I speak to you I do not speak on My own authority; but the Father who dwells in Me does the works. John 14:10*

In Jesus, the veil that kept us from God was torn and the reason for our dullness in hearing God has been completely removed. We are brand new and we have the Spirit of God living within us, enabling us to have full communication with Him once again.

**God's desire is to fellowship with mankind freely.**

# God's Methods of Communicating

## Day 13

The Bible—the Written Revelation of God:
The Bible is a love-letter from God to man. The Bible contains all the knowledge needed for life and godliness (2 Peter 1:3-4). The Holy Spirit gave the Bible to us so that we can know God and live by His standards.

There is a difference in simply reading the Bible and reading it under the inspiration of the Holy Spirit. In many of our prayer meetings, we begin to read the word out loud and the atmosphere changes where we all can hear from God personally through the reading of the word. Then the Holy Spirit expands what the word is saying through prophetic prayers, or prophetic insight and revelation.

The Holy Spirit:
*And I will pray the Father, and He will give you another Helper, that He may abide with you forever— the Spirit of Truth, whom the world cannot receive because it neither sees Him nor knows Him; but you know Him, for He dwells with you and will be in you. I will not leave you orphans; I will come to you... John 14:16-18*

Since He is the Spirit of Truth, He can reveal things to you that will cut between the soul and the spirit. The person you are ministering to may be projecting one thing, but you will know the truth and the truth will have the ability to set them free (if they so desire). After Jesus ascended into Heaven, He sent the Holy Spirit to dwell within us. The Holy Spirit speaks directly to our hearts. It is the Holy Spirit who illuminates the Bible to our understanding.

*That the God of our Lord Jesus Christ, the Father of glory, may give unto you the spirit of wisdom and revelation in the knowledge of him: The eyes of your understanding being enlightened; that ye may know what is the hope of his calling, and what the riches of the glory of his inheritance in the saints, And what is the exceeding greatness of his power to usward who believe, according to the working of his mighty power... Ephesians 1:17-19*

**The Holy Spirit speaks directly to our hearts. It is the Holy Spirit who illuminates the Bible to our understanding.**

# God's Methods of Communicating

## Day 14

The Holy Spirit leads us into all truth so that we properly understand and apply God's written Word, as well as His spoken Word.

*However, when He, the Spirit of truth, has come, He will guide you into all truth; for He will not speak on His own authority, but whatever He hears He will speak; and He will tell you things to come. He will glorify Me, for He will take of what is Mine and declare it to you. John 16:13-14*

What's He going to do with truth? Declare it unto you.

The Holy Spirit writes God's ways on our hearts.

God desires to walk and talk with us, the members of His body, in an individual, personal, and intimate relationship. The vast majority (90%) of our hearing from God should be personal, by His Holy Spirit and through the Bible. However, God knows our need and has ordained our interdependence within the Body of Christ and has set the ministry of the Prophet as His special voice. He has given the gift of prophecy as His voice in the Body.

Today, take the time to activate the voice of God in your life. Remember, God speaks in all different ways. Whether you have never heard from God or are a seasoned prophet, there is always a deeper relationship that can be built with God and a greater ability to hear and speak with the Holy Spirit. I am always seeking another level in the prophetic with God and there is always more to hear from God. He is God, there is no way that you could ever know all things that are on His heart, but you can always know more than before.

Now, choose one of these methods to hear from God today...

1. Through the Word of God (revelation in the Bible)
2. The prophetic Word from Jesus – "The Lord says …"
3. Prophetic Prayer – you may not be at a place where you can receive or feel comfortable with receiving a "prophetic word" but will receive a prayer from God … just make it prophetic!

*He has given the gift of prophecy as His voice in the Body.*

# The Power of a Seed

## Day 15

We must see and think differently, we must have a heavenly perspective. We must look at things according to the importance that God has put on them. What are His thoughts that He put a priority on? What did He keep reiterating all through the Bible?

*And God said, "Let the earth bring forth grass, the herb yielding seed, and the fruit tree yielding fruit after his kind, whose seed is in itself, upon the earth:" and it was so. And the earth brought forth grass, and herb yielding seed after his kind, and the tree yielding fruit, whose seed was in itself, after his kind: and God saw that it was good. Genesis 1:11-12 KJV*

In the beginning, God introduced seeds. Seeds that had everything they needed on the inside of themselves to produce after their own kind. God was releasing seed and He was germinating the earth with the potential to reproduce. He made a way and then He let us know the importance of seed throughout His Word. When we begin to look at things from a different viewpoint from the Word of God, we can begin to realize the significance of a seed and the power of a seed. Let's start at the very beginning.

God started out with seed in the form of His own words being spoken. He made a proclamation, and released the ability for it to bring back the harvest it was sent out to do. God also warned us that there are not only godly seeds that would be available. (Genesis 3:15) Here we find God is stating that both have seeds. Both have the potential to reproduce after their own kind. We can see the results of the seeds and how they have lodged in different people and brought forth different harvests. Those that have sown good seeds have made a difference for others, affecting lives and producing a harvest that is worth having and looking forward to. Those that have sown bad seeds have also made a difference for others, providing them a platform of choice for a harvest that will adversely affect not only their own life, but also the lives they touch.

*Those that have sown good seeds have made a difference for others, affecting lives and producing a harvest that is worth having and looking forward to.*

## The Power of a Seed

### Day 16

Think about this, God made us in His image and in His likeness. When He did this He put His seed within us. His very own seed. A seed that has power has potential to reproduce after its own kind. We are His workmanship He has provided a plan, provided a part of Himself to be deposited within us and He has also provided seeds for us. We need to understand how the kingdom works. Everyone has seed.

*And the LORD appeared unto him the same night, and said, "I am the God of Abraham thy father: fear not, for I am with thee, and will bless thee, and multiply thy seed for my servant Abraham's sake." Genesis 26:24 KJV*

What did He promise Abraham He would bless?
His seed! What is his seed?

*And the LORD will grant you plenty of goods, in the fruit of your body, in the increase of your livestock, and in the produce of your ground, in the land of which the LORD swore to your fathers to give you. The LORD will open to you His good treasure, the heavens, to give the rain to your land in its season, and to bless all the work of your hand. You shall lend to many nations, but you shall not borrow. Deuteronomy 28:11-12*

You see, a seed had been given to Abraham. A seed that came from the Word of the Lord. A promise that he would be the father of many nations. God had given Abraham a precious gift. If Abraham could see the power of the seed, he could possess the promise of the seed. In the world's system, if you work hard, if you connive, if you beg, borrow, steal ... if you can manipulate, then maybe you can get ahead. In God's system, He provides for you because He loves you and He wants you to have all you will need to succeed. God doesn't even make us find a seed. He provides the seed for us.

*"For as the rain comes down, and the snow from heaven, and do not return there, but water the earth, and make it bring forth and bud, that it may give seed to the sower and bread to the eater." Isaiah 55:10*

### A seed that has power has potential to reproduce after its own kind.

## The Power of a Seed

### Day 17

God spoke to Abraham and now the seed of promise was in him. It was for him and all his seeds after him. God didn't just address his children; he was addressing everything that pertained to seed. Everything he would honor God with, would become a part of an everlasting covenant and everlasting possession. The blessing would go on and on.

*And the LORD appeared unto Abram, and said, "Unto thy seed will I give this land:" and there builded he an altar unto the LORD, who appeared unto him. Genesis 12:7 KJV*

Abraham acted on the seed of promise by building an altar where he would present himself, his prayers and his sacrifices before the Lord. He was honoring the power of the seed. How and to whom are you sowing seeds? How are you honoring the seeds of promise? We all want to feast at the banquet table, yet God continues to ask, what have you done with what I have given? How are you planting your seed and to whom?

- Family – kind words, deeds, forgiveness, love
- Finances – tithes, offerings - obedience
- Friendship – time, love, communication, faithful, honesty
- Faith – agreement with word, increasing, exercising,

Do you recognize the seed that is within you? Have you recognized the potential of what the seed of promise can do for you? What specific seed are you sowing today and for what? You must consistently be looking for and expecting your harvest. If you are sincere about developing the lifestyle of a sower, the Lord will make certain you have something to sow, and will provide even if it takes a miracle. Not only will God furnish "starter" seed, He will sustain you.

*Now he who supplies seed to the sower and bread for food will also supply and increase your store of seed and will enlarge the harvest of your righteousness. You will be made rich in every way so that you can be generous on every occasion, and through us your generosity will result in thanksgiving to God. 2 Corinthians 9:10-11 NIV*

**You must consistently be looking for and expecting your harvest.**

## THE POWER OF A SEED

### Day 18

When we speak with faith and under the inspiration of the Holy Spirit, we are sowing the kind of seed that God blesses and multiplies. Remember, we have the ability to put things in motion, according to the way we respond to what God has made available to us. Seeds, good or bad, have eternal residences.

*Be not deceived; God is not mocked: for whatsoever a man soweth, that shall he also reap. For he that soweth to his flesh shall of the flesh reap corruption; but he that soweth to the Spirit shall of the Spirit reap life everlasting. Galatians 6:7-8 KJV*

What do you sow? Seeds!
What do you get a harvest from? Whatever seeds you sow. If we purposefully paid attention to all the seeds we sow, we could also know what our harvest would look like.

A farmer goes out to sow. He doesn't just go out and look at the ground, and think that it's going to bring the harvest. He goes out with seedlings. He puts them in the ground. He is doing it with conviction. He is expecting those seeds not to remain seeds. He is expecting them to reproduce after their own kind. If he is planting wheat, he is expecting wheat to grow, not an apple orchard. If he is planting apple seeds, then he isn't expecting corn to grow up.

Your words are seeds, your deeds are seeds, and your finances are seeds. Are you looking for good things to come your way? Then what are you planting in order for you to receive a harvest? Are you looking for a blessing? What is your seed that you have released for the blessing to come to you? Are you looking for healing? What seeds of healing are you planting to receive your harvest?

*For when God made promise to Abraham, because he could swear by no greater, he sware by himself, Saying, Surely blessing I will bless thee, and multiplying I will multiply thee. Hebrews 6:13-14 KJV*

***If we purposefully paid attention to all the seeds we sow, we could also know what our harvest would look like.***

# THE POWER OF A SEED

## Day 19

God's words are eternal. They are still running around the earth. Then ours must be also.

*So shall My word be that goes forth from My mouth; It shall not return to Me void, but it shall accomplish what I please, and it shall prosper in the thing for which I sent it. Isaiah 55:11*

The words God spoke and speaks are sent, and they WILL bring a harvest He intended for them to accomplish. Your words are also being utilized to bring something about. That is what makes your prayers so effective. The minute you pray God puts the seed inside of you for the answer to that prayer.

*And as for me, this is my covenant with them, saith Jehovah: my Spirit that is upon thee, and my words which I have put in thy mouth, shall not depart out of thy mouth, nor out of the mouth of thy seed, nor out of the mouth of thy seed's seed, saith Jehovah, from henceforth and for ever. Isaiah 59:21 ASV*

What is the seed here? The Spirit of God that has been given to you is the seed of promise. The seeds God has placed within you come with promises for you, for the seed of your children, for the seed of your children's children. Forever.

God has also given us power with the words that flow from our mouth. Just as He spoke, He spread seeds and produced a harvest. We must recognize that every word we speak is a seed sown. What flows out of your mouth not only reveals the content of your heart, it determines the course of your life. Our words are seeds. They go forth, they affect the atmosphere. Our words can help or hinder, bless or curse, heal or hurt.

What are you experiencing today, that is a result of the words you have been speaking? Today we have the power to plant seeds, because we have been provided seeds. We have our part to do, and God will do the rest.

*The words God spoke and speaks are sent, and they WILL bring a harvest He intended for them to accomplish.*

## THE POWER OF A SEED

### Day 20

How many of you have prayed for miracles to come through you? The minute you prayed that prayer, you put into motion the power of a seed that has been released to begin to bring you through a process to bring forth the harvest of those seeds. Miracles are a part of the harvest you can expect. How long does the promise of the seed exist?

*While the earth remaineth, seedtime and harvest, and cold and heat, and summer and winter, and day and night shall not cease.*
Genesis 8:22 KJV

Are we still on the earth? Yes, then it is still in place. Seed, time and the assurance of a harvest! He is doing things immediately in the background, all the while ensuring we get what He has already pre-prescribed for us. There are many seeds that are available to you, but you may have failed to recognize the seed, even when it is right in front of you.

Let's look at things from Jesus' perspective...

*Then he took the five loaves and the two fishes, and looking up to heaven, he blessed them, and brake, and gave to the disciples to set before the multitude. And they did eat, and were all filled: and there was taken up of fragments that remained to them twelve baskets.*
Luke 9:16-17 KJV

He didn't look at lack, He saw seed. He wasn't looking for someone that had the thousands of fish, thousands of loaves of bread. He knew He didn't have to look for the end result in its completion. All He had to have was the seed that was available at the time! That was all that would be needed in order to meet the apparent need at the time.

Jesus saw enough seed available in a boy's lunch to feed thousands. Look at the application Jesus used. It was Kingdom thinking. He asked about what was available. He wasn't looking at the need. He was looking for a seed. He knew that if He could get the seed that was already there among them, and if it was offered up to God, it would be a seed used to blessed others. He fully expected the multiplication. He gave thanks. He blessed it.

*He fully expected the multiplication. He gave thanks. He blessed it.*

## The Power of a Seed

**Day 21**

God wants us to begin to see things from a heavenly perspective. What you have today and what you have become is not by accident. It is a result of your actions yesterday. Of seeds that you have sown during your lifetime. You need to see yourself with seed in your hand. You have the seeds of promise within you. You have the seeds of blessing in you. You must see yourself as a person of blessing—with the very seed of God on the inside of you, and knowing that wherever you go, you bring the blessing of God with you.

You can't be concerned today with how things are going to come to you. The word says that "neither is he that planteth anything, neither he that watereth, but God that giveth the increase." We do our part, God will do His. God said to give and it shall be given to you. You have time, talent, energy and finances to make available to God in the form of a seed today.

When you give your offering (above your tithe), remember that time, talent, or effort can be offered to God along with your finances. Declare God's promises over your offering.

One of our young women was sharing with me that she is the one who takes up the offering at the youth service. She had been prophesied to that she wasn't just saying words over the offering, but that the words she had were causing her to become a part of the reality of the word concerning seed time and harvest. She experienced her books being paid for at school by someone unknown. She has received blessing after blessing and it is affecting her family. Why? The seeds of God's spoken Word activated the seed on the inside of her. She acted on it by giving, putting confidence in the seed by taking action. Now she is experiencing the power of a seed.

This is your opportunity today.

---

*You must see yourself as a person of blessing—with the very seed of God on the inside of you, and knowing that wherever you go, you bring the blessing of God with you.*

## THE POWER OF A SEED

### Day 22

As you release your tithe and offering see it as an opportunity for the fields to be ripe with your harvest. The harvest that you need. The harvest that God has promised you. It's really already inside of you. You possess your future right now; it is just in the form of a seed. Release the seed, with faith, with vision, with the understanding that if you release the seed, the Lord is faithful to release the harvest.

You see, you already possess abundance in the form of a seed today. Your supply for tomorrow will start with whatever you hold in your hand today. When you sow into God's ground by sowing seeds of faith into the kingdom, then your time of harvest will come. It will start something. It will ignite something. It will cause things to move in your direction. Giving God's way will result in a much higher return than you will ever receive from a financial institution. God doesn't add, He multiplies. See this not as a place of lack, but a place of opportunity.

Today Father, we are not looking at lack, we are looking at seed. There is enough seed here to meet the apparent need at the time and to bring about an overflow. It might look like a small lunch to some, but it is actually enough seed to feed thousands. We know that if we present the seed among us today, and we offer it up to you, it will be a seed used to bless others.

We fully expect the multiplication.
We give thanks. We bless it.
We present it before you, Father.

Our seed begins to cause the harvest to come into our life, today. We agree as touching this thing. We agree with our mouths, we release the seed in the name of Jesus and in faith that the seed we release today is affecting our lives today, and perpetually, in Jesus' mighty name.

*You possess your future right now; it is just in the form of a seed.*

## Time Worth Spending

**Day 23**

Transformation within our community does not happen overnight. It is not something that is completed through a one-time experience.

If we are going to experience the end-time transformation in our land, we are going to have to truthfully examine our own hearts. We must acknowledge the lack of "time" we have actually been willing to give to the presence of God's move.

The world is always talking about a life of leisure. We see billboards, commercials, and advertisements of every kind, but in reality we are so busy that even when we are done with one thing, we are racing to the next thing on our agenda.

We want God's presence to fit in our time slots and within the parameters of our current meeting times. "Show up God," we say, and please do it on Tuesday, Wednesday and/or Sunday, for I must have my "down time". Therefore, that is what many Christians receive – DOWN time. We are distracted by the world's system, pursuing the stuff of this world, and God is just one of the many things we juggle.

Revival is born out of passion.

If we want to see our communities transformed, we must seize the moment as He speaks, whenever that moment may be.

Examine your heart now and prepare yourself to answer the call of the Spirit. The time He requires from you will be worth it!

*Revival is born out of passion.*

# Elijah Then, Elijah Now

## Day 24

Elijah was an important prophet who shifted the atmospheres around him. He stood in an anointing to cause a shift in nations. He had many qualities that we will study out in this Kingdom Guide series and see how they apply to us today. So who was Elijah and what did he do? Though there is not extensive information on him, personally, we do know:

- Elijah's name means 'Yahweh is God'.
- He appeared at the beginning of 1 Kings 17, with no previous introduction.
- He lived about 100 years after King David, in the Northern Kingdom of Israel. – This is after the split into the two kingdoms of Judah and Israel.
- It's not a good time – the kings were unstable and the people were all over the place in what they believed and who they believed in.
- King Ahab married Jezebel who is very into Baal worship.
- Baal was the god supposedly responsible for reproduction and weather conditions. He would either punish with drought or bless with rain. (They would offer up their own children to Baal.)
- The people were constantly tempted to worship Baal instead of Yahweh. Elijah deals with the false god and the false prophets in one day.
- God answered Elijah by fire.
- At the end of his life Elijah went to heaven in an unusual way. – Horses and chariots of fire separated him from Elisha and then he was taken up in a whirlwind!

Quite a powerful man. Quite an unusual relationship with God. Quite an important impact he brought to the nation. What would set him apart in such a way, that he would have God's attention to the point that He whisked him away?

Obviously this was a man who knew God very well and trusted his life in God's hands. I want you to understand that Elijah was a man that we can learn a lot from. And as powerful as he was we must also remember that God said even greater things were "yet to come." (He was talking about us, today!)

***He stood in an anointing to cause a shift in nations.***

# Elijah Then, Elijah Now

**Day 25**

Elijah heard God and did what God wanted. The first we hear of him is this: *And Elijah the Tishbite, who was of the inhabitants of Gilead, said unto Ahab, As the LORD God of Israel liveth, before whom I stand, there shall not be dew nor rain these years, but according to my word.* 1 Kings 17:1 KJV

He makes an announcement for no rain, and no rain came. He makes the declaration that GOD is in him. Without rain there would be famine ... there would be suffering. God directs him and he is taken care of by ravens. He wasn't looking at his own discomfort, he was looking at what God was doing, and he wanted God to have His way in the earth. Then he is directed to go to the widow woman who is baking the last cake for her and her son so they can die. Not exactly a woman of faith. He tells her to make it and give to him first. Can you imagine having to obey like that? Sounds harsh, but it is because he understands God's voice, His commitment and His purpose will be fulfilled.

*Then the word of the LORD came to him, saying, "Arise, go to Zarephath, which belongs to Sidon, and dwell there. See, I have commanded a widow there to provide for you."* 1 Kings 17:8-9

Now he has been staying with the widow that God has provided oil for. Three years have passed and the word of the Lord came again to Elijah.

*And it came to pass after many days that the word of the LORD came to Elijah, in the third year, saying, "Go, present yourself to Ahab, and I will send rain on the earth."* 1 Kings 18:1

In the meantime Ahab has been killing off what he thought were all the prophets of God. He has especially been looking for Elijah, but has never been able to find him. Elijah knew the reputation of these people. But he also knew the reputation of his God. What did Elijah do? He went.

Has God ever called you to face down your fear face-to-face?

***He wasn't looking at his own discomfort, he was looking at what God was doing, and he wanted God to have His way in the earth.***

# Elijah Then, Elijah Now

## Day 26

*So Elijah went to present himself to Ahab; and there was a severe famine in Samaria. 1 Kings 18:2* Even though it was obvious in the natural that this would be risky to obey God, Elijah did it, and apparently without question. Immediate obedience! We don't actually know how the word of the Lord came to Elijah, maybe it wasn't in a way that we would hear God speaking, but when heard it he had instant obedience. Elijah had a great reputation.

*Now as Obadiah was on his way, suddenly Elijah met him; and he recognized him, and fell on his face, and said, "Is that you, my lord Elijah?" And he answered him, "It is I. Go, tell your master, 'Elijah is here.'" 1 Kings 18:7-8*

So we know that the servant of Ahab was also a servant of God and that he recognized and honored Elijah as a man of God. Elijah was on a mission. He told Obadiah that he needed to go get Ahab for them to have a meeting. Now we see the reputation of Ahab and the reputation of Elijah come out.

*So he said, "How have I sinned, that you are delivering your servant into the hand of Ahab, to kill me? As the LORD your God lives, there is no nation or kingdom where my master has not sent someone to hunt for you; and when they said, 'He is not here,' he took an oath from the kingdom or nation that they could not find you. And now you say, 'Go, tell your master, "Elijah is here!"' And it shall come to pass, as soon as I am gone from you, that the Spirit of the LORD will carry you to a place I do not know; so when I go and tell Ahab, and he cannot find you, he will kill me. But I your servant have feared the LORD from my youth." 1 Kings 18:9-12*

He is flipped out. He knows that Ahab will kill him. And the reason WHY is because he knows it is very possible that Elijah will just get carried away by the Spirit to some unknown place. Evidently this was common place for Elijah. And let us remember this is before the new and better covenant. This is before the Holy Spirit lived within. God was evident in Elijah's life. He had influence over society. That is for sure. The FBI couldn't have found him, unless God wanted him to be found.

### *Immediate obedience!*

# Elijah Then, Elijah Now

**Day 27**

Elijah was confident.

He let Obadiah know he would be safe for this was the plan of God. Today he would not be whisked away, he would meet with Ahab, he had business to take care of.

*Then Elijah said, "As the LORD of hosts lives, before whom I stand, I will surely present myself to him today." So Obadiah went to meet Ahab, and told him; and Ahab went to meet Elijah. Then it happened, when Ahab saw Elijah, that Ahab said to him, "Is that you, O troubler of Israel?" 1 Kings 18:15-17*

The enemy is always trying to flip the tables and accuse the godly for doing what is right. But Elijah isn't moved at all by his accusation. In fact, he just puts the record straight.

*And he answered, "I have not troubled Israel, but you and your father's house have, in that you have forsaken the commandments of the LORD and have followed the Baals." 1 Kings 18:18*

God's call had given him a confidence.

We have learned about confidence – it's empowering, it frees us up to do things we couldn't otherwise do.

God equips those He calls. Elijah knew that he had heard from Him, and if He said to do it, He would give him the ability and the confidence to do it.

As a father who watches over and loves his child, Elijah would not be alone at the face off.

Whatever it is that God has called you to do here on this earth you must be confident in His call. Confident that He said to do it; therefore, He will give you the ability and confidence to do it!

*God's call had given him a confidence.*

# Elijah Then, Elijah Now

## Day 28

Elijah had great strategies.

*"Now therefore, send and gather all Israel to me on Mount Carmel, the four hundred and fifty prophets of Baal, and the four hundred prophets of Asherah, who eat at Jezebel's table." 1 Kings 18:19*

It appears that this one prophet is up against a mound of false prophets. Think of all the demons in the arena. Think of how it would feel and how it would look. But Elijah, in the midst of the demon fest, was not moved. Instead he used it to challenge an entire nation to bring them back to truth.

*And Elijah came to all the people, and said, "How long will you falter between two opinions? If the LORD is God, follow Him; but if Baal, follow him." But the people answered him not a word. 1 Kings 18:21*

Yahweh one day, Baal the next ...

We don't think that we worship false gods today. But there is TV, sports, video games, I-Pads, your career etc.: Idols are those distractions that pull you away hours and hours a day from God ... away from your Bible, away from worship.

Elijah was at this pivotal point in Israel where it was time to put things in order.

He was telling them: It is time to put things in order. You can no longer serve both gods. You are going to be found out. It is time to set in place who you will serve. And who will you benefit from? You will see and decide who is God. It appears they were all intimidated by this man. When a man of God speaks with authority, they cannot say anything. Elijah knew who he was. He was not intimidated by 850 false prophets, full of demons.

It's easy to stand up for what's right and worship God at church in the midst of a crowd of others doing the same. But, would you be intimidated to do the same when it's only you in the midst of 850 who are against your God?

**It is time to set in place who you will serve.**

# Elijah Then, Elijah Now

## Day 29

The challenge is on...

*"Then you call on the name of your gods, and I will call on the name of the LORD; and the God who answers by fire, He is God." So all the people answered and said, "It is well spoken." 1 Kings 18:24*

When a man or woman of God stands before demons, with authority, they can't say anything.

A tactic of the spirit of Jezebel is to get you deceived and it actually makes you think you are doing the right thing. You're in derision. The people actually believed that Baal would win. Deception is a horrible spirit. I have sat with people in deception who could no longer hear my voice. They can no longer hear the voice of God.

It doesn't happen all of a sudden. It happens a little bit at a time, when you don't listen to God's inner voice, and you insist on having your own way, when you are selfish, when you take instead of give, when you frequent those places you shouldn't, and don't go where you should. It opens you up to be deceived and you cannot even tell the difference between good and evil anymore. You need intervention from God at this point.

All is not lost ... God can intervene.

I don't care what the spirit of Jezebel thinks, I care about what God says. If God is with us, who can be against us? One drop of the blood of Jesus is more powerful than any spirit.

Perfect set up, if you have heard from God. If you are put in a territory to set things right for God, then you have all of the strength and power of God backing you.

What is your set-up?

Where has God placed you to set things right?

*If God is with us, who can be against us?*

## Elijah Then, Elijah Now

### Day 30

Elijah had great faith.

*And he put the wood in order, cut the bull in pieces, and laid it on the wood, and said, "Fill four waterpots with water, and pour it on the burnt sacrifice and on the wood." Then he said, "Do it a second time," and they did it a second time; and he said, "Do it a third time," and they did it a third time. So the water ran all around the altar; and he also filled the trench with water. And it came to pass, at the time of the offering of the evening sacrifice, that Elijah the prophet came near and said, "LORD God of Abraham, Isaac, and Israel, let it be known this day that You are God in Israel and I am Your servant, and that I have done all these things at Your word." 1 Kings 18:33-36*

He stood in the office and authority of a prophet of God. He was confronting the spirits that had seized the minds of God's people. He knew that God would deliver His people. This was the show down. Elijah had a lot to lose if God didn't deliver, but Elijah trusted that God would do what He'd said He would. He trusted because of previous experience. He had a trusted relationship with his God.

He knew the reputation of his God who had led the people miraculously out of exile. And he knew if he stood for God, God would stand for him. He knew that the God who had taken care of the people in the desert and led them into the promised land would once again intervene for His people and give them a wake-up call. And he believed that the God who had called him to go and sort out the prophets of Baal and call the people back to Yahweh would again deliver His chosen people. And he was right!

Note that his prayer was not *"LORD God... Let it be known this day that...I WILL BE Your servant, and that I WILL DO all these things at Your word."* NO! You see, when we live right everyday in obedience, we don't need to beg God when we are in need. We are confident in who we are and who He is that we could pray...

*"LORD God... Let it be known this day that...I am Your servant, and that I have done all these things at Your word."*

# Elijah Then, Elijah Now

**Day 31**

Elijah had an end result in mind.

*Hear me, O LORD, hear me, that this people may know that thou art the LORD God, and that thou hast turned their heart back again. 1 Kings 18:37*

He got his assignment from God. This is it. It was all about restoration. It was about the hearts of the sons and daughters being turned back to the Father.

God's response? God's all-consuming fire fell from heaven.

*Then the fire of the LORD fell, and consumed the burnt sacrifice, and the wood, and the stones, and the dust, and licked up the water that was in the trench.* The water - the most precious commodity of the day (because of the famine and no rain) was ALL consumed. *And when all the people saw it, they fell on their faces: and they said, "The LORD, he is the God; the LORD, he is the God." 1 Kings 18:38-39*

Any questions? I guess not. Seems a nation was saved in a day, because Elijah was obedient; he was anointed. Because he acted out what He heard from God. He acted on the word of the Lord. That would be enough for some, but Elijah knew there was something else that needed to occur.

*And Elijah said to them, "Seize the prophets of Baal! Do not let one of them escape!" So they seized them; and Elijah brought them down to the Brook Kishon and executed them there. 1 Kings 18:40*

He understood something.

The enemy had to be destroyed. He had challenged the spirit that had reigned over that region and destroyed true worship, and he was not going to let the spirits continue to rebuild. He knew that he would have to destroy them ... to take a stand that would not be soon forgotten ... to show the power and determination of the Lord for purity to be restored.

***It was about the hearts of the sons and daughters being turned back to the Father.***

## Elijah Then, Elijah Now

**Day 32**

While he was sitting down, Elijah was showing us another important attribute of why God could use him in such a way. ELIJAH was a man of prayer. *"And Elijah went up to the top of Carmel; then he bowed down on the ground, and put his face between his knees,"* (posture of prayer). He went to his place of intimacy and he prayed until he heard that voice once again, for the instructions for the moment. I don't know how many hours you spend in prayer. We are told to pray without ceasing. Your communication with God is supposed to be 24/7. You can know the end result of God, without knowing how to get there.

*...and said to his servant, "Go up now, look toward the sea."* Elijah didn't get discouraged, he just kept sending the servant to look again, He knew something was about to occur. He was just staying in a place of expectancy.
*So he went up and looked, and said, "There is nothing." And seven times he said, "Go again." 1 Kings 18:43*

He tells him to go look again, and he comes back and says ... No building ... and he goes again ... and he comes back and says ... no car ... and he goes again ... and he comes back and says ... nothing in my bank account ... and he goes again ... and he comes back and says ... nothing happening in my family ... and he goes again ... And then something began to change.

*Then it came to pass the seventh time, that he said, "There is a cloud, as small as a man's hand, rising out of the sea!" 1 Kings 18:44*

He was about to bring the answer to the drought, an answer to the people's needs. You did not understand the first year, you did not understand it last year, there is an appointed time, but God's hand is going to appear — to stand in the gap to declare that they have heard His voice, and He is setting things in order. This is all he needed to hear. He didn't need to hear thunder or see lightning. He didn't need to have the rain before he knew the rain was there. It is in prayer that you know what is coming!

*He went to his place of intimacy and he prayed until he heard that voice once again, for the instructions for the moment.*

## Elijah Then, Elijah Now

### Day 33

He just was waiting for the hand of God to come. He was waiting for the sign God must have told him to look for. Because upon this report, he made another announcement,

*So he said, "Go up, say to Ahab, 'Prepare your chariot, and go down before the rain stops you.'" Now it happened in the meantime that the sky became black with clouds and wind, and there was a heavy rain. So Ahab rode away and went to Jezreel. Then the hand of the LORD came upon Elijah; and he girded up his loins and ran ahead of Ahab to the entrance of Jezreel. 1 Kings 18:44-46*

He had seen the outpouring. He knew this was a torrential outpouring on its way. It would be so much that it would stop chariots from travel.

Now the sky is responding (to the hand of God), and Ahab is riding just as fast as he can. Can you imagine? He must have been happy for the rain, but the rain is chasing him down. But that is not all. Okay, now this is just funny. God must have had great joy in this. Elijah, who has just faced the forces of evil down, and killed 450 men, grabs up his skirt and runs past Ahab in the chariot. That had to be a sight to see.

The man of God was energized, because that which he had seen in the spirit was now manifesting in the natural.

Why is this important? We have to realize that Elijah was called out of obscurity to be a prophet to change a nation.

He was really good at HEARING FROM GOD.

His obedience had caused him to have an anointing upon his life that was so strong it was transferable and continued after he was gone. His impact was from generation to generation!

---

*The man of God was energized, because that which he had seen in the spirit was now manifesting in the natural.*

## Elijah Then, Elijah Now

### Day 34

He was set apart for the kingdom to be displayed on the earth to make a difference.

He was surrendered to the Lord. He knew His voice. He obeyed Him. He loved him. He was in love with God and His ways.

You see... We are the Elijah's of this day!

*Elijah and those of the house of Liberty hear God and do what God wants.*

*Elijah and the house of Liberty have a great reputation.*

*Elijah and the house of Liberty are confident.*

*Elijah and the house of Liberty have great strategies.*

*Elijah and those of the house of Liberty have great faith.*

*Elijah and those of the house of Liberty have an end result in mind.*

*Elijah and those of the house of Liberty expose and destroy the enemy.*

*Elijah and those of the house of Liberty are people of prayer.*

*Elijah and the house of Liberty walk in supernatural strength and power and have the victory and declare that Yahweh is still God and He's not just any God – He's our God!*

And because of that, God has a word for us to hear in our ears today. Of this, you can be sure, what He says does matter.

Declare this today...

*I hear God and do what God wants... I have a great reputation.... I am confident... I have great strategies... I have great faith... I have an end result in mind... I expose and destroy the enemy... And I am a person of prayer.*

**You see... We are the Elijah's of this day!**

# CELEBRATION OF VICTORY!

## Day 35

*A prophetic word 9.18.11:*

We look not at that which is seen but we look at what is not seen; that which is not seen is what God has spoken. Faith is the substance of things hoped for; the evidence of things not seen. We haven't seen it yet, but God's word says it's there. Here's our evidence and here's our proof, and faith comes by hearing and hearing by the Word of God.

God says, I want you to see from my perspective. The prophet of old told his servant to go look to the sky and see what you can see. At first he could not see anything, but that didn't mean it wasn't there. Because my servant Elijah had heard from me. He had seen past the physical realm, he had even moved past the faith realm and had entered into the realm of the spirit where what he saw was more real than what the natural appeared to be. That is why he could say with confidence, to his servant, go look again. He didn't need the servant to look for his sake. He knew what was going to happen. It was going to rain. It was inevitable.

The devil couldn't stop it. Nature had to give way to my plan.

But he made him go seven times until the servant began to rise into agreement with the prophet. When he finally moved into a place where the prophet's confident faith had affected him, the servant also began to see what was occurring.

It was then that the manifestation began to be evident. But it had already occurred in God's heart. He had just shared His heart with His prophet. You are now seeing the manifestation of what my servant already saw in his spirit. You haven't been waiting on Me, I have been waiting on you. There had to be the place where you all came away from the apparent and submitted to the faith of the elder. Now you will rise into a new place as you inhabit a new place.

*You haven't been waiting on Me, I have been waiting on you.*

## Celebration of Victory!

### Day 36

For the tactic of the enemy was to put a damper on your faith ... to intimidate by the lack of rain (and reign) in your midst. But I see the rain coming because those who are called by My Name have stood, and have heard and there is now a knowing in the spirit that will be reinforced with agreement from the body along with My chosen vessels.

Satan thought he could stop my move. But just as he was powerless against the heavens opening for the rain to fall in times of drought, he is powerless against you, for you are entering into a new season of the (rain) reign.

My people have set their affections on Me and they are coming into unity as never before. That which has been heard in the spirit will manifest with a voice that will be heard that will shake the demonic realm down to dust and debris.

There is a little cloud, a carrier of the transference that is arising from the sea that I have created. It will rise and it will rise and it will unload upon you. You will begin to see the experience transfers. Transfers from darkness to light. Salvations are happening—lots of them as they are drawn by the Spirit to the place of safety from the storms.

The wisdom in this house is transferable. Don't miss this time of impartation. Come to every service with expectancy. I am for you. Those that have been praying for offspring will see suddenlies of the God kind to rescue them from the enemy's camp. There will be deliverance.

If you will dare to agree with Me, and to not get into your head, but lead from your heart, many will have ideas, concepts and vision that will cause the transference of wealth to come to them and to My Church. Please understand, this celebration is not only being celebrated on earth, but in heaven as well!

*My people have set their affections on Me and they are coming into unity as never before.*

# Celebration of Victory!

**Day 37**

Faithful witnesses applaud faithful witnesses and the gap closes as the rain releases the thunder needed to override the voice of the enemy. The diligence and the love that you have shown to Me has not gone unnoticed, and it will not be wasted, but it will be rewarded.

You have sacrificed; you have pressed past the depression, past the oppression, and have entered into the place of sacrificial giving.

What Satan meant to destroy you has backfired, for the fire has only refined you and caused you to focus intently on Me. Hear Me. Look forward. Make no small plans. You will look and see that which started as a small hand will have grown into an iron fist that no foe can penetrate.

Lift up your head, lift up your voice, for the Lord God Almighty is in your midst, and Lord Sabbaoth has won the battle.

Reign with Me, expecting nothing less than the miraculous — and you shall have it. Reign with Me, expecting nothing less than the miraculous — and you shall have it.

There is a sound. There is a sound. There is a sound. One voice, one shout, one orchestration that turns many into one. So shout the victory of the Lord in agreement with expectancy for I am with you for such a time is this.

*Lift up your head, lift up your voice,
for the Lord God Almighty is in your midst*

# It's All In Your Perspective

## Day 38

While I was on the plane coming home from ministering in Belize God began to say some things to me that I knew would be important directives for us to obey.

How many of you are currently in a condition that you never thought you would be in?

How many of you are facing a condition in your body?

How's the condition of your spiritual walk?

How's the condition of your relationships?

God said some things need to be put in order.

The most obvious thing would be, of course, that our focus needs to be on Him. But there is more than just looking to Him; there is even more than knowing He is there.

We must understand something vital today. Instead of focusing on our condition, we must start focusing on our position. It's all in your perspective.

Perspective means: "The state of one's ideas, the facts known to one, in having a meaningful interrelationship".

We all have our own ideas about relationship. That is why there are challenges in marriage. What one knows, the other doesn't, until there is interaction and communication that brings things into proper understanding and agreement.

We don't always see all the relevant data, just the FEAR factor, or "False Evidence Appearing Real."

For us to have a relationship with God and to live above conditions, we have to get out of our head (our reasoning) and into a positional understanding of who we are with Him.

***Instead of focusing on our condition,
we must start focusing on our position.***

# It's All In Your Perspective

## Day 39

Today we are going to take a look at Noah as an example. He was facing some conditions; he was the only righteous man alive in his generation. Today's difficult conditions aren't nearly as desperate as that. Though when it's happening to you, or your family, it seems to be desperate.

Jesus warned that in this dark world there would be trouble.

Moses even accused God of doing "nothing" just because he didn't see immediate results.

One of the most vivid examples we can use is Joseph. It was obvious that He had favor and position when he was wearing the robe of many colors, but when his conditions changed, and there was no evidence of that favor in the pit, or in the jail, it didn't change his true position.

For favor was still upon him. Blessing still followed him. Satan could make his arrangements to take away the blessing, but he couldn't stop God. And what was in Joseph always surfaced. He was able to keep a heavenly perspective because he had been with God in his dreams.

In the same way, what we see or don't see in the natural is never an indication of whether God is working. He always does what He promises.

*"God is not a man, so he does not lie. He is not human, so he does not change his mind. Has he ever spoken and failed to act? Has he ever promised and not carried it through?" (Numbers 23:19 NLT)*

So how do we keep the proper perspective so that we can overcome our current conditions? What needs to be in order?

Mainly, one thing: our mind.
We need to transform our thinking by concentrating on our position, so we can stop concentrating on our condition.

***What we see or don't see in the natural is never an indication of whether God is working.***

# It's All In Your Perspective

## Day 40

*"And Isaac called Jacob, and blessed him, and charged him, and said unto him, 'Thou shalt not take a wife of the daughters of Canaan.'" (Genesis 28:1 KJV)*

Today let me help change your perspective, as God changed Jacob's. What did Isaac do to Jacob? He blessed him. According to the meaning of this word, he installed the benefits of God upon him. And then he charged him with a directive. He told him who not to join himself to. Here we gain insight into why this was necessary: And Rebekah said to Isaac, *"I am weary of my life because of the daughters of Heth; if Jacob takes a wife of the daughters of Heth, like these who are the daughters of the land, what good will my life be to me?" (Genesis 27:46 NKJV)*

Heth means: terror, confusion, discouragement. Though Canaan would eventually be given as the land of promise for the Israelites, Jacob would have to separate himself from the spirit of the world that was controlling Canaan at the time and keep his seed pure.

*"Arise, go to Padan-aram, to the house of Bethuel thy mother's father; and take a wife from of the daughters of Laban thy mother's brother. And God Almighty bless thee, and make thee fruitful, and multiply thee, that thou may be a multitude of people; And give thee the blessing of Abraham, to you, and to your seed with you; that you may inherit the land where you are a stranger, which God gave unto Abraham." (Genesis 28:2-4 KJV)*

The blessing is re-iterated and expanded. Jacob had been blessed with an inheritance, and he began to move into obedience. He had to put himself in position to receive the blessing and we must do the same to receive our blessing. Though God has already declared His blessing on each one of our lives, it takes our decision to be in a position of obedience to receive.

We live in a world where terror, confusion, and discouragement are all around us. It is our choice whether we join ourselves to it or to God's GOOD will.

*He had to put himself in position to receive the blessing and we must do the same to receive our blessing.*

# It's All In Your Perspective

## Day 41

*"And Jacob went out from Beer-sheba, and went toward Haran. (The name Haran means to be angry, burn, dry, kindle.) And he lighted upon a certain place, and tarried there all night, because the sun was set; and he took of the stones of that place, and put them for his pillows, and lay down in that place to sleep." (Genesis 28:10 KJV)*

He didn't know it, but he was about ready to have a meltdown, to burn up some old mind-sets, and to begin to have an experience that would incite passion in him as never before. Conditions, not so good. He is in the middle of the desert. It's night, it's dark, his parents aren't there, his brother is mad. He is cold, alone with no pillows, just stones. But these were very special stones. These stones were of the place of burning. They were to be his own incinerator of his old ways of thinking. Here he would hear the voice of God and see beyond the natural to the unlimited blessings of the Lord. His perspective was going to begin to change.

*"And he dreamed, and behold a ladder set up on the earth, and the top of it reached to heaven: and behold the angels of God ascending and descending on it." (Genesis 28:12 KJV)*

From the place of the earth, a ladder extended to a place in heaven. And suddenly he was made aware that God had supernatural beings that were going from heaven to earth and earth to heaven. They were carrying out their orders to bring God's will to pass.

I think that we all can relate to Jacob at this point. Here he is being obedient to God and doing what he believes is right. He has turned away from the terror, confusion, and discouragement of Heth, and where does that lead him? In the middle of the desert, cold, alone, and TOTALLY UNCOMFORTABLE! But wait it doesn't end there … It is here at this moment that he has a supernatural experience with God! Is God trying to get you out of your comfort zone? Don't worry, God knows what you need and where you need to be and when … even if it doesn't make sense to you!

***Hear the voice of God and see beyond the natural to the unlimited blessings of the Lord.***

# It's All In Your Perspective

## Day 42

*"And behold, the LORD stood above it and said: 'I am the LORD God of Abraham your father and the God of Isaac; the land on which you lie I will give to you and your descendants. Also your descendants shall be as the dust of the earth; you shall spread abroad to the west and the east, to the north and the south; and in you and in your seed all the families of the earth shall be blessed.'" (Genesis 28:13-14 )*

Here he begins to understand that this blessing was not just words from his earthly father, but from His heavenly Father as well. God introduces Himself personally to Jacob as the same God of Abraham and Isaac.

These words begin to burn on the inside of Him. The voice of God, the visual of the invisible that had become more real than his natural senses, and had begun to work an effective work in his life. Now he began to see with different eyes, and his heart melted as he saw the words of the blessing stand before him. Descendants – lots of them – as many as the dust of the earth. And in them, and of that seed, would ALL the families of the earth be blessed. How far did he see into the future? Did he see us in this church today? How far did God allow him to see? I don't know, but I am sure that he saw as many as he needed to, to keep him focused on his POSITION with God instead of his CONDITIONS.

His perspective was changing. Then God says the most precious thing of all in verse 15: "Behold, I am with you and will keep you wherever you go, and will bring you back to this land; for I will not leave you until I have done what I have spoken to you."

"I am with you. I will keep you no matter what the conditions are, no matter where you are. I will bring you back to the land of promise." God's promise stands true today for you and your family! He will never leave you until all that He has promised has been accomplished!

*Now he began to see with different eyes, and his heart melted as he saw the words of the blessing stand before him.*

# It's All In Your Perspective

## Day 43

*"Then Jacob awoke from his sleep and said, 'Surely the LORD is in this place, and I did not know it.'" (Genesis 28:16)*

This is a new awareness for Jacob. Was God always involved in his life? Well, yes, God already had prepared his mother by letting her be aware that he was one of the nations that were inside of her as she carried him and his brother within. He told her that Jacob would be the one who would rule over the other. He knew his beginning from his end. Jacob must have known the story. But that is all it was, until it became personal. When God showed him WHO he really was, and what promises he really had upon his life, his mind began to change. His focus began to change. His heart began to be molded in a different way.

He would finally be able to understand that though God was always in this place, he just hadn't been aware of it before. Before he said "the Lord surely is in this place," he didn't know he would find God there. He thought he was just on a journey in the middle of the desert. He knew he had a destination, he just didn't realize that this was HIS destination.

God had said to me also on the plane that he had pre-determined destinations for us. I didn't quite understand that at the time. Much like Jacob, I was wondering how that would work. He also said there would be comings and goings, but with it would be security and focus. Jacob would seemingly leave the land of inheritance, but it was temporary. That would be a going, but indeed all of the nations would be blessed with the inheritance of the Lord, through Abraham, through Isaac and through Jacob. Glory to God!

His God was now HIS God and He would be with him. He had met with Him and His presence changed his mind. He was awakened to his old, stale way of thinking, and everything was new.

Have you ever just been going about your business only to realize "Surely the LORD is in this place, and I did not know it?" I think you just have to think back, and sometimes it takes a while before you realize it.

### *He would finally be able to understand that though God was always in this place, he just hadn't been aware of it before.*

## It's All In Your Perspective

### Day 44

*"And he was afraid and said, 'How awesome is this place! This is none other than the house of God, and this is the gate of heaven!"* Genesis 28:17

Afraid here means he was in reverence as he realized the awesomeness of God. He recognized who was in the house - God!! He understood that God was there, that angels were there. He just hadn't known it before.

*"Then Jacob rose early in the morning, and took the stone that he had put at his head, set it up as a pillar, and poured oil on top of it. And he called the name of that place Bethel; but the name of that city had been Luz previously." (Genesis 28:18 )*

He had taken the stone from the place that had changed his mind and he set it up for a memorial and then he poured oil on it. He was serious about remembering this place. He even named it. Not the house of Jacob and God, but the house of God almighty with His angels. Now his mind was changed. God had burned things out of him, and things into him, so he would never struggle again, right? Well, kind of ...

*Then Jacob made a vow, saying, "If God will be with me, and keep me in this way that I am going, and give me bread to eat and clothing to put on, so that I come back to my father's house in peace, then the LORD shall be my God. And this stone which I have set as a pillar shall be God's house, and of all that You give me I will surely give a tenth to You." (Genesis 28:20-22 )*

What did he just say? IF God will be with me, and keep me, and provide for me, and give me peace, and bring me back then he shall be my God. And then I will pay my tithe. Say, what?

God had just promised to be with him. To keep him safe no matter what the conditions were, no matter where he was. He promised he would bring him back to the land of promise.

Still relating to Jacob? Yeah, me too! It's amazing how easily we can give in to doubt over God's call on our lives

### *He promised he would bring him back to the land of promise.*

# It's All In Your Perspective

## Day 45

God had just promised He would never leave Jacob until all that He has promised has been accomplished. It sounds a little ridiculous but now Jacob is still questioning with the infamous "what if." But you have to understand, Jacob had just experienced his first real encounter with God. Much like us when we receive salvation; we believe in that moment that Jesus is the Son of God, that He took our sins and that He has offered us a new life with many new promises. But if we really don't know who Jesus is and what He has done for us, we often walk away from the reality of the inheritance of the blessing He has bestowed upon us.

We give God all these conditions for Him to meet so we will continue to call Him our God. But all the things we want, we desire, we demand that He prove to us, He has already provided for us. It was His intention to bless us from the beginning. No manipulation necessary. We must first understand our position in Christ if we are ever going to live from position instead of our conditions.

*"Therefore, if anyone is in Christ, he is a new creation; old things have passed away; behold, all things have become new." 2 Corinthians 5:17*

Is it true? Yes, it is. The curse is broken and the blessing is upon us. Our lives have just been positioned to walk in the fullness of the blessing by becoming sons and daughters of the Most High.

Then why don't we act like all things are new? You see, as a new creation in Christ we have a lot of spiritual possessions. Love, joy, peace, revelatory insight, and strength. You have also received a new POSITION as a child of God. If you believe in your position as a reality, then you must understand that ...

You are free from lack. You are free from having to measure up to someone else. You are free when wondering where you belong or what you are really like. You belong to Him; to the family of God. You are made in His image and in His likeness.

And you have promises. Many of them. There is much to realize!

*Then why don't we act like all things are new?*

# It's All In Your Perspective

## Day 46

Even the disciples got excited when they experienced the power God had shared with them.

*"Then the seventy returned with joy, saying, 'Lord, even the demons are subject to us in Your name.'"* (Luke 10:17)

What is subject to you? Demons, in His name. That is exciting. We like that part. We get excited when God uses us like that. Or when we see others used to cast out demons. It is awesome, right? Jesus – not so impressed. To this, He simply replies:

*"And He said to them, 'I saw Satan fall like lightning from heaven.'"* (Luke 10:18)

I think He was just trying to let them know that it was kind of an "of course" to Him. He was there when Satan was stripped of all power. He knew he could not hold those in his chains if we would take our position that He had provided. He continues to tell them the authority they were, and we are, to operate in:

*"Behold, I give you the authority to trample on serpents and scorpions, and over all the power of the enemy, and nothing shall by any means hurt you."* (Luke 10:19) Spooky, mean Satan and his power and his demons' powers cannot even hurt you. Nothing. Nada. Not at all. But then, Jesus says something that is often not quoted quite as much.

*"Nevertheless do not rejoice in this, that the spirits are subject to you, but rather rejoice because your names are written in heaven."* Luke 10:20

What message is He trying to convey to us? Not that you don't have authority over the devil, you do. But more importantly, the better focus is not on your experience with the demonic realm, but with the reality of your inheritance.

We are a part of God's royal family; we just need to change our mind-sets. We need to have a place where we lay our heads down on the stone, and we allow God to burn out the dross of our thinking.

**Focus on the reality of your inheritance.**

## It's All In Your Perspective

### Day 47

I was at a business conference at the beautiful Hillsborough Country Club. It was on the ocean. The rooms were spacious. The food would just suddenly appear in front of me at the right time. They had a cappuccino machine. I observed families the following day, enjoying the ocean, eating whenever they wanted, whatever they wanted. I listened to conversations from their children. They just expected these things, these fine conditions. They weren't begging their parents for food. They just charged it to their parents' account. If they wanted to play with a surf board or a bike, what did they do? Charged it to their parents' account. If they wanted anything, they just used their parents' name, and suddenly there were people and things put in motion to take care of them. It was effortless on the part of those who were living in the inheritance of their father's wealth. They had access to many benefits because of the sacrifice of their father.

Their position was a direct result of his position. What is your spiritual POSITION? Not your condition. We are sitting in heavenly places with Jesus Christ our Lord. We are with HIM. He paid the price; we have access to His account. However, you may be like Jacob, in process of coming to believe in God enough to trust Him with the honor of giving Him your first fruits. That, however, has not stopped His Word.

That has not affected His reality of who you are to Him. He had called Jacob. He had given him the promise of the future. He had seen him operating at a different level than he was currently operating at. But God knew what Jacob was just learning.

Jesus knew what His disciples were just in the process of learning. Their names were written in heaven. The Godhead had them on their mind, in their heart, and they had left them in their wills. And it didn't stop there; He wants you to know today. Demons are subject to you, but more importantly, your name is written in heaven.

*We are with HIM. He paid the price; we have access to His account.*

## It's All In Your Perspective

### Day 48

*"But as many as received Him, to them He gave the right to become children of God, to those who believe in His name." (John 1:12)*

You are His kid! If you believe in Him, if He is your Lord, then you have a right just like those children at the country club, but WAY better! They didn't have to act perfect to access daddy's money, influence or authority. They were a little loud sometimes, a little rebellious at times. They were a little unaware of the advantages they had been given. They took some things for granted. But not once did their fathers take away the blessing.

They had a position. That position was sonship. Those earthly fathers were focused more on who they belonged to, than their current actions or reactions.

They didn't have to be perfect to enjoy their inheritance.

They just had to know their name.

It's all in the perspective. They will grow, they will mature. They will eventually understand more that they have advantages that many around them don't have. Just like us. But God is working on things. Like He was with Jacob.

*So Jacob went on his way, and the angels of God met him. When Jacob saw them, he said, "This is God's camp." And he called the name of that place Mahanaim. (Genesis 32:1-2)*

Jacob has been married, worked for Laban, long and hard. He has seen God bless his livestock with spots, and with no spots. He has begun to understand the blessing is following him wherever he is and whatever he does. He is having an understanding that angels are there, with him, ministering to him and helping him and his family. He doesn't seem so alarmed by it any more. But he does still acknowledge it and that it is God's place.

***He has begun to understand the blessing is following him wherever he is and whatever he does.***

# It's All In Your Perspective

**Day 49**

You see, in the place where you know who you belong to, you know you are not alone. You are in a place of double camp. It is not you alone, God is with you. A new perspective.

Then you come to realize that angels are also ascending and descending, and there is an army that has formed around you. He has become more aware of the spiritual realm and its interactions. He is also aware in the natural that his brother is on his way to meet him after the great divide between them. Now Jacob begins to rehearse some things to his heavenly father. It appears he has been pondering some truths.

*Then Jacob said, "O God of my father Abraham and God of my father Isaac, the LORD who said to me, 'Return to your country and to your family, and I will deal well with you' I am not worthy of the least of all the mercies and of all the truth which You have shown Your servant; for I crossed over this Jordan with my staff, and now I have become two companies. Deliver me, I pray, from the hand of my brother, from the hand of Esau; for I fear him, lest he come and attack me and the mother with the children. For You said, 'I will surely treat you well, and make your descendants as the sand of the sea, which cannot be numbered for multitude." (Genesis 32:9-12)*

You almost have to laugh at this. Now in his time of trouble, he is experiencing fear. And suddenly he is desperate for God to remember the promise. But, God always did. Jacob is the one with the intermittent perspective. God is always seeing all the relevant data in your meaningful relationship with Him. What God has provided for you, though not seen with the human eye yet, doesn't mean it isn't manifesting in the spiritual realm.

God is always aware of the whole picture. Though you may be in the middle of your desert, your dark night of the soul, your eyes can be opened to the reality of what is reality to God.

*It is not you alone, God is with you. A new perspective.*

## It's All In Your Perspective

**Day 50**

The focus, the right perspective needs to be on WHO HE IS, AND WHAT HE HAS DONE FOR US. We can have an understanding of His commitment if we stay in His word. It has nothing to do with what we deserve.

Are you dealing with some doubt? Fear? Discouragement? Well, those may be the reality you are living in today, but it doesn't have to stay that way. You just need to change your perspective.

*"Blessed be the God and Father of our Lord Jesus Christ, who has blessed us with every spiritual blessing in the heavenly places in Christ, just as He chose us in Him before the foundation of the world, that we should be holy and without blame before Him in love, having predestined us to adoption as sons by Jesus Christ to Himself, according to the good pleasure of His will, to the praise of the glory of His grace, by which He has made us accepted in the Beloved." (Ephesians 1:3-6)*

Do you see anything in there about being accepted because of what we think, or how perfectly we behave?

No, it just talks about the blessing.

The irrevocable blessing that is following us in the same way it followed Jacob. He was a part of the lineage of the Lord Jesus Christ. So are you!

He had the blessing invoked on him, and so do we. We may be in process. But that does not affect God. It only affects us.

When we finally become aware that there is something keeping us from experiencing the fullness of the blessing, we can fight for all that is our own.

*The focus, the right perspective needs to be on:*
*WHO HE IS, AND WHAT HE HAS DONE FOR US.*

# It's All In Your Perspective

## Day 51

*"And he arose that night and took his two wives, his two female servants, and his eleven sons, and crossed over the ford of Jabbok. He took them, sent them over the brook, and sent over what he had. Then Jacob was left alone; and a Man wrestled with him until the breaking of day." (Genesis 32:22-24 )*

Jacob has his family where they need to be. And now he is alone again. But as we have discovered, he is never really alone. This sounds like a very strange story. Jacob seems to be in a wrestling match all night. It's strange unless it has happened to you. You're familiar with the nights where sleep doesn't come because you are wrestling in your own mind about something. You are trying to figure something out. You are trying to talk God into doing something for you. You are accusing Him of not doing something for you. You are asking forgiveness. Then you are angry. Then you are tired, but sleep won't come. Then you begin to remind God of what He has said. You begin to rehearse the things you know He has promised for you. And, all the while, God is there. He is fighting too. He is fighting for you to realize who you are and who He is.

*"Now when He saw that He did not prevail against him, He touched the socket of his hip; and the socket of Jacob's hip was out of joint as He wrestled with him." (Genesis 32:25)*

This means that he touched the soft part of him. God is determined to touch your soft spots. As He touched Jacob's, it could not stay in the same place it had been before, it had to move into a different position. Has God ever touched you and changed some soft spots in your life? Has He ever changed your position on something? Has He ever moved you? Never forget those times; they are landmarks in who you are becoming as a true, honored child of God.

Maybe there is a wrestling match awaiting you tonight? Are you willing to wrestle through in prayer for something? Are you willing to lose some sleep to gain God's touch?

**He is fighting for you to realize who you are and who He is.**

## It's All In Your Perspective

### Day 52

Jacob suddenly became aware of something. This was no ordinary wrestling match. This was a place he couldn't afford to let go of until he had what he knew was available and he would not let go. "And He said, 'Let Me go, for the day breaks.' But he said, 'I will not let You go unless You bless me!'" *(Genesis 32:26)*

AH-HA… Jacob knew something now. All through the night he must have wrestled with other thoughts in his mind. But when God touched him in his soft place, when things were put out of place, but really in order, he was looking for the blessing. He knew it was available and he knew it was accessible.

"So He said to him, 'What is your name?' And he said, 'Jacob.'" *(Genesis 32:27)* Jacob means supplanter. That means to take the place of another. He had become the firstborn before by being a heel catcher. But he had been through a process. He had experiences with God that had changed his focus and his perspective. "And He said, 'Your name shall no longer be called Jacob, but Israel; for you have struggled with God and with men, and have prevailed.'" *(Genesis 32:28)*

His name would be changed to match his new character. Israel, which here means, "He will rule as God." Because, as He is in this world, so was HE.

"Then Jacob asked, saying, 'Tell me Your name, I pray.'" (To which a question is asked of him). "And He said, 'Why is it that you ask about My name?'" *(Genesis 32:29)*

Why would he ask him that? Because he KNEW who he was. He was already familiar with Him. He was the blesser. And He blessed him there. I think you know Him too, we all do. We may have had different experiences and different names for Him, but deep down we know who He is … He is God Almighty, our heavenly Father, the One who loves us and blesses us!

*He was looking for the blessing.*
*He knew it was available and he knew it was accessible.*

# It's All In Your Perspective

## Day 53

*"And Jacob called the name of the place Peniel: 'For I have seen God face to face, and my life is preserved.'" (Genesis 32:30)*

"Peniel" means face of God. He did recognize him. I don't know what your perspective is right now (the state of one's ideas, the facts known to one, in having a meaningful interrelationship).

I don't know if your meaningful relationship with God is one-sided or two. I don't know if you really recognize that God is always with you. That He has angels assigned to you to bring about a heavenly perspective and a heavenly blessing. I don't know if at the time you are seeing clearly: If you have a pure mental view as you ought. Paul prayed for those in Ephesus because he knew they needed to change their perspective.

*"...That the God of our Lord Jesus Christ, the Father of glory, may give to you the spirit of wisdom and revelation in the knowledge of Him, the eyes of your understanding being enlightened; that you may know what is the hope of His calling, what are the riches of the glory of His inheritance in the saints..." (Ephesians 1:17-18)*

God is trying to touch you today ... to bring you to the place where the dross is burned off and you melt into the understanding of what the blessing means for you today.

He wants to touch your soft spots. The places where you have wrestled with your own emotions, and in your own strength you have tried your best to figure things out, to no avail. He wants to bring you to a place where you have the perspective that He has.

You are blessed.
Not because you feel it.
Not because you see it yet.
Not because you earned it.
Not because you deserve it.
Just because you are His children.

*He wants to bring you to a place where you have the perspective that He has.*

# It's All In Your Perspective

## Day 54

"The Spirit Himself bears witness with our spirit that we are children of God, and if children, then heirs--heirs of God and joint heirs with Christ..." (Romans 8:16)

You are a part of the inheritance of Jacob (not the supplanter but the one who is like God). He had a promise that came down from generation to generation.

"For when God made a promise to Abraham, because He could swear by no one greater, He swore by Himself, 14 saying, 'Surely blessing I will bless you, and multiplying I will multiply you.'" (Hebrews 6:13)

And so do we!

"... that the blessing of Abraham might come upon the Gentiles in Christ Jesus, that we might receive the promise of the Spirit through faith." (Galatians 3:14)

There was a young woman at a meeting yesterday. I saw her crying. Being a Pastor, I just had to make my way to her to see if I could help in some way. One of the ladies I had met that I felt was a divine connection was already with her, and to my surprise, she told me that those were not tears of sadness or need, but instead tears that came from the realization of a blessing. A 9-million dollar blessing! It obviously was not expected. Not by her.

But it was expected by God. He was just waiting for her perspective to line up with His. As He is with you today.

Today is the day the wrestling can be over. When you can quit asking His name, and realize that when you came to know Him face to face, the blessing was already yours.

And it will remain in effect. On the God side of things. When you realize He was there all the time, you can ask for the blessing, and realize the blessing.

*Realize that when you came to know Him face to face, the blessing was already yours.*

# It's All In Your Perspective

## Day 55

*"Then let us arise and go up to Bethel; and I will make an altar there to God, who answered me in the day of my distress and has been with me in the way which I have gone." (Genesis 35:3)*

(Just like He promised the very first time they interacted.)

*"Behold, I am with you and will keep you wherever you go, and will bring you back to this land; for I will not leave you until I have done what I have spoken to you." (Genesis 28:15)*

He will not leave you until He has done what He has spoken to you. Today let us make this prayer declaration:

In this place today, the place where we struggle, we set our hearts and our minds toward you God.

In these areas, I bring it to You and I give it to You and I set my mind on You. I receive Your perspective and I ask You to manifest Yourself to me today, to manifest Your glory to my heart today.

I want to love You in the areas of fear. Help my heart today. Interact with me so that my mind conforms and melts before You.

I want to be assured of Your plan. Confident in Your plan for me. And now before the throne of God … We have access to His heart …

Now is the time to put your head down in the desert place. In the cold place where you feel alone, and ask God to make you aware of what He has already put in place for you.

Ask Him to open your eyes to the things that He sees, that you have not yet seen, but are in place for your victory.

And change your begging into expecting His blessing.

You know Him. He's been there all along.

---

**Ask Him to open your eyes to the things that He sees, that you have not yet seen, but are in place for your victory.**

# Sowing Seed; Taking Ground

## Day 56

*Do not be deceived, God is not mocked; for whatever a man sows, that he will also reap. For he who sows to his flesh will of the flesh reap corruption, but he who sows to the Spirit will of the Spirit reap everlasting life. And let us not grow weary while doing good, for in due season we shall reap if we do not lose heart. Galatians 6:7-9*

Compelled to let go of the old by the words God has given us in this season, we move into a new dimension we never had before.

*Look upon Zion, the city of our appointed feasts; Your eyes will see Jerusalem, a quiet home, A tabernacle that will not be taken down; Not one of its stakes will ever be removed, Nor will any of its cords be broken. Isaiah 33:20*

We stake our claim firmly fixed!

As we sow our seeds, we declare with our stakes in the ground, we have released the power of the Kingdom of God and it will not be removed; our cords are going to be lengthened and we will experience the supernatural presence and power of this overflowing river, the river of life, the river that the enemy cannot enter into, the river of protection and provision.

This year, our family, our church, and we as individuals are going to enter into this season – that we will see what we've never seen before.

*<u>Declare</u>: Today as I sow my seed, Father, I declare Thy Kingdom come and Thy will be done. I yield myself to You that You will mature me; that You will cause me to grow spiritually, mentally and emotionally and in every arena of my life; that I may grow up in the stature of Christ; that I may operate in the Love of God; that I may obtain those things you've ordained for my life. That the world will see the difference that Christ has made in me by the life I live. I walk by faith and I believe for the impossible to be reality to me, for my family, for my church family and for the world, with great expectation. In Jesus' Name, AMEN!*

**That the world will see the difference that Christ has made in me by the life I live.**

# Unity Brings the Blessing

## Day 57

God is doing something in our midst and in the earth right now and we must be in a place where we allow God to work in our lives. We can produce in our lives those things that are necessary for us to be able to grow into that position where we can gather wealth. We can be the vehicles that God would use, by giving us ideas, concepts and strategies that will produce that which we have been promised. Remember, you can't give what you don't have, but you can allow God to mature you to the point that you are able to receive the secrets from God that will bring change to your situation, answers for others' problems, and be blessed with heaven's best.

*It is possible. How? till we all come to the unity of the faith and of the knowledge of the Son of God, to a perfect man, to the measure of the stature of the fullness of Christ; that we should no longer be children, tossed to and fro and carried about with every wind of doctrine, by the trickery of men, in the cunning craftiness of deceitful plotting, but, speaking the truth in love, may grow up in all things into Him who is the head—Christ— from whom the whole body, joined and knit together by what every joint supplies, according to the effective working by which every part does its share, causes growth of the body for the edifying of itself in love. Ephesians 4: 13-16*

How is it going to edify itself? In LOVE. He wants to bring us to a place of maturity. How? By coming together in UNITY. In unity (Psalm 133) God commands His blessings upon us forevermore, not just once in a while, but in every area of our lives. When we dare to come together in unity we allow God to mature us.

*Pray: Lord, I allow you to help me to grow up and become one with the body of Christ. As You do this, I pray you release the power of Your Kingdom so that I can hear the SOUND, SEE what I've never seen before, and HEAR what I've never heard before and make me mature enough to gather in the things that only You have told me to gather in.*

I want you to know that you can only receive from God what you allow yourself to mature into. The more you mature and grow in Him, the more you can receive from His Kingdom!

**Receive the secrets from God that will bring change to your situation, answers for others' problems, and be blessed with heaven's best.**

# STAKE YOUR CLAIM!

## Day 58

We are in a unique time where we have begun to experience God's presence in a way we have not known it. His Glory is becoming more real as we call out to Him. We love Him and that is what He is looking for. However, with all we are enjoying in God's presence we must also know that His presence is not just for when we are in church. We are the ones He is wanting to bless. We are the ones that He is wanting to shine through to bring heaven to earth. We must realize our role and what God's responsibility is and what ours is.

God has a system and satan has a system.

Satan needs sin to keep his system going. God just needs someone to agree with Him and display His realities to the earth.

We have not seen all that we know God has provided for us and we must know why so we can begin to rectify that which is holding us back from the fullness of the blessing.

We need to not only be doing something; we need to be doing something that has enough power to defeat the enemy every time. That brings strength. and favor to us. That causes the enemy to tremble and heaven to move into action on our behalf.

Would you like to know what that is?

*Let the words of my mouth and the meditation of my heart be acceptable in Your sight, O LORD, my strength and my Redeemer. Psalms 19:14*

Yes, the difference to receiving all that you are longing to receive and receiving it lies within your perspective.

*We are the ones that He is wanting to shine through to bring heaven to earth.*

# STAKE YOUR CLAIM!

## Day 59

*Let the words of my mouth and the meditation of my heart be acceptable in Your sight, O LORD, my strength and my Redeemer. Psalms 19:14*

Yes, the difference to all that you are longing to receive and receiving it lies within you. God has provided all we need. He has given us His Son. Washed away our sins by His sinless life. Given us the Holy Spirit to quicken our bodies, bring everything we need to remembrance and filled us with His power.

He has given us great and precious promises pertaining to every area of our life.

Our mind:

*For God hath not given us the spirit of fear; but of power, and of love, and of a sound (disciplined, self-controlled) mind. 2 Timothy 1:7 KJV*

Our bodies:

*But he was wounded for our transgressions, he was bruised for our iniquities: the chastisement of our peace was upon him; and with his stripes we are healed. Isaiah 53:5 KJV*

Our life:

*We have everything we need to live a life that pleases God. It was all given to us by God's own power, when we learned that he had invited us to share in his wonderful goodness. God made great and marvelous promises, so that his nature would become part of us. Then we could escape our evil desires and the corrupt influences of this world. 2 Peter 1:3-4 CEV*

Do you know that is the truth? It is the word!

Have you thought on those things continually?

Are your words in agreement with it?

**God has provided all we need. He has given us His Son.**

# Stake Your Claim!

## Day 60

We realize that Zion and Jerusalem in the Old Testament represents us, the church, in the New Testament. Knowing that, let us look and hear with ears that can help us to understand what the Spirit is saying to us in Isaiah.

This applies to us, right here, right now.

*Instead, you will see Zion (God's church) as a place of holy festivals (celebrations and offerings.) You will see Jerusalem (us), a city quiet and secure. It will be like a tent (a habitation) whose ropes are taut and whose stakes are firmly fixed.*
Isaiah 33:20-21 NLT

This is a tabernacle that cannot be taken down. Where is the tabernacle of God now? Inside of us.

And this verse is a promise to us that our stakes are not going to be removed! This year is like no other year. We are coming to understand who we are and whose we are. This is a year we are going to agree with God and confess with our mouth what belongs to us. This year we are driving our stakes down! We are announcing our rights.

We must stake our claim on what we are believing God for - this is a year of supernatural happenings. This year we're not going to back off; we're not going to move over; we are going to stake our claim!

And in this year He's said our stake will not be removed.

Declare:

He has secured me in this earth, in this place. It is time for me to take action that agrees with Him!

*He has secured me in this earth, in this place.*
*It is time for me to take action that agrees with Him!*

## Stake Your Claim!

### Day 61

The LORD will be our Mighty One. He will be like a wide river of protection that no enemy can cross, that no enemy ship can sail upon.

It doesn't matter what the enemy tries to do. He can't get into the river with us. He can't come into the stream of the God. He can't maneuver among us. Because we are not alone!

*For the LORD is our judge, our lawgiver, and our king. He will care for us and save us. The enemies' sails hang loose on broken masts with useless tackle. Their treasure will be divided by the people of God. Even the lame will take their share!*
Isaiah 33:22-23 (New Living Translation)

Do you get it? The enemy has been after us. But he isn't secure, and all that he has tried to build up against us, won't work. All the things he has stolen from us are being returned.

And even if we have been injured, even if we have been paralyzed, God has recovered all for us and we ALL, all of us, every single one of us, whether we have stayed strong or limped along, we are carrying off the plunder!

*The people of Israel will no longer say,*

*"We are sick and helpless,"*

*for the LORD will forgive their sins.*

Isaiah 33:24 (New Living Translation)

We are in the midst of miracles; we are forgiven in this river of God. Get this in your spirits! What you are willing to believe God for is not going to be removed!

---

***We are in the midst of miracles; we are forgiven in this river of God.***

# Stake Your Claim!

## Day 62

What you're believing for is not going to be held back; this is a year of miracles. I want you to begin to move into that place where you are thinking supernatural thoughts; not thinking in normal, natural things but in the supernatural, because this year the supernatural has been released upon you, upon me and all who will call upon the Name of the Lord.

We are being compelled to let go of the old by the words God has given us in this season, and we are able to move into a new dimension like we've never had before.

We have everything we need to do so.

We need to understand that God has already established the authority necessary. It was set by himself. He has chosen to delegate it to us, and it is time to live our life operating in a higher authority than satan's system.

In fact the authority we have been given to operate in supersedes:

*The system of the world*

*Our governmental system*

*The white house.*

*The earth's supreme court because it is ruled by a heavenly supreme court*

*It's the authority that comes from God and we, the church of the living God, represents.*

You see, God has big plans for you. He has big plans for the body of Christ. The body has been living beneath its potential.

Jesus didn't come to repair a broken system.

He came to replace it.

*It is time to live our life operating in a higher authority.*

# Stake Your Claim!

## Day 63

I had to go home one night and pray and the Lord kept telling me: * Renew * Restore * Revival *

That got my spirit going.

Then He dropped this scripture in my spirit:

"The just shall live by faith."

*Behold, his soul which is lifted up is not upright in him: but the just shall live by his faith. Habakkuk 2:4 KJV*

So living by faith restores, renews us and gets us in a place of revival. We are longing for revival, and the way to get it to manifest is for us to live a life of faith.

There is a higher authority but that authority is diminished when we stop looking into the mirror of God's Word and forget who we are and who we belong to. But it's not too late; God is the God of second chances. But God said we are going to have exponential potential.

Exponential: *expressible or approximately expressible by an exponential function especially characterized by or being an extremely rapid increase (as in size or extent)*

### Declare:

*God has given me this promise... That through Him I may have...*

*Everything that pertains to our life.*

*Everything that helps us to show that our God is the one and only true God to affect others with truth.*

*Everything we can find a promise on in the word of God.*

*Everything we already have on the inside of us that we have allowed to lie dormant.*

---

**We are longing for revival, and the way to get it to manifest is for us to live a life of faith.**

## Stake Your Claim!

### Day 64

If you don't know who you are, you live in fear, and fear is the open door that allows satan to mess with you and your goods and your inheritance.

*An hypocrite with his mouth destroyeth his neighbour: but through knowledge shall the just be delivered. Proverbs 11:9 KJV*

We just need to know what we know. You have to decide what the will of God is and then act according to the will of God. This is not the unknown, this is the known because we have the word of God. What is God's word on your healing?

*But He was wounded for our transgressions, He was bruised for our guilt and iniquities; the chastisement [needful to obtain] peace and well-being for us was upon Him, and with the stripes [that wounded] Him we are healed and made whole. Isaiah 53:5 AMP*

By His stripes you are what? Healed! What is His will on you prospering? *Let them shout for joy, and be glad, that favour my righteous cause: yea, let them say continually, Let the LORD be magnified, which hath pleasure in the prosperity of his servant. Psalms 35:27 KJV*

What's His will on you being blessed in everything? *"Now it shall come to pass, if you diligently obey the voice of the LORD your God, to observe carefully all His commandments which I command you today, that the LORD your God will set you high above all nations of the earth. And all these blessings shall come upon you and overtake you, because you obey the voice of the LORD your God: Deuteronomy 28:1-2*

You have to put the word of God in you in order for you to have that be the ruling force of your life. Whatever is in a person is that which is produced out of a person.

Let me say it this way. Whatever is the MOST in a person is that which is predominant and it will come out of the person.

A man with sin in him can't produce a system of holiness.

**You have to decide what the will of God is and then act according to the will of God.**

## Stake Your Claim!

**Day 65**

Satan is afraid of sons of God because they bring in holiness and light and holiness is stronger than sin and light is stronger than darkness. His system will fall as the church rises into their own position and begin to live righteously and stand in their position of influence in the earth. As we do what is right, as we proclaim truth, as we invade dark places with His life and His light, satan will lose his ability to hold people in his deception.

If you doubt it can happen, let's see what God did during the 16th Century Breakthrough: In 1559 a general revival broke out in Scotland. The conversions were so rapid that John Knox wrote, 'God did so multiply our number that it appeared as if men had rained from the clouds.' Describing the spiritual hunger of the Scottish people he adds, 'Now forty days and more, hath God used my tongue in my native country, to the manifestation of His glory…The thirst of the poor people, as well as of the nobility here, is wondrous great…' One Scottish church historian writes 'in Scotland the whole nation was converted by lump; and within ten years…there were not ten persons of quality to be found in it who did not profess the true reformed religion, and so it was among the commons in proportion. Lo! Here a nation born in one day!'

You see satan wants us to focus on the fact that we may have, at times, fallen short of bringing the glory of God to the earth, but now is the time to focus on this fact: His glory is overtaking us. He has been yearning for this time, when we will live in an understanding that is higher, where there is an open revelation of what it means that He is the living God.

Heavens reality is coming to earth and God is making us more and more aware of our dominion and what He wanted the sons of God to operate under. As believers our boundaries are unlimited.

The whole earth is groaning right now because the way things have been going, is not the way it was supposed to operate.

*Heaven's reality is coming to earth.*

# My Name

**Day 66**

The following is a prophetic word from the Lord:

This is my promise to you as an individual - I care about you. My name is revealed to you so that you can walk in the fullness of who I am on the earth. For you are My representation - you are those that are called by My name. If you know what My name means, you will know what you are representing to others.

Walk in the knowledge it. Walk in the ability of it. Walk in the anointing of it. For you see, as you pursue Me with passion, as you desire Me above all things, the revelation of the people that you read about — the ones that I have relationship with, the ones that I gave revelation to about who I was — will be yours also.

I love you the same. I'm available to you in the same way. I will give you a revelation revolution that will secure who I am on the inside of you. And you will begin to walk around knowing that the promises I have given all throughout My written word are alive to you right now. They are still secured to you by My name, by the investment that I have placed in My name, by Me honoring you, by bringing you into covenant with My name.

You need to call yourself by My name. Call upon My name and see if I won't show up – with dignity, with power, with ability, with all that you have need of. I am not mad at My people. I am desiring for them. I have not withheld from you. But I have given you all that I am.

Begin to take in the understanding. Begin to acknowledge Me for who I am. And you will see those facets of My personality come into place in your life. You will see the release of the things you've been of asking Me come into view, because I am the God who sees. But I not only see, I am able to meet your need. I am able to answer your cry. I am able to give you revelation that you need right now. As you begin to embrace Me for who I am, embrace all that I say I am, embrace all that My name means, embrace the fact that you are heirs, joint heirs, through My Son, you will be able to be partakers of the significance of My name

*I will give you a revelation revolution that will secure who I am on the inside of you.*

# My Name

Day 67

Even now I'm beginning to pour out healing in your midst. Even now I'm beginning to answer the heart cry of those who have said, 'I want to see healing come from my hands.' Even now I have heard your cries – you have called upon My name. You've called out to Me, the Lord Your God, and I am giving you an anointing to be carriers of the healing power of the cross.

As you call on the name of My Son, Jesus, as you call upon the name of the sacrificial Lamb, as you call upon the name of the One who took the stripes, so that you could be healed, so that they could be healed, you will begin to feel the revelation come into you. You will begin to have the effects of that flow through you, and you will lay hands on the sick and they SHALL recover. That ability was always in My name. And now you are a part of My family, a part of My covenant, a part of that ability. Believe it, walk in it. Look for opportunity. Apply My name – the Name above all names, and see if I won't move heaven and earth to bring forth the glory.

My name will be exalted – now, in this season, in this time, in this generation, in this city, in this land. For I am the Lord God – but I am the Lord your God, I am the Lord their God. So take My name to them. Take the revelation of My name to them. Use My name and you will see that I will back My name. I have always been. I will always be.

Prayer:

Lord, we just thank You for that – we thank You that You have invested enough – it's hard for us to believe that You would even trust us with that name – but You chose to, and therefore, we are partakers of all that it means. We will obey You. We will go into the highways and the byways. We will access what is in that name, and we will utilize it to bring heaven to earth.

We thank You for it!

*My name will be exalted – now, in this season, in this time, in this generation, in this city, in this land.*

# Being Confident

## Day 68

Today we will have to examine something to determine if we may be prey to the enemy. It is not that most people don't want to make a difference in their life to help others, but many are not as successful due to a lack of:

CONFIDENCE: Having strong belief, full assurance, sure of one's abilities, positive, unafraid, convinced

Confidence shows your true belief system. If you don't have confidence in someone, then you really can't trust them wholeheartedly. That affects the kind of relationship you will end up with in that relationship. That is why Satan works so hard at stealing your confidence in God.

I believe we all want to live our lives for Him. But how confident are we in Him? Can you say you always walk in full assurance of all that He is and all that He has promised?

We all know that Satan has set traps for us. He knows when and how we are most vulnerable. He designs challenges, to cause us to doubt the truth of the way God feels about us, and what He has provided for us. And yet, we know that God has made a way for us to live a victorious, secure life in Him. He has made a way for us to be confident, not unsure, not wavering in our belief and not wavering in our lifestyle where we can serve Him with all of our heart. We can be assured of who we are, and that our life counts for something.

We should have now realized that there is a higher place for us to function from. A place where we move past just loving God to being in love with Him. If we are to be confident, then we need to go over the main thing again. The main thing is the main thing. And God told us what the main thing is and was and always will be.

*Jesus said unto him, Thou shalt love the Lord thy God with all thy heart, and with all thy soul, and with all thy mind. This is the first and great commandment. Matthew 22:37-38 KJV*

**We can be assured of who we are, and that our life counts for something.**

# Being Confident

## Day 69

*Jesus said unto him, "Thou shalt love the Lord thy God with all thy heart, and with all thy soul, and with all thy mind. This is the first and great commandment." Matthew 22:37-38 KJV*

Our focus, our priority, our passion in life should be about this; for if we do that, then everything else will line up in our life accordingly. Since God is love, then we must realize that if something is missing in our lives, it isn't from His side. It must be ours. Jesus directly said this to us:

*And Jesus answering saith unto them, "Have faith in God." Mark 11:22 KJV*

This was not a suggestion. But it will take effort and engagement to accomplish.

*And we have known and believed the love that God has for us. God is love, and he who abides in love abides in God, and God in him. 1 John 4:15-16*

We have to be actively participating in our relationship.

Note that it actually says, he who abides "in love".

We have always seen that to mean "he who continues to walk in love", and though that is true and it is part of the correct interpretation, I believe the Holy Spirit is revealing more to us about the different levels of love.

As we learned, there is a difference between loving God and being in love with Him. If we abide "in love with Him", we will be aware of the God in us. If you truly were fully aware of what all that means, then there would be a lot more confidence and you would be able to obey instantly like Peter and John who declared to the lame, what I have, I give to you, rise up and walk.

*We have to be actively participating in our relationship.*

## BEING CONFIDENT

### Day 70

Miracles are just outward expressions of your confidence in God's promises. You must understand, you are not here by accident. Most people know that they are seeking something. But someone who knows they have a purpose adds actions and words that demonstrate they know who they are and where they are going.

God said previously that we are conquerors for heaven starting in 2011. That excited us. That speaks of victory. But it also speaks of conflict. If there is a conqueror, they must have had to conquer something. You'll find no real satisfaction or happiness in life without obstacles to conquer, goals to achieve and a purpose to accomplish.

The great evangelist Billy Sunday said, "More men fail through lack of purpose than lack of talent."

If you are not sure who you are, and who God is within you, you may end up in a frustrated place. A place where you are insecure, and not enjoying a successful life, and continually wondering if life has purpose at all. But God made us with all the ingredients necessary to be effective in this life.[1] However, to press forward and to do that, we must operate in a new place of understanding.

Alone we can do nothing of significance. But we, my friends, are not alone. We must really get a heart revelation that God is our Partner. Because of that we can believe larger, associate higher (with God) and do more than we ever could in our own strength. He simply has made a way for us to do that.

If He is indeed our partner, then our plans need to be big, because we do not serve a small God. If He is our partner, then we know our life has meaning. If He is partnering with us, then there is a reason and a goal that He knows we can reach.

*If He is indeed our partner, then our plans need to be big, because we do not serve a small God.*

# Being Confident

## Day 71

We need to be confident in the fact that we have God's amazing ability residing within us. If you believe that, you will then move into all the things He has set aside for you to do. Our definitions have helped us determine the difference in our spirit that will help make this a reality in our life.

Moving beyond loving Him to being IN LOVE with Him.

LOVE: It means… to have passionate affection for another. A feeling of warm, personal attachment with passion and desire. Beloved, sweetheart. Benevolent affection of God for His people, and the affection due from them to HIM.. To need or require.

You see, when you love someone, it is a truly deep feeling that goes beyond what the world has tried to make love look like. Contrary to what TV, movies, and peer pressure try to tell you, love is not casual passion. It is not liking something a lot.

True love takes relationship to another level. It brings about something that has happened to your heart into a place of action. You want to show the other person how you feel.

It is love for your sweetheart that makes you want to hug and cuddle with them. You have passion for being with them. You want to spend more time with them. You want to know them more intimately. That love takes it to the next level of being:

IN LOVE: This definition goes even deeper! It means...

to be infused with deep affection and passion, enamored with (to fill or inflame with love.) To captivate (to attract and hold the attention or interest of as by beauty or excellence).

When you move past just loving someone into being in love with them, you become totally captivated by them. That means they attract and hold your attention by their beauty or excellence.

That is our God.

*We need to be confident in the fact that we have God's amazing ability residing within us.*

# Being Confident

Day 72

When you are captivated by that kind of love, it causes you to do something for love's sake.

For love: Out of affection or liking, for pleasure: gratuitously. For the sake of (purpose or end, interest, benefit of)

Think of it. For the love of God means that because of the way we appreciate Him, and for the benefit of Him, and for the purposes that He desires, this is where we get our motivation to continue to move forward, not only in pursuing the love relationship we have with Him, but to pursue the very purposes for which we are alive.

We, as a people need security. It is one of the great needs of every individual that has to be fulfilled for us to enjoy our lives.

God made us that way and there is a security we find in the plan He has for us. Since God has an eternal purpose for each life, it is not a surprise that He also takes the initiative to come to the ones He has chosen to represent Him on the earth and reveal His love and unfold the direction for each life to take.

He knows we have to also be productive. Otherwise, the feelings of uselessness overtake us and we forget that we are made in His image and His likeness. We can then, because we have lost sight of truth, do things in our own strength, and we can miss out on all that God has preordained for us to walk in.

We are a part of the Kingdom of God. It is an upside-down kingdom. It is where we lay down our lives instead of living self-centered lives, because there is an understanding of higher things. It is because we have been affected by something that the world cannot offer. The world's system can't operate in it, because it is not comprehended by the world.

It is the system of unselfish love.

*It is where we lay down our lives instead of living self-centered lives, because there is an understanding of higher things.*

# Being Confident

**Day 73**

Let me refer again to Paul. It was the love of God and Christ's love for Paul that caused Paul to lay down his life for the sake of the gospel.

*For the love of Christ controls and urges and impels us, because we are of the opinion and conviction that [if] One died for all, then all died; And He died for all, so that all those who live might live no longer to and for themselves, but to and for Him Who died and was raised again for their sake. 2 Corinthians 5:14-15 AMP*

Our heart swells with appreciation for those who were willing to die to try to save one more life during the attacks on 9/11.

But Paul lived a life of being a first responder. Because he was compelled. Another translation says, "The love of Christ compels me." Paul experienced Christ's love and it made such an impact on his life, that he was willing to release his life to Christ and spend the rest of his life living for Him, and willing to die to self for others to live. Such personal love God had shown toward him, causing him to live his life in love with his Lord.

Paul realized the great love that took because he had been made aware of his mistaken identity. He had lived his life according to the identity of who he thought he was and with intentions of doing whatever was necessary to make things right. He had a revelation, but it was not altogether pure. He had a revelation that all must serve God. A revelation that anything else was unacceptable. Paul thought he was helping society and obeying God by killing Christians to rid the world of the enemy.

He failed to see that operating outside of love, you become the enemy of God's real purposes. But when he had a face-to-face encounter with God, he not only changed his life, but his life, revealed by his actions, demonstrated that the love he found in that encounter caused him to understand the reality of true purpose. He recognized he was chosen by God, on purpose, for purpose.

*Such personal love God had shown toward him, causing him to live his life in love with his Lord.*

# Being Confident

**Day 74**

When Paul saw what he had done to destroy lives "in the name of God", he realized that he was the chief of sinners. So he was aware of how badly he had behaved, and yet in the midst of it, God made Himself and His love real to him.

The word tells us that to whom little is forgiven, the same loves little. Then to whom much is forgiven, the same loves much!

You see, once the truth of God's unconditional love is a reality in someone's life, their life should never be the same. You should never encounter life, or people or circumstances without confidence in the God who loves you, who has chosen you, and who is working in your life now with purpose.

You are a special person. You are not an accident. You were not created to just wander through life without any direction or focus or reality of your worth. You have been made to be somebody important and a part of a wonderful family.

*Just as He chose us in Him before the foundation of the world, that we should be holy and without blame before Him in love, having predestined us to adoption as sons by Jesus Christ to Himself, according to the good pleasure of His will, to the praise of the glory of His grace, by which He made us accepted in the Beloved. Ephesians 1:4-6*

You belong to Him. You are just as much His sons and daughters as Jesus is. When God looks at you, He sees His blood, He sees His son looking back, for He has made us to be like Him.

Some have come to a higher reality of this. They are the ones that have fearless testimonies. They are the ones that are impacting others' lives simply by being who God made them to be - without apology. They are the witnesses.

*You have been made to be somebody important and a part of a wonderful family.*

# Being Confident

## Day 75

When you have experienced a love that has caused you to be more in love, captivated by the very essence of God's presence, you have confidence in God. Then Satan cannot torment you with fear for you are keeping your eyes on the things that will last throughout eternity. History is full of just this kind of testimony. You see, the greater the awareness and experience of God's love, the deeper the motivation and determination to serve the Lord, no matter what. Then you can walk in full awareness and confidence of your call. For we are all called to do something that will impact lives.

Confidence will come alive in you when you can recognize that He didn't just choose Paul and Abraham and Billy Graham.

He chose YOU! I love knowing that, don't you? We are not to live an aimless life with nothing really accomplished. I cannot tell you how many times I have prayed with a heart of gratefulness acknowledging the fact, that with all my flaws, and all the mistakes I have made and in spite of all the contributing factors that would say the opposite, God CHOSE ME to love Him. God CHOSE me to love others with HIM.

Oh I am so grateful. I am so happy with that knowledge. I know then, that though I may play a small part in God's eternal plan for the world, I have a part!

And so do you!! I know I cannot do it alone, I am not supposed to. You are not supposed to. Perhaps that is why this scripture is so very important to each of us.

*For He Himself has said, "I will never leave you nor forsake you." So we may boldly say:*

*"The LORD is my helper; I will not fear. What can man do to me?"*

Hebrews 13:5-6

---

***You see, the greater the awareness and experience of God's love, the deeper the motivation and determination to serve the Lord, no matter what.***

# Being Confident

## Day 76

When you are confident in the trust of His word, then you realize He is ALWAYS with you. He isn't going anywhere and leaving you behind.

When you were little, did you ever get separated from your parent?

I remember one time when I was little we were shopping. We were out on a busy sidewalk and I was following behind my mother, I was intent on following her shoes through the crowd. I followed as close as I could, but then I looked up and though those shoes looked like my mothers, the person I was following was not my mother.

I was so afraid I began to cry. My mother was not far, and she heard my cry and came and rescued me from fear.

The word promises us this as well.

*"and there is a friend that sticketh closer than a brother."*
Proverbs 18:24 KJV

Then I guess we could also safely say, He sticks closer than a mother. The point is, that since God will never leave us or forsake us, so we can have confidence that we are not left in this life, alone, ever. He has chosen us, He has committed Himself to us, and He has become our Father and our friend.

It is this knowledge that gives us the WANT to display AND SHARE His love to others. It is this relationship with our heavenly Father that causes us to do whatever it takes to live a life that makes a difference. We can be guided by Him, and our life can be more than a "dash" on a tombstone when we die.

*It is this relationship with our heavenly Father that causes us to do whatever it takes to live a life that makes a difference.*

# BEING CONFIDENT

Day 77

If we have experienced His unconditional love, then we must also understand that we are a vital link between Him and this troubled, lost world outside. We love Him because He first loved us. But now has He become the center of our life? You must realize nothing else can ever take His place in our life. When you acknowledge Him, your value system changes.

The world's value system is:

"What can we do for ourselves? What can we get for ourselves? What can we accomplish that will give us fame and fortune?"

The most popular things on TV now are competitions where the prize is fame and fortune and an "opportunity for you to pursue what makes you happy". But at the end of that road, if God isn't on it, they will still find it leaves them empty.

But when we have received God's expression of love to us through Jesus and we continue in our pursuit of Him, we will soon discover that our values have changed as our faith level has changed because it has responded to love.

*For in Christ Jesus neither circumcision nor uncircumcision has any value. The only thing that counts is faith expressing itself through love.*
Galatians 5:6 NIV

Faith here means: persuasion, i.e. credence; moral conviction (of religious truth, or the truthfulness of God or a religious teacher), especially reliance upon Christ for salvation;

*KJV - assurance, belief, believe, faith, fidelity.*

So confidence is vitally important. What we believe must be backed by WHO we believe. It's the only thing that counts.

Our faith will come alive and be active if we truly can trust God with every aspect of our lives.

*What we believe must be backed by WHO we believe.*

# Being Confident

## Day 78

Do you know the secret to making your faith count?

Our faith according to this scripture has an active ingredient: It works by, and is effective when it, the secret ingredient, is activated. What does it work by? Love!

If He is the reason we exist and we can't breathe without knowing Him more each day, we are not just loving Him, we are in love with Him. That very relationship causes our ears to open to what He is saying. It causes us to be aware of the things that are important to Him. It makes His priorities our priorities, and that compels us to love others and tell them about the experiences He wants to have with them.

When you are confident in Him, you have gone past the relationship we used to have with Him. So now, let's move a little further in the realization of our purpose. Are you ready?

*Love has been perfected among us in this: that we may have boldness in the day of judgment; because as He is, so are we in this world. 1 John 4:17*

If we know Jesus then love is made perfect among us and it has given us something we never knew we could have. Boldness. And that love has made us something else... It has made us like Him.

Did you get it?

As He is – so are we in this world.

This is the answer to Jesus' prayer.

*As You sent Me into the world, I also have sent them into the world. John 17:18*

**It makes His priorities our priorities**

# Being Confident

Day 79

*As You sent Me into the world, I also have sent them into the world... And the glory which You gave Me I have given them, that they may be one just as We are one: I in them, and You in Me; that they may be made perfect in one, and that the world may know that You have sent Me, and have loved them as You have loved Me. John 17:18,21-23*

That the world will know. That as it is in heaven, so it will be here. Glory revealed, through you, through me.

You see, God didn't just raise Jesus from the dead, He raised us from our dead, dormant, ineffective, useless lives. We are indeed sitting in heavenly places WITH Him; we keep an eternal perspective. Our lives look very different when we see them from God's perspective.

If we look at our lives through our circumstances, we will have a distorted view.

*But God, who is rich in mercy, because of His great love with which He loved us Ephesians 2:4*

There is that love thing again.

*even when we were dead in trespasses, made us alive together with Christ (by grace you have been saved), Ephesians 2:5*

He saw us alive before we were. He saw us saved before we were. He saw the effect of grace on our lives. And He provided a beautiful future for us together as sons and daughters. He made a place for us.

**He provided a beautiful future for us together as sons and daughters.**

# Being Confident

**Day 80**

*Not of works, lest anyone should boast. Ephesians 2:9*

No pride allowed. It won't get put down beside our name, but beside the name of Jesus, signed in blood. All of the confidence we need to have in Him to complete the call of God on our everyday lives is available to us. For purpose.

We were made by him. WE are LIKE Him.
As He is in this world, so are we!

*For we are His workmanship, created in Christ Jesus for good works, which God prepared beforehand that we should walk in them. Ephesians 2:10*

So what is He in this world?

*...and what is the exceeding greatness of His power toward us who believe, according to the working of His mighty power Ephesians 1:19*

He is the mighty power that is working in this world.

*...which He worked in Christ when He raised Him from the dead and seated Him at His right hand in the heavenly places, far above all principality and power and might and dominion, and every name that is named, not only in this age but also in that which is to come. Ephesians 1:20-21*

He is the one that is raised up,

He is the one that is above:

Every other principality.

Every other might.

Every other dominion.

Every other name.

Right now, here, and in that which is to come.

And as He is in this world, so are we.

We are the fullness of Him. !

**We were made by him. WE are LIKE Him.**

# Being Confident

Day 81

*To the intent that now unto the principalities and powers in heavenly places might be known by the church the manifold wisdom of God, We have his wisdom, we have his power, we are his extension, his representation. We are in the process of changing the mindsets of the church into kingdom. Kingdom people understand the bigger picture, they are living for eternal purposes. According to the eternal purpose which he purposed in Christ Jesus our Lord: In whom we have boldness and access with confidence by the faith of him. Ephesians 3:10 KJV*

The eternal purpose of God was that we would have so much confidence in who He is, that we operate in boldness, and we realize the access to all the powers of heaven to work on our behalf and for the benefit of others whose lives will be touched and changed by our faith in Him.

We must have a higher IDENTIFICATION AND AWARENESS of who we are and what we can do. THERE IS A HIGHER PLACE OF GLORY AND POWER He wants to show forth to the world, and He has chosen us for that purpose. WHAT WE MUST BE AWARE OF is that WE ARE STRONGER THAN Satan. GOD CHOSE us and made us POWERFUL (not by natural wisdom, but by simple gospel mixed with our own personality mixed with His power).

Today, we need to appreciate this greatness He has given us. We need to go past where we have been in our understanding into where we can be. With Him, there are still many things to experience that will be the best things that ever happened to you.

There are so many wonderful things He has for you to do with Him.

*GOD CHOSE us and made us POWERFUL.*

# Being Confident

## Day 82

How exciting. How else would we like to live our lives?

And there is more good news. We can have confidence in something even further.

*being confident of this very thing, that He who has begun a good work in you will complete it until the day of Jesus Christ; Philippians 1:6*

We can be confident that there will be nothing lacking on God's part in performing the work He has started in you when you gave your heart to the Lord Jesus. It will continue as long as you continue to be in love with Him.

Today we need to acknowledge His power. Not only what He works for us, but what He works IN us and through us. We don't lack the power to be happy, fulfilled, successful conquerors.

We need to repent of our lack of faith and lack of confidence and we need to assume our proper place of spiritual authority again.

With the understanding that our purposes for which we are designed to be like Him will be fulfilled, as we stand CONFIDENTLY...

- Having strong belief in Him
- Full assurance of His love
- Sure of His abilities and OUR abilities
- Positive
- Unafraid
- Convinced

*We don't lack the power to be happy, fulfilled, successful conquerors.*

## Being Confident

### Day 83

*For I am persuaded beyond doubt (am sure) that neither death nor life, nor angels nor principalities, nor things impending and threatening nor things to come, nor powers, Nor height nor depth, nor anything else in all creation will be able to separate us from the love of God which is in Christ Jesus our Lord. Romans 8:38-40 (AMP)*

We may not know if tomorrow we will live or die, but we can be confident in this. No matter what the enemy has planned, if we live our life in love with him, there is no threat in death. For even in that, we win. We will always have Gods love, in the here and now to make a difference. And we will still have His love when we pass from this life. It truly is the great win, win situation.

Friends, God is the same yesterday, today and forever.

God is the same in our lives today as He was yesterday in the lives of the prophets; God is real. God is in our midst; God wants to perform great and mighty things in your lives. So let's bring Him into the NOW and begin to live by faith. Faith is that foundation stone by which we come to God and we live by it and we believe it and operate in that dimension that separates us from the world's system.

*But without faith it is impossible to please Him, for he who comes to God must believe that He is, and that He is a rewarder of those who diligently seek Him. Hebrews 11:6*

From this we see that without faith you cannot please God; you're not going to make God happy or satisfied if you're not living by faith. He's created you to be a vehicle of faith. It also says he that comes to God must believe that He is.

You've got to have faith and believe that God is truly in existence today. God is not some abstract thing; God is real, He's alive, He's in our world today! You have to believe that He is and that He truly exists and that He is a rewarder to them that diligently seek Him.

### *He's created you to be a vehicle of faith.*

# Being Confident

## Day 84

Today we must realize that not only is God in existence but because He's in existence He will bless you. God does not exist to bless you or me but because God is real and He's here today and He is just altogether love, blessing will be a part of your life.

He's our heavenly father and He does not want to withhold any good thing from us. Your confidence in Him will increase your faith and your faith will bring rewards into your life

There may be an emergency today. If you don't know God, it is an emergency — for there are no guarantees how long you will live here on this earth. If you don't really love God with all your heart, it is an emergency, for your life is aimless. If you are not living your life with God's purpose, it is an emergency, because you are wasting precious time.

God is looking for some first responders today. The ones who are willing to lay down their lives for another, who will realize the need to acknowledge the truth of God's word by living for Him.

Will you respond with confidence that God's word is true?

*But whoever keeps His word, truly the love of God is perfected in him. By this we know that we are in Him. He who says he abides in Him ought himself also to walk just as He walked. 1 John 2:5-6*

Will you live for Him?

Will you lay down your doubts and fears and embrace the confidence He has made available to you today?

---

*If you are not living your life with God's purpose, it is an emergency, because you are wasting precious time.*

# Arise and Build!

**Day 85**

"Arise and Build" is a prophetic word that God gave me for this time, this season, and this generation:

Here is what the Spirit is saying:

It is time for you to quit looking through the eyes of the natural and look into the spiritual realm and survey the damage.

It is time for you to understand that there are walls that have been broken down. It is time for you to under-stand that there are people who are supposed to have the presence of God in their temple, and they no longer have a house where He can dwell.

It is time for you to understand that it's time for you to rise up and build and do something about it. It will not happen without prayer and intercession. But with prayer and intercession and getting the heavenly perspective of what I am able to do, things will begin to shift and things will begin to change and come into alignment with my divine will and there will be nothing that will hold you back from the provision, from the protection and from the divine alignment that I have for you. Because I have positioned you on the earth for such a time as this.

It is time for the Church to come together as an aid for one another. It is time for the Church to survey the damage and to stand in the gap. It is time for you to believe Me for favor. It is time for you to gather the people and make a declaration and call them together until they become as one voice. It is time for a sound to arise.

It is time for you to give Me My proper position back on earth. It will happen and it will occur as you begin to see yourself no longer as someone who just has a job, but someone who has been put in a position to govern this earth.

For there are strategies that I have laid aside for such a time as this. There is power that I have laid aside for such a time as this. There is passion that I have laid aside for such a time as this.

*I have positioned you on the earth for such a time as this.*

# Arise and Build!

## Day 86

I am the God who will provide you with all of the tools necessary in the spiritual realm, as well as that which is in the natural. Do not say that your God is dead. Do not believe the lies of the enemy. Do not let the Church anymore look like an abomination. Do not allow those that are called by My name to walk around in disarray and to have poverty thinking. Do not allow those that have walls broken down and have a broken heart to remain that way.

For I have given you the power that is instilled in your very being to arise and to take charge and to govern over people and cities and nations. If you will agree with Me and come into the place where you will arise out of the position of thinking you are insignificant, you will cause significance to arise not only within yourself but within all of those that are around you, for I am building a mighty army that will display Me properly on the earth.

For this is the time and this is the season for the Church to look like the blessed people that they are, so that it causes a jealousy to arise of those that do not know Me by name. When they see those things that you have been able to accomplish and when they see those things that you have been able to do when you come together as one, they will surely come and they will bow their knee or they will lose their inheritance.

The blessing is yours. The inheritance is yours. Do not doubt what I am able to do, for My call is on you. It is on My Church. It is time for the Church to be shaken and to arise into a new awareness of their power. It will occur as they are passionate about Me, passionate about what is on My heart. Compassionate for the people who are on their way to eternal fire. For there will be a day of judgment and it is not so far away, lest you think all of this is just for fun and games. There is a place of eternal fire where people will spend eternity. It is time for My Church to arise and to build… to be the conquerors that I have made them to be, but this is the purpose: that you would grab a-hold of the hand of those who have flames licking at their feet even now. And to pull them out of the flames and set them in a right place.

*The blessing is yours. The inheritance is yours.*

# Arise and Build!

Day 87

Because you have displayed My power and My favor because you have won My heart.

I'm looking for those people even now. I'm looking for those who will dare to be different, those who will not care what it looks like to others, or what their title will be. This is your title: son and daughter. This is how you are supposed to function: king and priest. Settle the issue and do that which has been pre-described to you. For I've seen already those things that you are supposed to accomplish. Do not agree with the enemy that says that you are insignificant. For you are significant to Me. You are significant on this earth, and you are significant for the end times. You are significant for eternity.

So lay not aside the things that have true value. But pick up the tools and pick up the gifts and pick up the people and cause them to come into a place again where they recognize who they are in Me so that the world may know that I am still God and that you are still My people and that I am still offering My plan of salvation.

*I'm looking for those who will dare to be different, those who will not care what it looks like to others, or what their title will be.*

# Arise and Build!

## Day 88

If we can examine ourselves today, and focus on things that will matter, really matter, then at the end of our life, whenever and however that happens, we can be satisfied that we accomplished something that was worthwhile. That we have made a difference and that we are leaving marks upon people's hearts and lives with indelible ink that will forever continue.

How many of you feel like you are satisfied that you have accomplished that at this time?

Maybe some are not quite certain of what you should concentrate on to feel that sense of accomplishment in your life. Some may be unsure of your relationship with God. Maybe you feel you have disappointed Him and so you feel a little ashamed to be with Him.

Maybe you feel like you have done your best, and it still isn't good enough, so what is the use?

Maybe you feel like God has made Himself more real to others than He has to you. Maybe you feel like your circumstances in life have so overwhelmed you that you are not able to plug into God or live a Christian life successfully and so you seem to be at a standstill.

Well, I want to help you today by renewing your mind to the truth of what God has already done for you.

We don't lack the power to be happy, fulfilled, successful conquerors. We may live under the threat of an enemy. He may want to steal, kill and destroy us.

But God… But God… But God.

Our God has given us many promises. He has provided everything we need to live a life that will make a difference.

*Our God has given us many promises. He has provided everything we need to live a life that will make a difference.*

# Let's Take a Look from God's Perspective

**Day 89**

Today I want to talk you about the End of the Beginning. God sees everything from His final perspective and then He works backwards and invites us into His plan.

*Declaring the end from the beginning, and from ancient times the things that are not yet done, saying, My counsel shall stand, and I will do all my pleasure. Isaiah 46:10 KJV*

Nothing is a surprise to Him. God was not surprised that man would choose sin and cause a separation from Him. He had already prepared the remedy - the remedy that would be the end to the beginning of that separation.

> God always has a plan.
> A plan for you, a plan for me.
> A divine plan that will stand.
> Your life is not a surprise.
> What your destiny is - is no surprise to Him.
> He loves you.
> He has chosen you.
> He has formed you for greatness.

That may be a surprise to us, but it is not to Him. He has made you in His likeness for a reason. Genesis tells us that God created man in His image and in His likeness. It was a purposeful decision. Why? God wanted man to know His love.

When you have so much love for someone, what do you want to do? You want to express it. You want them to know it. You want to share in that love. God wanted us to be able to interact with Him, our creator, in a personal way.

*Action Step: Today, try and see God's perspective over you. He loved you, He loves you, and He is going to love you in the end. How does this change your actions and thoughts toward God?*

---

**God wanted us to be able to interact with Him, our creator, in a personal way.**

## Let's Take a Look From God's Perspective

### Day 90

Jesus was always Plan A not Plan B

*And all the inhabitants of the earth will fall down in adoration and pay him homage, everyone whose name has not been recorded in the Book of Life of the Lamb that was slain [in sacrifice] from the foundation of the world. Revelation 13:8 AMP*

He was slain when? From the foundation of the world He was fully aware of what man would choose, and fully aware of the cost it would be to redeem them back into full relationship with the Father. However, Jesus was committed. Committed to the point that it pushed Him far past that which anyone should endure. It was not because He deserved it, for He stayed as a pure lamb. One that was sinless. Even those around Him could see the difference in the sacrifice. One of the thieves who hung on the cross next to Him declared, "I deserve what they are doing to me, I have sinned. But you are dying unjustly, you have not sinned, please just remember me when you come into your kingdom."

Jesus died, not having sinned, but taking on our sin because He was compelled by a love that we cannot comprehend.

Those touched by it may not have known how much it affected them at the moment, but they would as the days followed. Suddenly, they would find themselves driven by something new. Something they hadn't been aware of before. They would see with different eyes. They would feel with a depth they had never known before. They would respond against the natural, as they moved according to a love that had touched their lives in a way that cannot be explained in human terms. For eternity had brushed up against them, and they would never be the same.

How has this defining love touched you? This kind of love, the love of Jesus requires transformation. You cannot be touched by it and stay the same. Can you recall how it changed you?

*For eternity had brushed up against them, and they would never be the same.*

# Let's Take a Look From God's Perspective

## Day 91

The scripture tells us that Jesus was always looking for <u>SEEKERS OF TRUTH.</u> They would be the ones that would be able to receive the reality of His unconditional love. One such woman was Mary Magdalene. Jesus cast seven devils out of her according to Mark 16:9. Now, there is a dynamic you won't easily forget. The enemy of Mary's soul had taken residence inside of her. She was driven to do things she wouldn't ordinarily do. She had to be horrified at her own actions, but she was powerless to change. Then … in steps a man. But not an ordinary man. A man on a mission. A man who was moved by her need. What did He see as He looked at her? Jesus didn't look so much at the obvious; He looked at the final product. He was looking at the end result of what was about to occur for her. She was about to experience His unconditional love:

<u>IT WOULD TOUCH HER</u>
<u>IT WOULD FREE HER</u>
<u>IT WOULD LEAVE A DEPOSIT IN HER</u>
<u>IT WOULD CHANGE HER LIFE FOREVER</u>

Changed beyond what she would have imagined. For she would follow Him. She would learn from Him. And she would show up in places where many others had left, for fear of what would happen to them if they continued to follow this man from Galilee.

A once looked-down-on, rejected person who had nothing to offer in the natural, had caught the attention of the disciples who would record the happenings of the cross and the truth that God would unfold. Mary. A very common name. A very insignificant person to so very many. But not insignificant to the Father, who led Jesus to her. Not insignificant to Jesus who responded, not in judgment, but in love and power, to set her free.

<u>SEEK THE TRUTH TODAY. SEEK NOT WHAT YOU THINK ABOUT YOURSELF BUT WHAT JESUS SEES WHEN HE LOOKS AT YOU.</u>

*Jesus didn't look so much at the obvious;*
*He looked at the final product.*

# Embracing God's Love

## Day 92

Do you know the words that define Liberty Life Center?

*<u>Embracing, displaying and sharing God's love.</u>*

It's what drives our church; however, it's not just for our church, it's God's heart so it's really for everyone, especially those who say they are Christian. Over the next series we are going to delve into this declaration and mission. It is my prayer that we will come to a greater understanding of our purpose, destiny, and strategy to fulfill the call on our lives. So let's talk today about embracing His love. Would you like to know God's love even more? Is it your desire to have a vibrant, close relationship with God? Then you must be compelled by your passion, to spend time with Him. When you are confident in His love, then your PASSION and your love for God will drive you to spend time with Him, to get His heart and to do what He says. Some people think prayer is nothing more than listing petitions to God as though He were some kind of genie, to where if we plead or bargain with Him long enough, He'll give in to our wishes. Prayer is not so much gritting your teeth as it is "falling in love."

Jesus said *"And you shall love the LORD your God with all your heart, with all your soul, with all your mind, and with all your strength. This is the first commandment."* Mark 12:30

The truth is that when you are passionate about something or someone, you have no problem wanting to spend time with them. To do that, you must enter into a new place with your desire to spend time with Him in prayer. Just as in any relationship, communication is IMPERATIVE! That's what prayer is: communication with God, both speaking and listening.

If we are going to really embrace His love, then we must TRANSITION from knowledge of Him into a real and intimate relationship with Him.

Many of us do mental gymnastics with God. We say we believe Him, we say we believe in Him, we say we know Him, we even say we love Him. And though that may be true, we must be honest in how hungry we are to know Him in a deeper manner.

*That's what prayer is: communication with God, both speaking and listening.*

# Embracing God's Love

## Day 93

The world is desperate right now. They are looking for answers. There is trouble seemingly all around, but it is not so different than it was when the apostles were alive. *Now while Paul waited for them at Athens, his spirit was provoked within him when he saw that the city was given over to idols. Acts 17:16*

Something happened to Paul when he saw the idols. He didn't get mad in the flesh. He didn't try to fit in with what they were doing. The same Spirit that raised Christ from the dead that lived inside of him began to be awakened, provoked. He was seeing that the glory that belonged to God was being shared with other gods, who really weren't gods at all. He realized if they had a lot of idols that they had erected, they were seekers.

They were looking for answers, but they hadn't been able to find the truth. Paul was filled with compassion for these souls. He saw the bondage they were in, and how Satan had taken hunger and had used it to enslave them. He was grieved. So the first thing we notice about Paul is that when he was able to discern the atmosphere, he began to do something to change it. He didn't just get agitated. He got stirred up. He knew he was there for a reason. The reason was to change their reasoning into relationship.

*Therefore he reasoned in the synagogue with the Jews and with the Gentile worshipers, and in the marketplace daily with those who happened to be there. Acts 17:17* He went to where the people were. The ones in the church, and the ones in the marketplace. He hung out with them, he had conversations with them. He wasn't just barking at them his truth, he was listening to them, and then he would pray and take it to God and ask for wisdom and love and the proper timing.

## Action Step

*In your journey today at work, in school, or wherever you may end up, take note of the people around you. Take time to genuinely listen to them, be praying and ask God, as Paul did, to give you the wisdom, love, and proper timing to reveal the truth to them.*

***They were looking for answers,
but they hadn't been able to find the truth.***

# Embracing God's Love

## Day 94

As Paul spent time among the philosophers of the day he could see that many of them had religious thinking, and then there were the other ones with just thinking. They needed a "new think".

*Then certain Epicurean and Stoic philosophers encountered him. And some said, "What does this babbler want to say?" Acts 17:18.* This was a crowd of people who were steeped in deep thinking. Thinking that was at times even contrary to Christ. So Paul began to place himself within their midst. He just connected with God, got saturated in Him, and then he would go out and build relationship with them. He had plans to engage them into an encounter that would lead to another kind of encounter. Others said, "He seems to be a proclaimer of foreign gods," because he preached to them Jesus and the resurrection.

They didn't understand what he was talking about because their eyes were still blinded to the truth. But that didn't stop him from preaching the truth. He was telling them about the Savior of the World, and His sacrifice, His death AND His resurrection. Now even though they did not understand, they were interested. They decided they would bring him to the town square to hear what this passionate man had to say about this new doctrine of his.

*And they took him and brought him to the Areopagus, saying, "May we know what this new doctrine is of which you speak? For you are bringing some strange things to our ears. Therefore we want to know what these things mean." Acts 17:19-20* This was a "new think". His words were different, something they hadn't heard before, something they were finally willing to acknowledge that they wanted to know more about.

### ACTION STEP

Listen to the discussions and concerns of your friends and co-workers. What are some of the philosophies of the day that you hear? What are the questions that they are seeking answers to? What "new thinking" do you have to reveal?

*This was a "new think".*

# Embracing God's Love

## Day 95

*For all the Athenians and the foreigners who were there spent their time in nothing else but either to tell or to hear some new thing. Acts 17:21*

That is what they did. They just went around and listened to different doctrines. But Paul was not going to miss this moment; he was going to seize this opportunity.

*Then Paul stood in the midst of the Areopagus and said, "Men of Athens, I perceive that in all things you are very religious; Acts 17:22*

He wasn't insulting them, he was just stating the truth. They probably took that as a compliment, though we would recognize now, religion is just a form, not a relationship. But he is about to shake their world.

*for as I was passing through and considering the objects of your worship, I even found an altar with this inscription: 'TO THE UNKNOWN GOD.' Acts 17:23*

They had erected an idol to the "the unknown God". These poor people just didn't get it. They were trying to desperately figure out what god was THE god. And so they built an idol to this one that they did not know, or did not know well. Some may have gotten closer to the truth than others, but they hadn't found him. But there was a real God who was about to make Himself known. They knew there was something and someone more to know. They were building something with their own hands that was showing the outward cry of an inward need.

Prayer:

*Lord, I know that you have placed me in this life at this time and I pray that you begin to open my eyes to the people that you have placed me in the midst of. I pray that you open my ears to not just hear what they say they are looking for, but that you open my ears to hear what their heart is seeking. You are all-knowing and you know the answers to life that they are in need of. I pray that you teach me to love them so purely that I am kept from any judgments against them and love them so courageously that I can speak freely the truth and testimony that you have given me.*

**But there was a real God who was about to make Himself known.**

# Embracing God's Love

## Day 96

*Therefore, the One whom you worship without knowing, Him I proclaim to you: Acts 17:23*

Paul is telling them that he doesn't just recognize the truth; he knows the one that is the truth. Many today, just like then, are trying so hard to find "it." So many of the shows today that have competitions, the judges say, "you have 'it' whatever 'it' is - you have it." They can recognize the passion of a person in pursuit of their dream. And it becomes tangible — something that you can actually see and feel. It creates an atmosphere that others can visibly see that there is something different about that individual. It is intense. It is active. It has aggression. It has goals.

These people, like many today, were in pursuit of a dream. Their dream was to know gods. They knew there were many names for them. They knew that maybe they would find the one that could settle their arguments, and bring them satisfaction. So they kept looking, and seeking, and counseling with each other on what they had discovered. They thought about it, pondered it. If they thought it had any validity to it, they would just erect another idol to it. And move on to the next "think". I think, they think, she thinks, he thinks. Paul was about to give them a brand new "think". *"God, who made the world and everything in it, since He is Lord of heaven and earth, does not dwell in temples made with hands." Acts 17:24*

This God was different. He was the Lord over the heaven. He was the creator of the places above them, surrounding them. And He was the Lord over the earth. The globe. The place where they dwelled and all around them. Furthermore, He wasn't dwelling in temples made by humans.

Can you imagine this as a "new think" thought? Could you imagine how hard they would have been trying to figure out what in the world he was talking about?

*Furthermore, He wasn't dwelling in temples made by humans.*

# Embracing God's Love

## Day 97

*"Nor is He worshiped with men's hands, as though He needed anything, since He gives to all life, breath, and all things." Acts 17:25*

This God was beyond the gods they had heard about. None of the ones they had made with stone had any real power to perform. They had no strength. They just sat there. But this God, this one that Paul knew and spoke of from personal relationship, this God gave life and breath to everything. Our brains can't quite comprehend the statement, though our spirit within us bears witness to the fact that it is true. Now he was going to go even further... *"And He has made from one blood every nation of men to dwell on all the face of the earth," Acts 17:26*

Now we get into the meat of the matter. The blood of Jesus has brought everyone together. That Christ has made a way for them, and all to have access to the one true God... This would shake their thinking. This could change their lives, if they would allow the "new think" to bring new life to them. This new think would bring destiny into view if they would allow it, the rest of this scripture says... *"...and has determined their pre-appointed times and the boundaries of their dwellings," Acts 17:26*

Now Paul is letting them know that God has a determination. He knows the times that have been set aside for each one of them as individuals. He knows them inside and out. He knows the boundaries they have set; He knows the boundaries, the territories that He has laid out for them also. *"...so that they should seek the Lord, in the hope that they might grope for Him and find Him, though He is not far from each one of us" Acts 17:27*

*God has put a desire in each one, to seek Him.*

*The unknown God could be known by them.*

*How much more then, can we enjoy intimacy with God?*

---

**Our brains can't quite comprehend the statement, though our spirit within us bears witness to the fact that it is true.**

# Embracing God's Love

## Day 98

One Sunday service in particular, God came to meet us. Some fell on their face, some went on their knees, others just bowed their heads at their seats but His presence was tangible and available to all. There were some who stayed and cried out for Him until 2:00 in the afternoon. Oh such glory. Such intimacy. Such awesome presence. We were tired, but we were happy.

But that was last Sunday. We had been with Him, but it was for purpose. And it was not so we could look back and remember what had happened. No, you must realize that He has a perfect time and place for you to find Him on a daily basis.

Paul had been with Him. Not once, not twice, not a week ago. He had spent time with Him. That is why his words carried weight. That is why he operated in faith. No fear of man could intimidate him. He didn't care how much knowledge they had, he had knowledge of the One he spoke of from personal experience.

His God was not a God he thought about, his was a God that he spoke to daily, that he lived to please.

In order for you to embrace His love, you must move past your mental assent. We think the people in Athens were ridiculous, yet we have been known to operate in the same capacity.

Even as good Christians, we can fall back on knowing what we already know, not seeking Him further for a more intimate moment than we have ever had before.

What moves us into the place of being able to embrace Him the way we need to so that we can display Him properly?

Perhaps it is the groping for Him. It is the place where you grab hold of God. For when you grab hold of Him, blessings begin to come your way.

*For when you grab hold of Him, blessings begin to come your way.*

# Embracing God's Love

## Day 99

Old cycles break. Restoration begins and brings you back into the place where you are no longer talking about an unknown God... But the God, the one you know ... the one you seek with all your heart.

Not the God that we just go after when we want a good life, a good job, an easy answer. But God who has proven He is good to us and that all things turn around for good when we humble ourselves before Him in prayer. God who has a way of knowing all about you and is even able to find your boundaries, the places you may have walled Him out of. The places His presence needs to invade.

We don't need idols. Yet we as the church can name all the idols that have gone before us. Even the ones that have accomplished great things for God. We need to forget the names, but remember the outcome. We need to quit worrying about who we quote, and just live in the truth of what was said under the anointing of almighty God.

I have heard people say, I know so-and-so personally (some big shot in the kingdom). Esther said it to Pastor Christie and I one day. She said, "We don't need a big name to come to our Made For More conference, we all have names, we need HIM (our God) to come."

How can we be one nation under God if the church can't even let go of their idols? When church allows idols, it opens doors to demons. In our arrogance have we forgotten our commitment to keep Him first? Is it possible for us to have gone from knowing Him to Him being the unknown God to us?

*Is your heart burning within you for Him to come closer to you than ever before? Have you taken things into your hands and tried to work the system by your own power?*

<u>DOES HE MISS THE DAYS WHEN YOU USED TO TRUST HIM FOR EVERYTHING?</u>

**You are no longer talking about an unknown God... But the God, the one you know ... the one you seek with all your heart.**

# Conquest For Heaven (1 of 10)

## Day 100

Today's Kingdom Guide is a series from our 2011 Prophetic Word from the Lord. Though the year has passed, the word of God still stands true. Sometimes His promises take minutes before we see them come to pass and sometimes they take years. It is our job to meditate on what He has spoken, recognize with thanksgiving what has been accomplished, pray for what has yet to come and find what our job is to see it through here on earth!

*In those things which seem to have fought against you, it has only caused you to understand my grace, my mercy, and obeying me and trusting me at a higher level. For in that place of trust you lost your self-confidence and you have become more confident in Me. You recognize that your ability to take care of yourself was not really able to conquer the things that would come your way. But let not your heart be troubled for in the midst of adverse circumstances I have built you as conquerors. For we have much Kingdom business to do. I have conquests for you. I have victory for you. But there is much activity that will be done in 2011 for you see it's the year of preparation. It's the year to prepare for the Kingdom completion. The things that have been talked about, the things that have been said, the things that have been declared, the things that have been decreed, even those things that have been warred over in the past are all being compressed into this time frame now where you will begin to understand like you've never understood before. The kings in my court will be the counselors of the kings of the world. For wisdom and revelation is going to be given to you at a higher level as you continue to press into me. Even the things that have come against you, even the things that tried to take you out, that tried to corner you, that tried to keep you from obeying Me. Those things have become a stepping stool now that you can rise into a higher place, into a higher level, into a higher place of understanding of the reasons why. You see, I've already won the victory, and yet I need you to walk this through with Me. I need you to conquer for those around you, I need you to see with my eyes and to spot the enemy before he arises. I need you to keep him under your feet. I need you to walk across territory knowing who you are and declaring the truth of what I've given you.*

*I've expanded your borders, and I'm expanding them more even now!*

# Conquest For Heaven

**Day 101**

*You see, after death comes a resurrection. And the same way that I was resurrected from the dead, I am resurrecting my church into a new place, a new awareness, and a new amount of the ability to battle against the enemy and have victory on every side. The weapons of your warfare are not carnal but they are mighty to the pulling down of the strongholds of the enemy – and it shall come by love. You see love conquers all. It is the love that you have for Me that will turn you inside out. It is the love that you receive from Me that will cause you to be able to conquer the enemy and the things in your life. The disappointments really come from fear. Fear that I am unable, ill-equipped, not standing by My word, not bringing truth to you, not bringing you to the place of victory that I've promised. But now you understand, I was there all along, I was there in your darkness, I was there in your corner, I was there when you seemingly gave up. I never gave up on you. You see, I've already pre-written every day of your life. I've already seen every step you're going to take. I've already positioned angels there for you. Equipment there for you. Victory there for you. Fear is bowing its knee because of love. My perfect love casts it out. My perfect love, that's what I've deposited on the inside of you. That's what will keep you going in the right direction. That's what will cause my compassion to come upon you. And instead of being able to see it all mapped out before you as you have demanded in the past, there will have to be instant obedience because I like it that way. And this is the time frame you're in now – instant obedience, where you hear, you see, you obey, you win.*

*Fear is bowing its knee because of love. My perfect love casts it out.*

# Conquest For Heaven

## Day 102

*So much infirmity, so many needs. Satan has tried to say there is no hope, there are no answers, oh but he's tried that before. But I am the answer to every need, and I have provided already. I've been waiting on you and you thought you were waiting on Me. It seems so hard, it seemed as though it was like I was deaf and ignoring your prayers, and the church began to cry out for redemption, for restoration for the things that they had need of, but it's exactly what I wanted. It's what I've been waiting for is for my church, my church, My people called by my name to humble themselves and to pray and to turn, turn, turn, turn from the wickedness. Turn away from the contamination and turn once again to Me, and cry out for mercy. And the healing has begun. My church is now beginning to understand as I've healed their broken hearts, and dried away their tears as they run into the mane of the lion of Judah. And they have allowed Me to wash away their tears and to war for them and to protect them. As they see who they really are with, that I've already warred and already won. That my protection is there as they knelt before Me, as they looked into my eyes and they began to see the love that's never changed, the love that was there all along, the love that would direct them and redirect them, the love that would kiss away their fears, the love that would clean them up and put them back on the path of righteousness. And now my church is crying out for glory, you'll hear it again and again and again, the glory, the glory, the glory. And I've left glory inside of you, and it's time for you to understand there is a dynamic going on, until the glory that is within you is so strong, that it goes inside out and reflects Me to the earth. Oh there'll have to be some readjusting, there'll have to be some reevaluating, there'll have to be some reinstitution of those things that you have let go of because of despair, of disappointment. Oh, but church, my church, don't you know I've already written this time. It is a time of victory, it is a time of hope. It is a time where you will see that you will be able to do more than you've ever even imagined because your trust has returned to Me. In the midst of your darkness, in the midst of what seemed like there were no answers, you found the answers alive in Me again.*

### Turn away from the contamination and turn once again to Me

# Conquest For Heaven

## Day 103

*Deliberation – there's deliberation for a deliberate plan to conquer. Deliberation means to think about, discuss, to make your decisions carefully. It's being able to have a discussion with those you trust before you reach a decision. It's unhurried, it's steady, it's thorough. It's individual action. It's deliberation for a deliberate place. I am asking you to live deliberately. I am asking you to talk deliberately. I'm asking you to go forward deliberately. One foot in front of the other. The race is won by deliberation with Me. I've put you in this place because I can trust you, I've caused you to be conquerors and winners already, but I'm looking for the round table of those who have won some things, the ones that have already fought and won and have victory under their belt, they are strong, they know how to press through the darkness and know that there is light on the other side. For I have caused you to be light to the world, I've told you that you are the light to the world. While I was in the world, I was light. Now that light resides inside of you. Now that light has to be set on a hill so that it will be seen and known. Now that which is on the inside of you will bring out the light among men so that they may see and partake of the light and come out of the darkness. More souls, more souls will come. Those that have cried out and not given up, you'll see them come to you unexpectedly. Be ready, prepare yourself, have yourself full of my word and full of my love, full of my ability. Walk according to the spirit, not according to some written out plan. They want to know your life story. They want to know My life story. They want to know how they intersected and how they can be there too. The world is desperate. In your desperation you found the answer. In their desperation, they're searching for you. The answer is inside. The answer is inside. The answer is inside.*

---

*Be ready, prepare yourself, have yourself full of my word and full of my love, full of my ability.*

# Conquest For Heaven

## Day 104

There's a reconditioning going on. A reconditioning that the spirit will do for you. It's as if you've become dry and worn out like leather in a car, and you've got to allow the moisture of the spirit to come and to be rubbed into every place that has been dry and weary. Restoration will come, refurburation will come. I'm doing it even now by my spirit. I'm doing it even now by my spirit. It is in the place of praise. It is in the place of honoring Me that you will receive the blessing. That's why there's been an increase in pressing through to worship. That's why there's an increase in pressing through in prayer and fasting will be a part of your life as you surrender the flesh to Me.

It's not that you change my mind by fasting, it's that you change yours. It's that you empty yourself out of the things that the flesh really wants, and as you kill it, I enter. Oh there was death going on in 2010, Satan thought it was to take you out, but the death was really of self-will. It was to get you to cry out "Not my will but Yours be done".

*Cry out... "Not my will but Yours be done."*

Now it's time to move along. It's time to pick up your weapons, your tools, that which you've learned through the hard spots. Those things that you have grabbed a hold of even through the places you thought were dysfunctional. I'm making you functional again. You will have to see yourself as a warring church again. I called you freedom for reason, you had to get there first. And there is a fight when there is freedom declared. Oh but life has returned. I'm blowing fresh breath back into you. Examine yourself and see, don't you feel different right now? The clock has ticked, the time has come, a new season, a new reason to be alive, a new reason to fight, the synergy of life has come back, of unity, all of those things I've asked you to do, all of those things I've asked you to be, being one with Me and one with each other, it brings life. And now you will have new encounters in the spirit realm. Now you will be able to see and hear oh so succinctly, and short sentences will set you free. Don't underestimate my power or My strength, or My time frames, because in an instant of time, things can change. There will be suddenly's. Suddenly's for you. There is a restoration process. I am restoring what the canker worm has stolen if you continue to agree with Me. Agree, agree with the heavenly realm. Agree with the heavenly realm.

*There is a new reason to be alive, a new reason to fight.*

# Conquest For Heaven

## Day 106

*Provision will come but not as you've seen it before. It is pro-vision. It's the visionaries, the people that will be sought after. People will have to return to the proactive, to being proactive about vision, going after those that carry it, after the vision of God, after the heart of having a vision and picking it up again. Some of you have left the place of vision in 2010. You've given up, you gave away your territory. But I'm offering it back. Who will stand and who will take back the territory? You can have it back in a moment, but you will have to take provision back, you will have to trust Me now for that which you've tried to trust Me for before. There will be no more trying, there will be determination. Draw the line, never ever look back again. Don't question Me on this again. Let your vision return, right now. Covenant has never changed, promises have never change, My word has never changed. Agree again with Me. And see what I will do supernaturally to bring it to past. The signs, the wonders, the miracles, well where have they been? They've been locked up on the inside of you. But now I'm giving you the keys to the kingdom, and as you humble yourself and as you seek Me and as you love Me and as you receive My love, you'll see there was nothing the disciples could do to make the time come faster because I already saw the day it was going to occur. I already knew the time, and now the time has come again for my church.*

*The time has come again for the church to understand and to display my glory and my power as never before. It's transitioning, it's positioning, it's translating things from heaven to earth. The potential that has been on the inside of you is now going to be exponential potential realized. But only if you're willing to lay down the things and pick up the things necessary.*

**I'm giving you the keys to the Kingdom.**

## Conquest For Heaven (8 of 10)

### Day 107

*You'll begin to realize more the individual call now upon your lives. You'll tap in and press into the corporate vision like never before, it will be easier because there will be more vision. Be pro the vision. Come into agreement with the house, come into agreement corporately and you will see that I will cause things to happen for your vision to take place individually. It's going to be more precise. You'll see the things that I've called you to come into play, you'll be able to recognize it and call it by name. You'll be able to see why you're in this race and the part you have to play. It's a day of joy. It's a day of peace, it's a day of declaration. The rejoicing that went on, on D-Day, the declaration went up and the people rejoiced. They still had to walk forward, but they knew the battle had been won. I declare to you the battle has been won. Walk it through to the end of victory. Walk with me as I've declared you're never alone, you'll never be alone, you've just got to live from the inside out. More of heaven is yours.*

*The nations are calling. The nations are calling. And the nations are coming. It's two sided. They're calling and some will go, we're calling and some will come. Diversity within this house. Thanks God. You asked and I said I'd give you the nations for your inheritance. And you just keep asking for it, so I'm going to bring it. Now be ready for the diversity, be ready for your inheritance, for this is the inherited time. Multiplication. Multiplication because you finally will be settled on who you are and quit apologizing for it. Never be afraid to go into the deep, I've called you to the deep. And deep will call unto deep. Those people who are passionate, those people who are desperate, that is who needs you, that is who will come and that is who will be comfortable in this atmosphere. There is a desperate people with a desperate call. Let them be desperate with you for Me. Just invite them into the stream and they will swim along side.*

**Never be afraid to go into the deep, I've called you to the deep.**

# Day 108

*I'm giving you ideas. You'll see that some of you will be able to see the beginning of the fulfillment of it. You've already had thoughts, you've already had things that have dropped into your spirit and some are asking for more still. Some of you already have things that need to be walked out. The things that I've talked about, the things that you know, the things that I've dropped on the inside, go forward with them now. Now is the time. Now is the time. And I will bring more. I will bring more. You're beginning to understand and see some effortless victories. Now I'll make more come still. The effort, the effort isn't trying to get them, the effort is staying in the spirit and coming after me. Just as you saw happen tonight, from the outer court, to the inner court, to the holy of holies, there was a battle going on. It took time and determination, it took a warring spirit and it took some warfare, it took my warriors being determined. But you got there. Now do it again, and again, and again, and again. The effort is getting into the holy of holies with me. And being willing to spend the time until you make it there, and once you're there, the victory is won. Because with Me, it's already victory time. Fight, fight for your time with Me, fight with my word, fight with my promise and fight with each other for victory. Side by side. Conquerors. Receive it again. You are conquerors. Conquests have to be made. Pre-assigned to you, pre-assigned to Liberty Life Center. Receive it and then do it.*

*Step by step, vision by vision, be pro-vision. It's time to put a demand upon the seed you've sown. I've had you hear and learn and understand sowing and reaping for reason. Now the seeds that you've sown in the past are still there. Begin to declare the harvest. Begin to expect it, begin to look for it. And be immovable about it and you'll see it come to pass.*

**Because with Me, it's already victory time.**

# Conquest For Heaven

Many of the things that Satan had planned had already been stopped even by those when you weren't aware of it, those prayers that you prayed against the terrorists have stopped many attacks. The things that you have declared and decreed from years ago actually stopped things from happening in 2010. You're not aware of it, but I am. Allow your faith to arise again that even in the midst of what seemed like desperation and destitution, there were still things that were being fulfilled and harvests that were occurring even during 2010 when you didn't realize it. Now you'll begin to understand it and as you walk forward and as you look at the past, you will understand that those things really did happen even though you weren't aware of them because I do not waste things. I do not waste prayers. I do not discard those things that you have brought before Me in the heavenly realm. So come again and win the war for those that are around you. Win it for the future and win it in the present. Oh it's a time of victory. Oh I want you to hear my heart. I've seen these days ahead of you. I've seen what you can do, I've already equipped you well. Oh the things you already know. The things I've already deposited inside of you. The things that are going to explode now. It's like the poppers. You will pop and the inside of you will come out and it will have Jesus written all over it. It will cause a noise that will be loud and strong and will infiltrate the darkness and cause those to hear sounds that they've never heard before, to feel things they've never sensed before and to know that your God is real. Your God is real.

There will be new rivers in the dessert for those that have been in the dry places. Even the things of the natural have been showing the things that will happen in the spirit. The flooding that has occurred, although it was devastating in the natural, the flood that I have will be devastating to the enemy and bring about that which will turn things around in the spiritual force, in the spiritual realm to bring about rivers of living waters on the earth.

### Day 109

*I do not discard those things that you have brought before Me in the heavenly realm.*

# Embracing God's Love

## Day 110

Throughout all generations there has been idol worship. Idol worship is using illegitimate people, places, or things that people look to for help. It is the things that are looked to satisfy the longing in every heart, but it replaces the longing for God Himself ... His will, His ways. When that occurs, even those that once knew Him begin to lose step with Him, as they get dazed trying to satisfy by the outward things rather than being stirred up in the inside with truth that changes cities and places and people.

When we stop realizing where the truth comes from ...Where the power comes from ...Who deserves all the glory ...Then we become an ineffective people group that are just as bewildered by the media and the reports of the day as the world is.

It's time for church to go "public" too. Everyone else is. Tony Evans said it this way (paraphrased), "God is calling His church to a time of repentance. It's time to exit the places where we have allowed our minds to agree with Satan and to determine once again to agree with God. He is right we are wrong. The good news is that as we exit there is a 'grace overpass' that we can take that will bring us to the 'restoration ramp' where we can once again be on our way to the proper destination."

God isn't concerned about our sins, if we confess them before Him. He wasn't sending Paul out for nothing. He isn't sending us out for nothing either. He is moved by people who were at least looking for something more. We need to always be wanting more of Him. He looks for those who will grope after Him. Even we, in our lack of true knowledge, or mixed knowledge, can find Him there, for He is waiting for us to reach out to Him. He is waiting for you right now.

<u>HE WANTS MORE OF YOU TODAY THAN YOU GAVE HIM YESTERDAY.</u>

<u>DO YOU WANT MORE OF HIM TODAY THAN YOU HAD YESTERDAY?</u>

**We need to always be wanting more of Him.**

## Embracing God's Love

**Day 111**

We may have woke up thanking God for His presence on Sunday, but on Monday, our prayer needs to be, "God help me to experience you even more today." You can move His heart. He is after your heart. When we respond in love, it moves our heart towards Him, it moves His heart to us.

Our first calling is to love Him. We can't love God in the humanistic culture today without Jesus - it will not work. Jesus and relationship with Him is the only way. Those are God's terms and Jesus defined love as rooted in the spirit of obedience.

It is impossible to love Him without pursuing a life of obedience. Not just in our behavior. All His commandments are related to love. The more we obey the more we respond to His love. Love requires that we have allegiance to Jesus. There is a crisis of truth today in our land. In the name of tolerance and even in the name of love, there are those that are redefining what love is. But for Him, we must speak as Paul did, confident because of relationship, boldly yet tenderly. Jesus is God and there is no other. All the world's religions can say whatever they want to say, but there is no other way.

We must be totally loyal to Him in terms of the way of salvation. There is no salvation outside of Him. None other than Jesus lived perfectly and offered Himself for the sins of the world. There just is no other standard of truth. The words that the known God speaks, define morality, marriage, life, and righteousness.

*In our allegiance to Him we must say what He says.*

*It is time to come out in the open, to go public regardless of what it costs us. We love you, Jesus! No matter what that costs us.*

**Our first calling is to love Him.**

# Embracing God's Love

## Day 112

The Church should be modeling the answers to the world's problems. No one person is the answer. But God does have a plan. You see, God never forgets about the blood. He is ever mindful of the blood. The sacrifice that was made that ripped the wall of partition in two. The One that gave access to Himself to every hungry-hearted person. But on certain days, in certain ways, we tend to forget about the blood. About the sacrifice that has given us access behind the veil.

God promised Jesus a partner. He promised Him someone that would be committed to Him to the end. Someone that would love Him with all their heart, soul and mind. He is still looking for that bride, the one whose eyes are fixed on one thing. When we touch Him, He will touch us. When that occurs, the dynamic of heaven and earth coming together actually occurs. It is in this place where we are able to "come to ourselves" with the original DNA of God for us in His plan.

Within the knowledge of HIM, we find the ability to defeat the plans of the enemy that would cause us to not reach our purpose. We need to continue to pray and cry out for mercy upon those things that are necessary to be changed in our own life.

*"Search me, O God, and know my heart: try me, and know my thoughts; and see if there be any wicked way in me, and lead me in the way everlasting." Psalm 139:23-24 ASV*

### Is this the cry of your heart?

*This is where the dynamic of heaven and earth coming together actually occurs. Make this the cry of your heart today… and all of your days. It is the answer to your problems and the solution that the world is in need of.*

*"Search me, O God, and know my heart: try me, and know my thoughts; and see if there be any wicked way in me, and lead me in the way everlasting."*

**He is still looking for that bride,
the one whose eyes are fixed on one thing.**

## Embracing God's Love

### Day 113

The Word the Lord gave me is that we need to "relinquish" everything but Him. When we let go of everything but Him, we discover the truth of what He has always wanted for us.

God's plan in creating us was to be with Him in the glory cloud. The place where everything was flourishing, where our needs are met by Him. Where our souls are satisfied by His presence. Where His knowledge floods the earth and flows within and out of us. The third person of the trinity enables us to once again embrace our God.

Heart to heart, spirit to spirit, mind to mind.

We can come into a place where the things that are of the Spirit of the living God are so much more real than the temporal things. Where the things of this world lose their place in our minds and hearts. Where being with Him is the priority because we have not just groped, but through our reaching, we have discovered Him. We have found a place with Him that is available if we seek Him continually.

For in Him is the power that we are searching for.

In Him the glory we have cried out for is found.

In Him, we will understand the Kingdom that has been set up to last forever and ever.

*Yours, O LORD, is the greatness, The power and the glory, The victory and the majesty; For all that is in heaven and in earth is Yours; Yours is the kingdom, O LORD, And You are exalted as head over all. Both riches and honor come from You, And You reign over all. In Your hand is power and might; In Your hand it is to make great And to give strength to all. 1 Chronicles 29:11-12*

*Heart to heart, spirit to spirit, mind to mind.*

# Embracing God's Love

## Day 114

God is available for us to know. He can give us strength. We are to walk in His purposes. He is able to do more than we can ask or even think if we continue to grope after Him, and desire to know truth.

Recently, many of us gathered at the church for prayer some for a full 6 hours, and it felt like it swiftly fleeted by. Because when you are communing with God, His time takes over. Do you recall that a few years ago I had a vision? In the vision I heard people from all the nations saying, "Come Lord Jesus come." I thought they meant for the rapture, but then I came to realize, no it was just come, LORD Jesus, come to us. Intervene for us. Be with us. Give us your heart. Come before you come. I believe that is what is happening. I watched Bill Johnson and a lot of people on Friday night that were crying out the same thing. I heard that group of believers saying the same things that the groups of believers said yesterday, and that we are saying collectively, here, and with the other churches we are in relationship with.

God is beginning to bring us to the place where the next great awakening can occur. That place of desperation where we meet with Him in prayer, and there is no distance between the spirit and the soul. Where the Spirit is so full with the presence of God that we can't deny His presence is real, nor would we dare to.

We prayed for the curses to be broken and for God's intervention by praying and seeking and finding Him in the midst of the storm. Other people around the world had joined us in prayer for our nation as we humbled ourselves and repented of our sins and the sins of the nation. The God that has become unknown to many, is now making Himself known again.

Are you a part of this?
Will you join in the cry of God's people all across the globe?
Will you cry out with us "Come Lord Jesus come!"

*Where the Spirit is so full with the presence of God that we can't deny His presence is real, nor would we dare to.*

# Exposing

**Day 115**

I began to ask God what He has been laying out before us and what is occurring in our atmosphere. He said He has been exposing the enemy, but now He will be exposing Himself to us in new ways.

Exposing: to make known: bring to light, to cause to be visible or open to view: to display

The exposure of Satan enables us to be wiser in defeating him.

The exposure of God Himself in our lives, will make us love Him more.

If we can see Him in a closer view, if He displays Himself to us in such a way that things are brought to light for us, we will also have an awareness of the way God sees things and we will be able to align our thinking to His.

As we do that, the mandate on our lives and church will be brought to a place of new ability. But, as always, the renewing of our minds is key to bringing transformation.

How can we transform cities so that nations can be transformed?

How can we make the necessary impact that brings needed change?

Different thinking produces different actions.

We all have a role to play to affect change from rebellious, dark attitudes to humble honor of God, which will touch people's hearts and thinking towards God.

Nations will be transformed when cities are transformed.

Cities will be transformed when individuals are being transformed.

*The exposure of God Himself in our lives, will make us love Him more.*

## Evaluating His Significance

### Day 116

I want to talk to you today about your part in the end time revival. (Or movement, or whatever.)
It is evaluating God's significance to your life.
Are the things He counts important, important to you?
Are the things He hates, the same as the things you hate?

*I love them that love me; and those that seek me early shall find me.*
*Proverbs 8:17 KJV*

In prayer one night, we had a mandate to ask God for His heart. I also instructed everyone to please pray only by the Spirit. As people felt led to take the mic, and prayed in the Spirit, each one cried out to God, and they found Him. There were many personal reports saying it changed their life forever.

• One had been struggling with being able to pray where he could feel the presence of God. Tuesday night He not only felt His presence, he heard His voice and he lifted his with the others, and had a personal breakthrough that was better than what he had experienced in his life before this.

• Another reported that they felt the prayers kept escalating until they brought them to a place that they felt as though God had brought him, and us to an old-time wash tub, where we were washed and cleansed and then squeezed out 'til we came out on the other side clean and new and born again... again.

• Another said: It was about desperation: To be desperate personally, it intensified her own desperation. There was a desperation because the time is short before the catching away and the wave of darkness... It was very fierce and desperate and aware of the desperate times that are arising For "whatever" — there was a desperation for whatever is on God's heart.

As they prayed, God was showing me the significance of each other to reach His heart so that we could all experience what is important to Him in a different way. I realized why we must pray, and why corporate prayer is vitally important for us individually to be a part as well as for the purposes of changing the world. You do believe prayer changes things, don't you?

*There was a desperation for whatever is on God's heart.*

# Evaluating His Significance

## Day 117

It is evident that many who call themselves Christians today are not living holy lives that are pleasing to Him. We want His blessings, but we aren't so sure we want to do right all the time.

*Psalm 84:11 says, "For the Lord God is a sun and shield; the Lord will give grace and glory; no good thing will He withhold from those who walk uprightly".*

To those who do what? Walk uprightly. God said He is going to reveal those areas that are not pleasing to Him. It isn't so we can feel bad, it is so we can repent and turn from whatever is holding us back from joy and productivity in the Kingdom. If Satan can get us to focus on our needs, then our focus isn't on God. If he can get us to focus on our own strength, then we are not focusing on our dependence on God. If he can get us to focus on what the world says is important, we lose the value of the things that are eternal.

*And He said to me, "My grace is sufficient for you, for My strength is made perfect in weakness." Therefore most gladly I will rather boast in my infirmities, that the power of Christ may rest upon me. Therefore I take pleasure in infirmities, in reproaches, in needs, in persecutions, in distresses, for Christ's sake. For when I am weak, then I am strong. 2 Corinthians 12:9-10*

It is when you recognize you can't do it, and you lean to the grace of God for empowerment, that you begin to live again with understanding of the Spirit

*greater is he that is in you, than he that is in the world.*
*1 John 4:4 KJV*

Greater is He that is in you than he that is in the world! Bigger, larger, more powerful is He that is in you. Not you, but he that is within you. You are to live in a holy place with Him so you can be holy like Him. You have to be aware of the power that has already been given you.

*It is when you recognize you can't do it, and you lean to the grace of God for empowerment, that you begin to live again with understanding of the Spirit.*

## Evaluating His Significance

### Day 118

One night during prayer one of our leaders came up and just kept declaring, "The same Spirit that raised Christ from the dead dwells in you." The atmosphere changed to a place where we began to actually believe and trust and become confident in that as fact and not just wished. Coming into agreement with that word does two things:

It takes away reliance in our own ability (which isn't working out too good for us, now is it?) and it makes us aware of His ability within us.

Yes you can do all things. But it is through Christ who strengthens you. When you recognize your weakness and your infirmities, rejoice over the fact that you can release the empowering presence of God to operate in your life. As long as you take credit for it, God can't operate in it, but the moment you cast your care upon Him, God releases His power, and His grace is sufficient to overcome the obstacles of the enemy and to defeat them in every area of your life!

You can be aware of your own failures. You can admit that you have weaknesses, without using them as excuses to partially surrender and partially obey.

The moment you are willing to recognize and admit it, and look to God instead of yourself for the answers, you can begin to celebrate that when you are willing to admit this failure and recognize your weaknesses or inabilities, you release the power of God and His grace NOW to do what you cannot do.

By the awareness of His love and grace you will walk in success and victory. By His grace you are able to overcome; you're able to defeat and you're able to walk in His strength. You can live a life that reflects His glory to others, that lives in holiness and purity. We must get to the place where our sufficiency is found by being with Him.

*release the power of God and His grace NOW to do what you cannot do.*

## Evaluating His Significance

**Day 119**

I have good news for you today that God in Christ, as He is, even the fullest and brightest displays of His glory, grace, and goodness, are to be found by us, spirit to spirit.

Begin to speak this out loud:

I am…
Shifting now from soul to spirit as never before.
Shifting now from occasional love to consistent love.
Shifting now from part-time commitment to full-on commitment.
Walking in power, by love.
Walking in presence by consistent time with Him.

God has made His holiness "absorbable." We can absorb this holiness that surrounds Him by lingering in His living glory – much like Moses who stood before Him until he became so much a part of Him, God's glory was on him so much His essence was tangibly seen. See Exodus 34:29-35.

Moses absorbed a measure of the glory of God's holiness in such a way that he released deliverance to a nation.

I believe that "absorbable" holiness will fill a generation of deliverers soon to be dispatched to the nations.

David had the ability to be king and lead a nation because he was a man after God's own heart.

Moses cried out to know Him, and God called him His friend.

Abraham believed God because he had spent time with Him and had absorbed the essence needed to go to a new level of faith.

Saul was in a trance – in a place with God for 3 days and nights and came out as Paul.

*God has made His holiness "absorbable."*

## Evaluating His Significance

**Day 120**

God is looking for a people who are hungry for Him. People who count being with Him a priority as well as a privilege.

Will you remain in the holy presence until you "catch" it? Become a part of Him so that everyone that sees you will know you have been with Him. God's kingdom will come and "His will" will manifest itself, not based upon your natural ability, but upon the ability that Christ has infused you with the grace of God, in Jesus. See Ephesians 1:4-5.

Again, we see that He chose us, and He chose that we would be holy. "Holy" comes from the root word: qadash (kaw-dash') - which means: to be clean (ceremonially or morally): appoint, consecrate, dedicate, keep, prepare, proclaim, purify, sanctify (oneself), wholly.

Please understand this today, He loved us in advance. He is making mysteries open to us.

We are living in the maturity of time. The climax of the ages. And God's plan is to unify us. How? By living in the Spirit. By spending time with His heart, and getting His essence abiding in us. It will make us aware of our inheritance and we will bring forth His glory to the earth.

Today we must evaluate His significance in our lives. Is He an afterthought or our first thought? Is His will important to us? Are His ways important to us? Do we remember His love towards us, or are we experiencing that love on a daily basis because we make time for Him? Are we willing to love as He loves? Are we willing to lay down the things that are keeping us from His best overtaking our lives? He loves you today, He wants you to know your significance to Him. He wants you to honor His holiness and give Him top priority.

**HOW GREAT IS OUR GOD?**

*We are living in the maturity of time. The climax of the ages*

# A Heavenly Perspective

**Day 121**

*"Blessed be the God and Father of our Lord Jesus Christ, who has blessed us with every spiritual blessing in the heavenly places in Christ." Ephesians 1:3*

He has blessed us with spiritual blessings - the most important blessings of all. Spiritual means that He has breathed His Spirit within us and that He has given us a renovated, higher nature. He breathed His divine breath into us. He changed us. We are no longer bound to our sinful nature. We no longer have to be subject to simply responding to the circumstances and pressures around us. We have the very nature of God within us, breath to breath, with the Creator of the universe.

Here is a new perspective for you:
Where does the blessing begin? In the beginning.

*"... just as He chose us in Him before the foundation of the world, that we should be holy and without blame before Him in love..." Ephesians 1:4*

Just as the Word tells us that Jesus was slain before the foundation of the world, He chose us IN HIM before the foundation of the world. And He made a way for us to be holy and without blame in His presence. Do we have access to come to Him because of good deeds? Perfect actions? No, perfect LOVE. *"... having predestined us to adoption as sons by Jesus Christ to Himself, according to the good pleasure of His will... to the praise of the glory of His grace, by which He has made us accepted in the Beloved." Ephesians 1:5-6*

Understand, then, that in the beginning of the beginning, which always was, God's blessing was upon you. He had planned His divine influence and its effect on your life. He planned it so that you could grasp this. And as you continue to be transformed by your new mind, as you change your perspective, you will have a heart full of gratitude, not for what you may be experiencing in life, but because you understand His love for you and His ultimate plan of blessing for your life.

*We have the very nature of God within us, breath to breath, with the Creator of the universe.*

## A Heavenly Perspective

### Day 122

We can hardly take it in, because we are so caught up in a slot-machine mindset in our life. If we desire something from others, we always feel as though we must earn it by our behavior or some form of payment that must be made. But in this scripture, do you see anything in there about being accepted because of what we think, or how perfectly we behave, or a payment we must make? *"... to the praise of the glory of His grace, by which He has made us accepted in the Beloved." (Ephesians 1:6).* No, it just talks about the blessing, the irrevocable blessing that is following us in the same way it followed Jacob. He was a part of the lineage of the Lord Jesus Christ. So are you. He had the blessing invoked on him, and so do we. We may be in process, but that does not affect God. It only affects us.

No matter how many times I preach this, no matter how many times we all hear it, no matter how many times we hope we understand, we must come to the understanding that our own mental assent will never get us to the place of assurance we need. To get out of our minds, we need help of the supernatural kind. Good news. We have it. It is the Spirit of God. No wonder Jesus said He would have to go away so He could be the one to influence us from the inside out.

*" ... that the God of our Lord Jesus Christ, the Father of glory, may give to you the spirit of wisdom and revelation in the knowledge of Him ..." Ephesians 1:17*

The Spirit, the breath of God, will come and give you wisdom that transcends the natural. It's higher. It can be spiritual and worldly knowledge but it's higher than what you can understand in the natural, carnal realm. The Spirit of God who lives inside of us will give us the revelation of Him that we need. In the definition of revelation here it means, "He takes off the cover," and reveals the things about God and about our relationship with Him that we can't otherwise comprehend. Because God has a reason for it; He has something planned for you.

***He would hear the voice of God and see beyond the natural to the unlimited blessings of the Lord.***

## A Heavenly Perspective

### Day 123

*" ... the eyes of your understanding being enlightened; that you may know what is the hope of His calling, what are the riches of the glory of His inheritance in the saints ..." Ephesians 1:18*

He wants us to be illuminated, to enable us see the hope of our calling. This is the hope of our invitation. It is a hope with pleasure, with expectation. You see, He won't force His inheritance on you, but not only has He invoked the blessing on you, He has given His Holy Spirit to make it a reality for you so that you can anticipate it with pleasure, having confidence in Him taking care of all the things that pertain to our life.

So then, we know that it is only by the Spirit of God that we can identify with what our inheritance really is.

There may be some saying, "Well the Spirit may know, but I still haven't figured out how that applies to my life." Here is how that works:

*"The Spirit Himself [thus] testifies together with our own spirit, [assuring us] that we are children of God." Romans 8:16 AMP*

We know it, not by the natural circumstances or evidence. Not because it makes any sense logically, not because we can even convey it with natural words or natural means, but we are SPIRIT, soul and body. Our spirit man is assured by the very Spirit of God that we belong to HIM. Our spirit-to-spirit experiences cause us to testify jointly, that it is indeed a fact that we have the blessing of God on our life, and the power of God upon us that has made us one with Him. Not an afterthought, but a desired child, chosen by Him.

*Our spirit man is assured by the very Spirit of God that we belong to HIM.*

# A Heavenly Perspective

## Day 124

God wanted us to have everything we would need to give us a blessed life. That is why Jesus came to earth. Jesus Himself has felt everything we feel. He knows what it is like to hear a good report. *"And there came a voice from heaven, saying, Thou art my beloved Son, in whom I am well pleased." Mark 1:11 KJV*

And a bad report – *"For as Jonas was three days and three nights in the whale's belly; so shall the Son of man be three days and three nights in the heart of the earth." Matthew 12:40 KJV*

That's a little uncomfortable. But Jesus knew it would be necessary for Him to understand exactly what we would need to bring us through to the other side. *"For we do not have a High Priest who cannot sympathize with our weaknesses, but was in all points tempted as we are, yet without sin." Hebrews 4:15*

He has been in the same place you have been. He has had to fight temptation, confusion, and wanting to question His circumstances. But He didn't give in to temptation; He kept focused on eternal things so He could overcome the confusion and not question His father, but rather, just obey Him. He knew He had to stay connected to Dad to be able to do what was necessary and what was right. But He gave us the same instructions, so we could do what He did when He was fighting the enemy.

*"Let us therefore come boldly to the throne of grace, that we may obtain mercy and find grace to help in time of need." Hebrews 4:16*

Jesus relates to our weaknesses in our minds and our bodies because He was tempted in everything like us. There is nothing we can ever experience that He didn't already win the battle over. All, any, every, thing. All manner of whatever's. Every one, every way, as many things that can happen. Thoroughly, whatever, and whoever.

### *Jesus Himself has felt everything we feel.*

# A Heavenly Perspective

**Day 125**

Are you beginning to get a new perspective? Do you have some things you are working through? Still need help? Then all you have to do is to take a walk. *"Let us therefore come boldly unto the throne of grace, that we may obtain mercy, and find grace to help in time of need." Hebrews 4:16 KJV*

Time to move towards God—not away from Him. Come closer, approach worship, go nearer. Not timidly, as a beggar, but boldly as a son or daughter. My kids don't have a problem speaking openly and plainly to me. They know I will love them through their words, even if they are not exactly the ones I wanted to hear. You must understand you are not shocking God by your honest conversations with Him. You need to run to Him and be completely honest in His presence. Run to God, to His throne. That is His power seat. And you will find just what you need: it is the throne of grace. It's here we find help. A life-line for a lifetime. So, let's go back to Romans, and see what is the proper perspective to have when we face FEAR: False Evidence Appearing Real. We go to Him, and He wraps His love around us to hold on to. Then we take on a new perspective on purpose.

*"[But what of that?] For I consider that the sufferings of this present time (this present life) are not worth being compared with the glory that is about to be revealed to us and in us and for us and conferred on us!" Romans 8:18 AMP*

This does not say we suffer here, that our bodies will be in pain, or that there will be no hope until the resurrection. No. There has already been a resurrection. Jesus rose from the dead on the third day, and whatever the tactic of distraction is of the enemy today… NOTHING we face compares to the glory that is about to be revealed TO us, IN us, FOR us, and CONFERRED (bestowed upon as a gift, favor, honor) on us. Hallelujah! We just need to understand who we really are in Christ. We need to understand our significance … how much meaning our life really has.

***NOTHING we face compares to the glory that is about to be revealed TO us, IN us, FOR us, and CONFERRED on us.***

## A Heavenly Perspective

### Day 126

*"For [even the whole] creation (all nature) waits expectantly and longs earnestly for God's sons to be made known [waits for the revealing, the disclosing of their sonship]." Romans 8:19 AMP*

You see, it's not about what we need, it's about what we haven't received as a personal revelation on the inside yet. For once you really know what you know and Who you know it from, then it is settled. God has given us everything we need. SPIRIT, soul and body. *And not only the creation, but we ourselves too, who have and enjoy the firstfruits of the [Holy] Spirit [a foretaste of the blissful things to come] groan inwardly as we wait for the redemption of our bodies [from sensuality and the grave, which will reveal] our adoption (our manifestation as God's sons)." Romans 8:23 AMP*

See, we have joined as spirit to spirit and we can know the blissful things to come as we get a revelation of our adoption. A married couple in our church had it in their heart to become foster parents. They took classes. They did what they needed to do to help another life become a part of their life. In the meantime, this kid, this boy from the church just kept showing up in their home. One day, a light bulb went off in their hearts. They no longer saw him as a friend, a visitor, a nice boy, not even as a foster child, but as their child.

The boy wasn't perfect. But their hearts melded together. How do you explain that in the natural? He doesn't even look like them - he has a different nationality and a different skin color ... but it didn't matter! He had and has access to them, not as a person, but as a son. What day did the boy realize that his longing for a family had come to an end? That he had found a place that came with an inheritance that he never had to do anything to deserve? I think there are still days he struggles with feeling the full effect of that. When he makes mistakes, he may think their love changes. He may think his inheritance is in jeopardy. But it's not. It's intact, because, his parents don't just like him. They made covenant with him. He is now experiencing more of what it means to be in that kind of covenant relationship with them, with us at Liberty, and more importantly, with his God.

***He had and has access to them, not as a person, but as a son.***

# A Heavenly Perspective

## Day 127

An orphan waits for the day of his adoption. He has hope. But he hasn't seen it yet. He hasn't seen the one walk through the door, like Pastor Bill and Esther when they laid eyes on Sarah, and said, "Oh yeah! We have enough love for her." Orphans have hope for what they will experience because they haven't really had the full experience yet. It was the same for us. We knew there was a higher love, a higher place of acceptance that we needed; we just hadn't experienced it before salvation, though we longed for it.

*"For in [this] hope we were saved. But hope [the object of] which is seen is not hope. For how can one hope for what he already sees?" (Romans 8:24 AMP)* We who are Christians hoped that our life could be different. But we needed a true father. Then someone offered us the gospel of salvation. We accepted Jesus and our life was changed. We became a part of the family of God. Our hope turned to reality.

On the day of their adoption, those children's hope changed to reality. But it took them a while to fully understand the benefit package that was theirs. Once they belonged to a family, they no longer had to hope. They had it. They saw the love in their eyes. They saw them cry when they cried. They experienced their correction and direction, and they had the blessing whether they felt like it was a blessing or not. Many of us still are hanging on to a rope to have hope for things to change in our circumstances. That is where faith comes in. We had to believe in Jesus, not because it was logical to do so, but because the Spirit of God joined with our spirit in revelation of truth. On that day, we were adopted. And hope mixed with faith, became reality. Some of the things God has provided may still not be fully manifested in the natural, but that doesn't mean it hasn't occurred. What are you to do in the meantime? *"But if we hope for what is still unseen by us, we wait for it with patience and composure." Romans 8:25 AMP*

"Are you serious, Pastor Dawn? I can't do that. Patience and composure … I can't do that." Correct, you can't do it, on your own. But you are NOT alone. You have the Holy Spirit who will help you. Today, ask the Holy Spirit for the patience and composure that you need. Stop for a second and dwell upon the fact that you were once orphaned and today you are a child of God! How does that change the way you see today?

### *we haven't really had the full experience yet.*

# A Heavenly Perspective

## Day 128

*"So the [Holy] Spirit comes to our aid and bears us up in our weakness; for we do not know what prayer to offer nor how to offer it worthily as we ought, but the Spirit Himself goes to meet our supplication and pleads in our behalf with unspeakable yearnings and groanings too deep for utterance. And He Who searches the hearts of men knows what is in the mind of the [Holy] Spirit [what His intent is], because the Spirit intercedes and pleads [before God] in behalf of the saints according to and in harmony with God's will. We are assured and know that [God being a partner in their labor] all things work together and are [fitting into a plan] for good to and for those who love God and are called according to [His] design and purpose." Romans 8:26-28 AMP*

We are a partner with God. We are His family. We have been adopted in. We are sons and daughters. We see that we are not only predestined for glory, but we are preserved for glory. Therefore, No Foe Should Intimidate You! You need never fear any enemy that might come against you because you are forevermore guarded by the grace of God. God's promotion package: *"Moreover whom He predestined, these He also called; whom He called, these He also justified; and whom He justified, these He also glorified." Romans 8:30*

He called you. That is when you knew He called your name and you responded with salvation. He justified you. This is when He made you clean, just as if you never sinned. Then He glorified you. He esteemed you and let you become one with His glory, to have a different reputation. That is a great package, and it boils down to this: *"What then shall we say to these things? If God is for us, who can be against us? He who did not spare His own Son, but delivered Him up for us all, how shall He not with Him also freely give us all things? Who shall bring a charge against God's elect? It is God who justifies." Romans 8:31-33*

So, who are you up against today? What obstacles are you facing in your life? Call them out to God. One of the greatest strategies of warfare is to know your enemy. Recognize what is working against you, but don't stop there, now realize who it is that your enemy is facing. Is it just you? No! It is you and God! Now let me make this equation very simple for you ... YOU + GOD = VICTORY!

*YOU + GOD = VICTORY!*

# A Heavenly Perspective

## Day 129

If anyone or any demon picks on you, they are picking on Jesus.

*"Who is he who condemns? It is Christ who died, and furthermore is also risen, who is even at the right hand of God, who also makes intercession for us." Romans 8:34*

Do you think your prayers are answered? Then do you also think Jesus' prayers are answered? Jesus took care of it, by love. When He said no weapon formed against you would prosper, it is spelled out for us in the next verse. *"Who shall separate us from the love of Christ? Shall tribulation, or distress, or persecution, or famine, or nakedness, or peril, or sword?" (Romans 8:35 ).* This is actually a rhetorical question that gives a definitive answer no matter how the question is asked.

To the question "who?" the answer is: nobody can be against us.
To the question "what?" nothing can be against us.
To the question "when?" never can anything be against us.
To the question "where?" nowhere can anything be against us.
One of the greatest lessons taught in the Bible that you will ever learn is this: God plus one equals a majority.
Because the who, what, when and where has come up against a force much greater than they can succeed against.
- Joseph learned that lesson in prison.
- Joshua learned that lesson at Jericho.
- Jonah learned that lesson in the belly of a whale.
- Moses learned that lesson at the Red Sea.
- Paul and Silas learned that lesson in jail.
- David learned that lesson against Goliath.
- Daniel learned that lesson in the lion's den.

You and God are a majority. All the things you may face, He has already won the victory for. God has just allowed your inheritance to come to the reality that you are a winner. You have a lot to look forward to.

Start your day today in victory, knowing you have already overcome whatever and whoever may come against you today. No, not because you are all that great ... we're human, we can fail, but our God is a great God and nothing can stop Him!

***God plus one equals a majority.***

# A Heavenly Perspective

## Day 130

The power of God and the kingdom of God is not a fairy tale. It is a reality. We are not to live in FEAR. We can't be in fear of Wall Street or our street. We can't worry about tornadoes, or hurricanes or oppression or natural things. Because we have a supernatural Daddy who has made covenant with us. God is a good God. He loves you; He blessed you with an irrevocable blessing. God has provided healing ... for you ... in your spirit, soul and body.

Instead of being bound up by your circumstances, looking at your present situations, look instead at who God is, look back to the Word, and let it change your perspective. Look to Jesus - the author and finisher of our faith. Stop talking about the circumstance or the problem and talk about Jesus.

—He is the Christ
—The Son of the Living God
—The Healer of your body
—The One who has provided everything you need
—The miracle man
—The One who brings total restoration to your family

Go to the throne, go to the mercy seat, where the breath of God will assure your spirit that what you don't see is more real than what you can see in the natural. The Word of God is more powerful than the word of a man. The Word of God is more powerful than the name of a disease. With the Word of God you can walk out of every situation, and every circumstance that satan has come against you with. Get a different perspective. Don't entertain the voice of circumstance, but listen to the voice of God's Word. It is life to you and health and healing to all your body. It is the reality you need to experience victory and freedom. The Word of God is the most powerful agent that you can cooperate with.

The Spirit gives you revelation of what God has provided.

The Spirit empowers us with understanding and wisdom of God's word, but it's His WORD that He gave us to heal us. Do you meditate on the Word of God? What are you standing on today?

*The Word of God is the most powerful agent that you can cooperate with.*

## A Heavenly Perspective

**Day 131**

You can't change your perspective without changing your thoughts. Do your thoughts sound like this:

- "OMG what am I going to do?"
- "I don't see how this can be for my good."
- "I prayed and I don't see any difference."
- "I don't feel any difference."

Or do your thoughts sound like this?

- "I am expecting the healing power to flow through my life and into by being."
- "I will not settle for sickness."
- "I will not settle for lack."
- "I will not settle for confusion."
- "I will not settle for depression."
- "I will not settle for stealing, killing and destruction, for He has come to give me life and life more abundantly."
- "I have a contract, a covenant."

Read the following scriptures out loud and listen to what the Word of God says about the words of God, and get a heavenly perspective:

*Psalm 119:89: Forever, O, Lord, Your Word is settled in heaven.*
*Psalm 119:105: Your Word is a lamp unto my feet, and a light unto my path.*
*Psalm 119:160: Your Word is true from the beginning: and every one of Your righteous judgments endures forever.*
*Psalm 119:162: I rejoice at Your Word, as one that finds great spoil.*
*Isaiah 40:8: The grass withers, the flower fades: but the Word of our God shall stand forever.*
*Jeremiah 23:29: Is not My word like a fire? says the Lord; and like a hammer that breaks the rock in pieces.*
*Matthew 4:4: It is written, Man shall not live by bread alone, but by every word that proceeds out of the mouth of God.*
*Matthew 24:35: Heaven and earth shall pass away, but My Words shall not pass away.*

***You can't change your perspective without changing your thoughts.***

## POTENTIAL OF A SEED

**Day 132**

All seeds have the potential for a hundredfold return, but not all realize the hundredfold return. What is the difference? Today we will look at the potential of a seed. Potential = a worthwhile possibility; a latent ability that may not have been developed How do we get our seed to reach its full potential? In this series we will review the 4 prerequisites to potential.

**1. You can't misjudge God and His intentions for the potential of the seed He has given you.**

You can't think that God gave you seed and He is wanting you to give more to Him because He is trying to get something from you. The seed you sow has the ability to expand your borders, and the seed you sow has the ability to provide a place of destiny that God has already prepared for you. Lets' look at the parable of the talents (Matthew 25:14-23) to discover more about what the Kingdom is like.

The potential of the seed they had been given had been used to multiply and reach that potential. They had doubled what they had been given, but it wasn't over. They were given more; they were given more territory to go to, with the ability to multiply. The seeding would continue, and so would the harvesting.

They all had been given seed. They all had power in their seeds. Their seeds all had the potential that God had intended for them to reach. You are planting seeds in life, whether you are paying attention to them or not.

Seeds, good or bad, both have eternal residences. So there is a significant difference in which kingdom we are sowing into. God's intention for you is to live an abundant life, here and now and throughout eternity. And He wants you to share what you have been given. Therefore, you have to believe the seed is not only for God's harvest, but for your harvest as well.

*You are planting seeds in life,
whether you are paying attention to them or not.*

# Potential Of A Seed

**Day 133**

*Now may He who supplies seed to the sower, and bread for food, supply and multiply the seed you have sown and increase the fruits of your righteousness, while you are enriched in everything for all liberality, which causes thanksgiving through us to God. For the administration of this service not only supplies the needs of the saints, but also is abounding through many thanksgivings to God. 2 Corinthians 9:10-12*

The potential of a seed! If you can see it the way He sees it in its final form, it has not only caused you to be supplied and increased, it has enriched you to be liberal in all things. Notice that it causes thanksgiving to occur. Have you ever experienced the joy of giving?

Imagine if no one ever experienced the potential of a seed and no one ever gave anything to anyone, ever. The end result is a joyless society with no power of their own. That is what the world's system is becoming—joyless, for they no longer want to help their company to thrive, they want to take from the company. The companies no longer sow seed to their employees. They try to squeeze more work out of them for less pay because they know they are desperate just to have a job. It has become a joyless tragedy, for seeds of trust and goodwill and giving are being withheld. Selfishness negates love.

The opposite is how the Kingdom of God works. It is the upside-down Kingdom. It is pure joy to give, expecting nothing in return from the person you seeded to, but instead, expecting God to honor the potential of the seed sown and providing even more seed because you have sown.

It is joy unspeakable, and it brings glory to God. For you realize whatever you have sown is nothing in comparison to how much God is going to do with it. The potential of a seed is exponential.

Exponential: expressible or approximately expressible by an exponential function especially characterized by or being an extremely rapid increase (as in size or extent) – growth rate.

**The opposite is how the Kingdom of God works.**

# POTENTIAL OF A SEED

## Day 134

The second thing you must do if you want your seed to reach its potential is this:

**2. You must settle it for yourself that IT IS GOD'S WILL FOR YOU TO PROSPER.**

*Let them shout for joy and be glad, Who favor my righteous cause; And let them say continually, "Let the LORD be magnified, Who has pleasure in the prosperity of His servant." Psalm 35:27*

Prosperity: This word in the Greek is shalowm (shaw-lome'); or shalom (shaw-lome'); Most of you will recognize this as a word that means peace. And it does. Amazing! Prosperity means peace. Because when you prosper it causes storms to cease, not only for you, but for others.

We must really get the heart of the Lord concerning how He feels about you having all that you need. You need peace, you need joy, you need health and you need money. So let's understand His heart today as we get the word into us. Be willing to embrace the word, no matter what life has dictated to you at this time.

*The blessing of the LORD makes one rich, and He adds no sorrow with it. Proverbs 10:22*

I want you to know what rich means here, it means: "to accumulate; or to grow (causatively, make) rich". For every need you encounter, God has a seed to meet that need. You already possess abundance. It's just that it may still be in the form of a seed now.

*Through wisdom a house is built; By understanding it is established; By knowledge the rooms are filled with precious and pleasant riches. Proverbs 24:3-4*

There is a whole different mentality we must operate from. Kingdom thinking comes from the King and the way He thinks. We do have access to it.

**God has a seed to meet that need.**

# POTENTIAL OF A SEED

**Day 135**

Let us examine the Kingdom mentality that was in Elijah.

*And the word of the LORD came unto him, saying, Arise, get thee to Zarephath, which belongeth to Zidon, and dwell there: behold, I have commanded a widow woman there to sustain thee. So he arose and went to Zarephath. And when he came to the gate of the city, behold, the widow woman was there gathering of sticks: and he called to her, and said, Fetch me, I pray thee, a little water in a vessel, that I may drink. And as she was going to fetch it, he called to her, and said, Bring me, I pray thee, a morsel of bread in thine hand. And she said, As the LORD thy God liveth, I have not a cake, but an handful of meal in a barrel, and a little oil in a cruse: and, behold, I am gathering two sticks, that I may go in and dress it for me and my son, that we may eat it, and die. 1 Kings 17:8-12*

The widow had no faith in what she had. She had faith that it was the last of her provision before total loss – death. But Elijah was operating out of Kingdom mentality. He saw things from a different perspective. He didn't see it as the last, but as the potential, not only for her and her son to be sustained and provided for, but that it would multiply and reach its potential by providing for him and them, continually.

He had to see it that way or he couldn't have asked for it from her. If you don't settle the fact that seed is the way to the harvest in the Kingdom of God, you can resent what appears to be selfish according to the dictates of the world's way of thinking. But we are not to operate the same way. You have to really believe the benefit of God's Kingdom economy or you will be stifled from helping people to receive all that God has in store for them.

There is no way Elijah could have asked for her last little bit of meal and oil if he didn't have a clear understanding of the potential of what she held in her hand. She didn't have a little. It appeared to be a little, but in God's economic system, she had just exactly what was necessary. A seed that had potential. But it would never reach its potential to provide for her need until it was released.

*operating out of Kingdom mentality*

## POTENTIAL OF A SEED

### Day 136

Elijah had faith in God. He had faith in the promise. He had faith in the power of the seed. He didn't see this as a disaster; he didn't get stressed out about it, because he had tapped into a different level. He was looking from another view. He saw this as an opportunity for her to prosper and get her needs met, as well as his. Just like Jesus did with the loaves and fishes. He didn't need a grocery store; he needed a willing heart with a seed in her hand. You see if you begin to operate in Kingdom mentality, you will not see this as, "How mean is the prophet" or even, "How mean is God to require her to give the very last thing she had to give." NO! If you allow God to change your thinking and your vision, you will see this quite differently.

How wonderful is our God that He sought out a woman who had a great need—a desperate need—and give her the opportunity to allow the seed she had in her hand to provide and multiply and to keep the word of the Lord going. She wasn't just sowing seed; she was sowing into the future provision for the prophet and for her household. You see, this seed would provide a way for the word of the Lord to continue.

Elijah was operating with the wisdom of heaven's knowledge. He saw the bigger picture, so he didn't see this as asking too much from her. He saw it as the answer to her need. His faith was operating, and his faith would help her to overcome her own fear.

*And Elijah said unto her, Fear not; go and do as thou hast said: but make me thereof a little cake first, and bring it unto me, and after make for thee and for thy son. 1 Kings 17:13 KJV*

He made her plant a seed first, because He had the secret of heaven's revelation on the inside of Him. If she planted, if she gave to him the seed she had in her hand, it would provide first for him (seed has to be given to multiply back to you) then back to her and her son.

***He had the secret of heaven's revelation on the inside of Him.***

# Potential Of A Seed

**Day 137**

*For thus saith the LORD God of Israel, The barrel of meal shall not waste, neither shall the cruse of oil fail, until the day that the LORD sendeth rain upon the earth. 1 Kings 17:14 KJV*

Elijah was speaking the truths of heaven under the anointing of Almighty God. This is God Jehovah, eternal God. He was in charge, and He would stay in charge. This announcement would cause faith to arise in the widows heart. I don't believe this woman suffered in the decision-making. I believe when the prophet spoke, it released the atmosphere of heaven's reality and there was an excitement in the expectancy. She was taking the meal, and mixing the oil. But instead of seeing it as just enough to die with, it was seen as enough to live with and to provide for others with. Can you see her as she mixed the ingredients together and it began to multiply right in front of her?

*1 Kings 17:15 KJV: And she went and did according to the saying of Elijah: and she, and he, and her house, did eat many days.*

If we can grab hold of this, we will not only see us being able to provide for our families but we will see the potential of the seed realized in our heart. Our eyes will see the faces of those who will be provided for by the seed being multiplied.

*And the barrel of meal wasted not, neither did the cruse of oil fail, according to the word of the LORD, which he spake by Elijah. 1 Kings 17:16 KJV*

*You shall remember the Lord your God, for it is He who gives you power to get wealth that He may establish His covenant which He swore by your fathers as it is this day... Deuteronomy 8:18*

God wants you to understand His heart towards you. He wants to provide abundantly for you. He doesn't want you to be without and He doesn't want others to be without. He wants to be the answer to your need, and He wants you to be the answer to their need.

*He wants to be the answer to your need, and He wants you to be the answer to their need.*

## POTENTIAL OF A SEED

**Day 138**

The third thing you must do for your seed to reach its potential is...

3. **You have to think the way God thinks for your faith to cause your seed to reach its potential.**

Say out loud, "Every seed has potential."

Faith is the ingredient that can cause your seed to multiply back to you the hundred-fold return. We need to release our seed with faith. Your hundred-fold return will require you seeing things from heaven's perspective.

Can you SEE YOURSELF WALKING IN ABUNDANCE?

*As a man thinketh in His heart so is He... Proverbs 23:7*

*I would have fainted if I did not believe to see the goodness of the Lord in the land of the living. Psalms 27:13*

We must understand that FAITH is an action of obedience which will create a manifestation of your expectation.

God doesn't react to need alone. He reacts with compassion, but somebody has to exercise their faith for the answer to their need.

- Choose to think His thoughts concerning seed, time and harvest.
- Choose to think about your hundred-fold return.
- Choose to think about what you will do with it.
- Choose to think about the ability of God concerning your seed.
- Choose to think of the potential of the seed being realized as you add the ingredient of faith.

*Every seed has potential.*

# POTENTIAL OF A SEED

**Day 139**

The fourth thing you must do for your seed to reach its potential is…

4. **You have to be committed and purposeful in your sowing of the seed with expectancy.**

*Most assuredly, I say to you, unless a grain of wheat falls into the ground and dies, it remains alone; but if it dies, it produces much grain. John 12:24*

Have you thought about how much God is committed to seed, time and harvest?

*For God so loved the world, that he gave his only begotten Son, that whosoever believeth in him should not perish, but have everlasting life. For God sent not his Son into the world to condemn the world; but that the world through him might be saved. John 3:16-17 KJV*

God is so committed to the system He put in place, He gave seed. Not just any seed, but the most precious seed that He had. The Son who was like Him, the Son who had His heart. But God wasn't asking us to do something He wasn't willing to do Himself. He was sowing His Son to reap many sons.

*But we see Jesus, who was made a little lower than the angels, for the suffering of death crowned with glory and honor, that He, by the grace of God, might taste death for everyone. For it was fitting for Him, for whom are all things and by whom are all things, in bringing many sons to glory, to make the captain of their salvation perfect through sufferings. Hebrews 2:9-10*

Jesus isn't expecting anything out of you that He hasn't already been willing to do Himself. He is committed to seedtime and harvest. He provided seed for the sower through His death. He laid down His life, no one took it from Him. No one can take your life from you; you have to lay it down. No one can force the seed you possess today out of your hand, but there is an opportunity for the seed you have to reach its potential.

***Jesus isn't expecting anything out of you that He hasn't already been willing to do Himself.***

# Potential Of A Seed

## Day 140

If you want your seed to reach its potential the questions set before you today are these:

1. Have you misjudged God and His intentions for the potential of the seed He has given you?

2. Have you settled it for yourself that: IT IS GOD'S WILL FOR YOU TO PROSPER?

3. Are you thinking the way He thinks for your faith to cause your seed to reach its potential?

4. Are you committed and purposeful in your sowing of seed with expectancy?

If you haven't been able to answer yes to these questions, now is the time to do so.

Don't be ashamed
– but be willing to turn the tide of your heart today.

If you have misjudged God as a withholder and consider Him hard to serve there is an easy remedy: repent.

If you have not settled it in your heart that it is God's will for YOU to prosper, search and meditate on those scriptures, and come into agreement with God.

Make a declaration of faith that will cause your seed to reach its full potential.

Release your seeds today with purposeful intention and full commitment to the seed, to the perseverance to receive it through the timing of God, and to sowing with expectancy.

*to the perseverance to receive it through the timing of God,*

## Prophetic Word of Hope

### Day 141

I was in prayer one week and God began to speak to me, and I began to type it out. His words were flooding my soul. I knew that I would have to record them to remember all of what He said, but part of what He said was this:

*"It is not people that used to love me that I am seeking for, but those with current love. Those that love me fresh and new each day as I love them fresh and new. The love I have is an awakening to each new day. I want them to love me the same way I love them. There is a heart of desperation that I have for you, for my people. I am desperate to share my love. I am looking for those that will reciprocate. It is birthed by the need, but it continues by desire.*

*I am picking up those who will allow me to. I will hold you, I will heal you, I will present you before my father so that you can receive the fullness of the glory that he has reserved for you as an individual. There is a reservoir of love, of peace, of gifting, that brings hope and love and peace and wisdom that have been set aside for you. It is in His presence as I carry you there by the wings of the Spirit you will experience those things that you never thought possible before. It is the greatest experiences of your life that you have been missing because you have been hitting and missing at being with Me.*

*In my hands, as I uphold you in my Father's presence, as you are presented, you will have new experiences that will take you beyond the places you have been before in Me. Now is the time, now is the season, and now is the reason why you were created to begin to take true form."*

Do you have ears to hear, can you imagine that He wants to hold you and present you before the Father?

Do you understand what is awaiting you there, in His presence?

### *I am picking up those who will allow me to.*

# Living By Faith

## Day 142

I began to ponder why there is so much trouble, so much attack on the Body of Christ in so many ways. I realized it comes down to two important things. We must operate in faith and faith operates by love.

**Operating in faith makes the impossible, possible.** But we can't grow in faith without understanding God's love. So let's start by looking at faith principles. We are in the season of God. Does that sound like a season of impossibilities or possibilities? Is God limited? Or are we limiting God?

Jesus told His disciples, after speaking to the fig tree,

*So Jesus answered and said to them, "Have faith in God. For assuredly, I say to you, whoever says to this mountain, 'Be removed and be cast into the sea,' and does not doubt in his heart, but believes that those things he says will be done, he will have whatever he says... Mark 11:22-23*

Jesus demonstrated and taught them about faith, and overcoming doubt with faith. Jesus operated in faith and He exercised the authority given Him that overrode the natural state of things. He promised His disciples they would operate that way too. This applies to us, His disciples today.

*Therefore I say to you, whatever things you ask when you pray, believe that you receive them, and you will have them. Mark 11:24*

In KJV it says "whatever things you desire". Now it's what you desire, what you ask for when you pray, what you believe you will have, you will have.

If you think that you are living in hard times, with hard circumstances, you may be correct. Some may be experiencing things that are more challenging than others, but we must understand that God has provided a way for us to live under the anointing of God, the favor of God and that the circumstances around us will not be able to dictate our ability to thrive.

*What you ask for when you pray, what you believe you will have, you will have.*

# LIVING BY FAITH

### Day 143

Let me ask you, if people who have received prayer for healing of a disease, and they say they believe they have their healing, but they continue to "go forward" for prayer, is that because they have weak faith? No!

It could appear that way, but you are looking at the outside and God is looking at the inside. They could be exercising their faith by agreeing with what the Word says, until the manifestation of their healing comes in totality. Maybe they need to be touched by His love so they can raise their level of faith.

God keeps telling us to trust Him, trust Him more, and trust Him higher. We, the church, can sometimes make people feel guilty because we have not totally understood faith because we haven't been saturated enough in His love.

Some people may hear a message and get inspired, but they will not really have faith for their circumstance yet. But if they continue listening, and stay around others with faith and if they stay close enough to feel God's love, they can grow their faith. While others who appear to be receiving may only be getting emotionally carried away, but when they will leave, they do nothing with what they heard.

Which one is living by faith?

*To live by faith, one has to continue to feed their faith.*

It is necessary to stay fixed on the truth of God's unfailing love. If they continue to allow the world to influence their thoughts and their actions, then they will not be able to continue to activate and operate in faith. Then they will say, "I tried that faith stuff and it does not work." BUT...

*FAITH WILL WORK FOR THOSE THAT WILL WORK IT*

Faith works by love.

**Trust Him, trust Him more, and trust Him higher.**

# Living By Faith

## Day 144

Faith works by love.

It's a choice of whether we believe it or not.

Does God know you? Does He care about you?

Does the One on the throne know your name, care about you?

Does He love you like He does Jesus? It takes faith to access the truth of that. But if you do, it will change your life because faith works by this love. When you can really believe His love for you, then you quit worrying about how it is going to work for you. You won't doubt that His love for you is real. You won't doubt healing is yours.

Herein is our love made perfect. It doesn't start out perfect, but it can be perfect. There is no fear in love, perfect love casts out fear.

### *Love displaces fear.*

Here is a visual: if you have some milk left in a glass, and you put it in the sink and begin to run the water, then it will become milky water. If you keep running the water, after a while, it's a mixture with just a little milk, and finally, it will run clear.

If you let the love of God come into you, and run into you, and over you, when it is fully developed, you won't be afraid of the devil or your pastor, or being mugged, or terrorist attacks, or cancer, or heart attacks, or plane crashes, or dying... Or ANY THING because you know that you know and you believe the love that your Father has for you and it comforts you.

### ACTION STEP:

*So be honest and ask yourself: Does God know you? Does He care about you? Does the One on the throne know your name, care about you? Does He love you like He does Jesus?*

**Love displaces fear.**

# Living By Faith

## Day 145

How do we measure what level of faith we have? Simply ask yourself: How much fear is still in you? Another word for fear is insecurity or dread.

God did not give us a spirit of fear, but He did give us a spirit of LOVE and it works a peaceful, stable, sound, secure mind. Not insecure! But a secure, sound mind. Christians that are upset all the time, can't sleep, are mostly irritated, angry, discouraged and complaining, because they are in need. But the answer to their need is to understand and access the love of God more. We have all had insecurities and fears, but we need to stop. We should stop! Instead, we need to think about how God loves us and talk about it. We should get up in the morning, and think about His love and thank Him for it; we should ponder it all day long. We should think about how He provides for us, and think about Him through the night until we are fully developed in it.

How much does God love you? Think about it, talk about it, share it with others, speak it until we are saturated with it. Nothing can separate us from that love unless we allow it.

Love has provided for us. Doubt may have stolen from us, and now fear may have some place in our lives, but I am telling you today, nothing can separate us from His love. No one, nothing can shake us because He is pouring His love on us until there is no mixture. He is pouring out the reality of our sonship until we are totally convinced.

When you are fearless, you are a problem for the devil. He can't do anything with you, because he can't scare you. If he can't scare you, he can't stop you, and you will be able to operate in immediate obedience. When we are fully aware of how God loves us, there will be no fear, no fear at all, none, just love.

### Action Step:

*Today: Hand out eviction notices to all the fears in your life!*

***God did not give us a spirit of fear, but He did give us a spirit of LOVE and it works a peaceful, stable, sound, secure mind.***

# Living By Faith

## Day 146

We must be a people who are fruitful and who will embrace change, and in order to do that, we must have faith in God, in God's Word, and do things God's way. What He has told us in His word should be our determining factor of how we live. Then it won't matter what anyone says won't happen. Is it possible for you to be free from your past, for God to use you? Is it possible for God to repair marriages and bring restoration in your relationships? Is it possible that even if you have acted irresponsibly and charged stuff excessively, for God to bring you to a place of good financial standing again?

## Who is it possible to? To those who believe!

Is it possible for those who have received a bad report from the doctor to be healed, for glands to change, bones to change, joints to change, for things to grow or disappear?

## Is it possible? Yes, to who? To those that believe!

Say, "I believe!!" All things are possible to those who believe. Jesus said that. People say, "Well, seeing is believing. I don't know about healing and miracles, I need to see it." NO, seeing miracles will not give you faith. You can see it and still leave in doubt. I have seen goiters fall off, people get up out of wheelchairs, others get deliverance on the spot, and people still walk out saying somehow it was fake. So just seeing it doesn't give you faith.

*I would have fainted unless I had believed to see the goodness of the Lord in the land of the living. Psalm 27:13*

He didn't faint because He believed to see the GOODNESS of the Lord! You have to believe to see the goodness. Come in faith believing to see He is good.

### Declare:
*I believe, today right now, He is good, and if I can believe that, I can experience His goodness covering my problem, right here, right now.*

## *All things are possible to those who believe.*

# Living By Faith

Day 147

Let us look at some people who moved according to faith, and not by sight. Others that had faith in God had tapped into this, do you remember Isaac?

*There was a famine in the land, besides the first famine that was in the days of Abraham. And Isaac went to Abimelech king of the Philistines, in Gerar. Genesis 26:1*

Famine: they were starving in the natural. But Isaac lived under a different system, and had a different reaction to present conditions.

*Then Isaac sowed in that land, and reaped in the same year a hundredfold; and the LORD blessed him. The man began to prosper, and continued prospering until he became very prosperous; for he had possessions of flocks and possessions of herds and a great number of servants. So the Philistines envied him. Genesis 26:12-14*

The reason that Isaac could sow in famine and reap a hundred fold was because He had faith in God. He was secure in His love. Therefore, famine had nothing to do with meeting his need or not meeting his need. His confidence was in the One who could and would bring to him the abundance of heaven, in spite of adverse circumstances.

We have a job to do!

Believe to see the goodness of the Lord right here, in this place, right now. Sometimes you get touched and you get better over time, but it's still a miracle. If it was impossible, and it takes time to change, but it changes, is it still a miracle? Yes, and some miracles happen in a moment of time.

Did God make the heavens and the earth?

Then why would it be hard for Him to touch you?

*Is Jesus the same, yesterday, today and forever? He loves you, and He wants you healed, free, and not struggling any longer.*

### He had faith in God. He was secure in His love.

# Living By Faith

## Day 148

*If you will believe, what is possible? ALL things.*

Do you believe Elijah was sustained by birds bringing in food every morning and night? Do you believe the woman who owed a debt she couldn't pay could take a pot and fill other borrowed pots until the oil paid off her debt and sustained her into the future?

Do you believe that an axe head swam? Can an axe head swim? If you believe the Bible, yes it can! Do you believe a leper can dip in a dirty river and then be clean like a baby's newborn skin? Then why wouldn't you believe that God can give you back your goods, heal your body, save your children, cleanse you of any infirmity? Do you believe that thousands can be fed from a little boy's lunch? Do you believe if you go fishing that a certain fish will grab on to your line that just happens to have enough coins in its mouth to pay taxes owed? Then, do you believe that God will give you money to pay off your bills?

Do you believe a man was conceived in a virgin without a human father, and do you believe He showed us how to live? Do you believe He died, and He resurrected and He was caught up into glory? Do you believe He is coming back at the trumpet sound and we will be caught up together and so we will ever be with the Lord?

If you believe that, then you can believe the lame can walk, and the blind can see, and that which is lost will be found. Because nothing is too hard for the Lord. AND nothing is impossible to them that believe!!

Focus on the Lord, focus on His love. Focus on the healer, the One who makes us whole in every way, anyway. There is healing in the name of the Lord. God will minister to us today as we look to Him in faith.

*There is healing in the name, there is restoration in the name, there are miracles in the name, of the Lord.*

*Focus on the Lord, focus on His love. Focus on the healer, the One who makes us whole in every way, anyway.*

# An Invitation From The Most High God

**Day 149**

"An Invitation From The Most High God" Is a prophetic word that conveys the cry of God's heart for the church of today.

The Lord says: Do you see it? Do you hear it? Do you see it? Do you hear it? If you hear it, you can do it. If you see it, you can be it. Do you see it? Can you hear it?

It's the cry from heaven. It's answering My cries. The hungriness of your hearts, the desperation that you have for more of Me. And because you have put out that desire and because you have honored Me above all things, I am bringing an invasion to this earth. I am going to invade this place with the miraculous in a new way. You're going to see it, and you're going to feel it, and you're going to be it.

For don't you understand that under the old way and under the Old Testament, and under the old covenant, they couldn't see and couldn't partake of all of My glory, because it would be too much for them. Oh, but I sent Jesus. I sent My son and He portrayed My glory upon the earth. And what a glory He portrayed. For He was the very essence, the very mirror of Me, the very image of the Father. He never did anything without checking with Me first. And He showed you how to do it. He could hear what I was saying, He could see what I was doing and He just simply carried it out. He saw through the eyes of the Spirit, and He heard through the ears that which comes from portals of heaven. He could hear the sounds echoing and reverberating through Him. And there was no doubt that I would do what I said I would do. So He walked with Me, and He talked with Me. And then He spoke My words and did My actions and brought about My glory and My Kingdom to earth.

And now I am looking and I'm watching and I'm seeing who will recognize. Who will recognize where the glory lies? For your eyes are looking to heaven, but if you look into the mirror of My Word you would understand that you sit there also. For did I not tell you that you are sitting in Christ already in heavenly places? Do you not understand the price that was paid through My Son has already provided you the fullness of My glory?

*If you hear it, you can do it. If you see it, you can be it.*

# An Invitation From The Most High God

## Day 150

Oh yes, it's a revelation revolution because My children are finally going to understand that it is not something that they are looking for, it is not something that they have to wait to have. But I have already made My deposits on the inside of you. It is your inheritance. I have made you to be kings and priests in My Kingdom already. You are containers of My glory. The only problem that you have is the places where you haven't surrendered. For My glory is available to anyone who would dare to ask and be willing to sacrifice. You must walk away from the things that have held you back before, on purpose, and draw the line, never to return. You must keep your eyes fixed on the road that is before you and not be pulled away by the circumstances or the plots of the enemy.

But My people who are called by My name, they will see by the eyes of the Spirit, they will hear what the Spirit has to say. They will see it happen before it happens and then there will be no fear. For all fear will be washed away with the truth that is from the higher place of thinking. For as you allow My mind to become your mind, as you have the mind of Christ, there is no room for fear. There is no room for doubt. There is no room for circumstantial evidence.

You will no longer see people that are sick; you will see the remedy for their sickness. You will no longer see the need, but you will see the provision that I have provided to come into their life. You will no longer see the lack, but you will see the abundance. You will no longer hold back those words that I have hidden on the inside of you, but they will roar through you like rivers of living waters. And it will cause those that are thirsty to be filled to overflowing.

You're running into My streams. You're beginning to understand. You're beginning to go deeper into the depths of My love. And therein lie the secrets that you've been waiting for. For as you hide under the shadow of My wings, as you understand that I am all those things that I've promised, and that I am in you, you will no longer doubt your ability to do the things that I told you you could do.

*For My glory is available to anyone who would dare to ask and be willing to sacrifice.*

# An Invitation From The Most High God

## Day 151

A revelation, a revolution. What is going to take place on the earth is going to take an army of people. An army that is not looking at the natural, not being held back by that which is seen, but is looking beyond those places and seeing the potential of what can be, and bringing to pass. Oh it will be a wonderful day. To see My army marching the way that they were always called to march. In unity -- with one voice, and one purpose. No longer worrying about the way that they are presented to others, or what people think or say, but only hearing My voice and not caring about that. For My voice thunders with many waters. It will clear out all of the debris and it will set you free to set others free. And there will be a joining together. That is why it is so important that you understand, that you value, that you honor those that have known this way before. You will not be the first; you will not be the last. But you will be those that are of the utmost importance for this time frame of history.

For I am coming back for a Bride without spot or wrinkle and you will help iron it out. You will lay the path of righteousness before others that they may walk in it. You will dive into the deep so that they will follow you, for someone always has to lead. And My heart's cry is crying out: Who will be the leaders of the movement of the latter days? Who will be a part and sign up to be a part of the army that I am raising up to release and to roar and to have fire and glory?

For don't you know that it is oh so easy, all you have to do is surrender. All you have to do is set aside those things, to put Me first in every place of your heart. For don't you know I am tired of vying for your attention. Don't you know that I'm looking past all of the things, and I see My glory deposited inside of you, and I so want you to value it. I so want you to respond properly to it, I want you to let it come forth. I want you to let go of all of the things that have hindered it and held you back. I want the river to flow once again and the fountain of My glory to be seen.

*You will be those that are of the utmost importance for this time frame of history.*

# An Invitation From The Most High God

## Day 152

Man tries to build their own Kingdom. They focus on themselves, they focus on their need, they focus on their own abilities. And they get caught up in thinking they could actually do this. But the only reason you can do anything is because you're Mine. Because of the deposits that I've laid on the inside of you. Because what I've already promised you is true. I've laid treasures inside each one. And this is the season that I will walk amongst My treasures. And I will pick them up and I will call them Mine again. My treasures. I'll pour more of Me inside of you, if you'll just let the glory out. It will be an intense time. A time where My fire will burn on the inside. A time where it will get rid of all the dross. A time where all of the things that have been eating at you will have no more power because you are letting the glory out from the inside.

Jesus was the firstborn among the brethren, carrying My glory to the earth. But have you not been born-again? Do you not already have the glory? You are crying out for the ability to see it but I am crying out for you to be it.

A revelation is necessary. A revelation that comes by My Spirit, not by the flesh. The flesh will burn away, and My Spirit will rise within. And My glory will be known and seen and you'll begin to wonder why: How can my hands do these things? How can my feet go those places? How can I understand the things I've never understood before? And yes you will. You will see your hands be laid on people and they will recover. You will begin to speak with authority and you will see the winds calm. You will see things rise and fall at your command because you're beginning to understand who you really are now: sons and daughters of the Most High God.

*A revelation is necessary.*

## An Invitation From The Most High God

**Day 153**

I am the Most High God.

I am the Most High God.

I am the MOST HIGH GOD.

Just let Me have My position in your life, in your thinking, in your walking, in your doing, in your portraying. I am the MOST HIGH GOD. If I am the MOST HIGH GOD in your life, then what is the hindrance? There will be no more hindrances for I am THE MOST HIGH GOD. I am high enough that it will wash away your sin, it will wash away your mindsets, it will wash away all of your frustration, it will wash away your fears, it will wash away your anger, it will wash away your need. I am the MOST HIGH GOD. And you are My people. You are the ones that I am looking to. I'm looking to you. I am opening up eyes that are hungry to see. Oh, you're going to see. It will be a time for the seers to come forth like never before. The people who don't even know, the new people. And the old people, the ones that are seasoned by the flavoring of My Spirit. The ones that have spent time already, that have seen all of the great men and women that have gone before them. That honor them and have partaken of their blessing and of their anointing and of their cup. And those that are brand new in Me, just babes, but dare to believe. For don't you know that the last shall be first, and the first shall be last?

Oh, I am having a good time watching my people come into their own, watching for this time of history to come to pass. For I am anxious for My Bride. I am preparing the table and soon I will cry to you to come home. But in the meantime, I want you to know who you are on earth. You are those that have been called to take dominion. You are those that are called to pull down, to root out, to destroy the works of the enemy. You are called to replant and to rebuild and to restructure.

*You are the ones that I am looking to.*

# An Invitation From The Most High God

## Day 154

I am going to invade your thought life with ideas that are from heaven. I am going to give you the ability to have wealth if you dare open your eyes. I am going to speak things into your spirit that are going to set you free from the bondages of slavery. But I need you to be a servant. I need you to have a mindset of humility. I need you to have the assurance that as you walk into the things that I have for you, the way to stay pure is to stay a servant. The way to stay big and to stay kingly and to stay in your proper position is to humble yourself at all times. To recognize that it is always Me that gets the glory although I have deposited it in you.

For you see if we would just work together this thing would all work out. For you give Me all the praise and the honor and the glory and I'll pour out more upon you and in you and through you. All I ask for is the acknowledgement. Because I am the MOST HIGH GOD. Now when I said I would not share my glory with another, that's what I mean. I want you to recognize that it all comes from Me. But I didn't withhold My glory from you, I put it inside of you with Jesus. I did it on purpose. I did it so that you could portray Me properly. And so the glory is coming, and the glory is here, and the glory is now, and the glory is in you. What will you do with it? What will you do with My glory?

Build the Kingdom. Build the Kingdom. I put it in you to build. I put it in you to lay foundations. I put it in you to raise up structures. See it, and be it. See it! See it! See it! And join yourself to it. If you can see it, if you can trust Me, you can build it. What does My Kingdom look like? It looks like a wonderful place full of satisfied people that have been healed and delivered and set free. Who are walking in fullness of who I am. They understand and they are walking and they are so glad that they obeyed. My Kingdom contains people who know how to praise Me. They know how to worship and honor Me. They know how to keep Me first in their life. My Kingdom is being built by those people. My Kingdom is a people who are without stress and without worry because their confidence and their trust has already been discovered inside of Me.

*I need you to have the assurance that as you walk into the things that I have for you, the way to stay pure is to stay a servant.*

# An Invitation From The Most High God

## Day 155

There is nothing that I will withhold from you if you just walk uprightly. Now you don't have to walk it alone. I told you I will be with you every step of the way. I will never ask you to do anything that I haven't already provided for you. I won't ask you to go anywhere I haven't already walked. I will ask you to do the impossible as you take hold of My hand, because with Me all things are possible. All I want you to do is join Me. All I want you to do is acknowledge Me as the MOST HIGH GOD. Be a part of My Kingdom. Build it.

Can you see it yet? Are you looking through your spirit eyes? I am in this place. I am opening up your spirit eyes. I am allowing you to see your future if you just look a little harder. What does your life look like in the Kingdom? What are you doing in the Kingdom? What deposits have I made inside of you already? What are you going to be doing with them? Look a little harder and you will see yourself on the road, on the pathway. It is a righteous road, it is a narrow road, but if you look you can see yourself there. Oh, it's a "worth it" road. It is a "worth it" road! It is where My glory is, it's where My power is, it's where My purity is, it's where My holiness is, it's where My freedom is, it's where My peace is, it's where My comfort is. Just choose it.

Do you see yourself? Can you see yourself walking righteously? Can you see yourself free from sin? Can you see yourself making a difference? Can you see yourself reaching your hands out to meet the needs of others? Can you see yourself in abundance? Look again! You don't have to do it; you just have to be it. You don't have to make it happen, I'll make it happen. Just look with spirit eyes. Just hear My voice and obey Me. The smallest details will bring about the biggest abundance. I am training you to hear Me in the small things. If you obey Me in the big things, it will bring you to a place where you will obey Me even in the smallest requests of My heart. And the smallest requests of My heart will bring you the biggest abundance of your life.

*You don't have to make it happen,*
*I'll make it happen.*
*Just look with spirit eyes.*

# An Invitation From The Most High God

## Day 156

You see, it is a time for you to see Me as THE MOST HIGH GOD. And to see Jesus as the King of Kings. And to see yourself as partakers of all of that. Be witnesses for Me. Witness who I am with your eyes. See it with spirit eyes and then tell them, just tell them what you see.

When you see Me in My fullness, when you see Me in My glory, when you understand My very nature and My character, when you are so well acquainted with Me that you can fully trust Me completely because you've abandoned yourself to My care and I've proven Myself strong, they too will see Me. They will see Me through you. The way it was always been meant to be. And the blind will see. And the mute will speak. And the dead will be raised. And the poor will be fed.

Separate yourself.

Separate yourself.

Separate yourself.

I have given you your will. You have to will it because I gave you that opportunity. But when your will aligns with Mine, there will be a release, there will be a happening. There will be a revolution. It's happening inside of you first and then it will happen on the outside. You'll understand things you've never understood. You will read My Word and it will be alive to you because it will be you and Me alone.

The revelations from heaven I am not withholding any longer.

I am pouring out an abundance of understanding, of wisdom. It will run all through the land and those who dare to drink of it will bring forth an ocean of love to the earth. An ocean of love. A tsunami of My greatness because I am THE MOST HIGH GOD.

**They will see Me through you.**

# LOVE IS A CHOICE

**Day 157**

Isaiah 61:1

*"The Spirit of the Lord GOD is upon Me, Because the LORD has anointed me to preach good tidings to the poor; He has sent Me to heal the brokenhearted, to proclaim liberty to the captives, and the opening of the prison to those who are bound..."*

In order to bring freedom to the world's captives, we need to walk in a new level of freedom ourselves. The call of God is not going to just happen by some kind of "magic" but by us coming together as a people that understand our call and our destiny and are reaching out to others.

We at Liberty Life Center have been experiencing:

> A new passion   A new freedom   A new environment

We have reached new levels because we've come together in prayer and continued to grow corporately in our ability to yield to the Holy Spirit.

We've learned that we must live to be with Him, to feel His arms of love around us, to be assured that He is good, to be secure that He has a plan for us and know that He will never forsake us. It is the greatest feeling in the world when He is the center of your life. But you have to fight for your place in Him.

Our first calling is to love Him; there is no place of peace without it. Nothing can fill His place in your heart and anything else will leave you empty. We have to love Him, seek Him, and be embraced by Him; then we will be in a proper position to display Him.

Love is a choice.

Love is the ability to make the right choice according to God's Word; it's choosing the highest good according to God's Word in every situation. Love never fails. It can't according to 1 Corinthians 13:13.

*Our first calling is to love Him; there is no place of peace without it.*

# I AM A SOUL-WINNER!

## Day 158

We are in a season of embracing the reality that God has placed us here on this earth, in this time frame of history, to individually and corporately make a difference. We make an impact by refusing to be compromised in our beliefs and in our actions. That is accomplished by having God's heart on the matter and settling before Him what we individually will and will not do.

We can't just be good, we must do good.

One way is to make a conscious effort to be aware of those who are already in our everyday lives and be bold enough to share the good news of Jesus. He has changed our lives and we love to talk about Him.

My nephew's church invited a guest to give his testimony. He was not someone well-known. He didn't care about being known by people, just God. He decided he would sit outside of the hospital and pray when God told him to. He has many testimonies including one of raising someone from the dead. I don't know all the details, but what I do know is that this man's testimony so affected my nephew's father-in-law, that he just determined he was going to be bold, be strong, and reach out. He owns a furniture store, so he has many people in his area of influence. Of course, he has owned the store for years, so he always had opportunity. He just hadn't recognized it and seized it fully. By his commitment, and just by being aware of the opportunities, he won 10 people to the Lord in one week!

*He has changed our lives and we love to talk about Him.*

# I AM A SOUL-WINNER!

## Day 159

The question then, isn't whether or not we should reach out. The question is, how do we reach them where they are? If we are to do that, we must begin to understand that God has put DNA in every individual. This will help us. If we know what everyone is made of, we can reach them with wisdom and meet their basic needs.

The following daily devotions will consist of three keys that will help you to be sensitive to others and help you to be a more effective witness.

Take the following declaration and declare it each day of this series and I pray it will empower you to realize the boldness you have through the love that is in you!

Declare:

I declare that I'm advancing the Kingdom of God; I'm not a hearer but a doer! I am loved and accepted by God. I love and accept others. I don't forget who I am. I know who I am and because of that I will be blessed in all that I do.

I am blessed to be a blessing. It is part of who God made me to be. I will give to others, and they will come to love Jesus because of my giving. I will be blessed, they will be blessed, my church will be blessed, and the Father's heart will be blessed. AMEN!

*I am blessed to be a blessing.*

# I AM A SOUL-WINNER!

**Day 160**

1. The first inherent need that everyone has is to be loved, because we have the DNA of God.

God IS LOVE. So now let's look at the beginning of man in a little different way: (Genesis 1:27) "Love created man in his own image, in the image of Love created he him, male and female created he them."

God is love. He created us in that image of love.

We can conclude then, that mankind is always seeking love, as well as having an inherent need to "Be Love" to others.

(1 John 4:17-18) Of course the perfected love this is referring to is Jesus. Because He is in us, we have boldness to be as He is in this world. How was He? (John 3:16)

So God is love, mankind was fashioned in His image and likeness; therefore, the basic DNA was love.

Jesus redeemed us after the fall, by being sent by love to bring love back to perfect union with God. Jesus brought reconciliation to mankind to God's original intent. (1 John 4:11)

There is no denying there is power in love. We needed it, we received it, we were changed by it. There are multitudes of people that need it, that need to be changed by it, and we can offer them His love and ours because we have embraced God's love … We must display God's love … and share God's love.

That is the primary tool of a soul winner. Love will reach them.

How do I know? It reached you. It reached me.

**We have the DNA of God.**

# I AM A SOUL-WINNER!

## Day 161

2. The second thing that is inherent in the need of man, is the need for acceptance.

As hard as it may be for many to understand, people join gangs, go through beatings of initiation to the point of death, obey outrageous demands, and are willing to give up their own life … all for one thing – acceptance.

Why? Mankind was made to belong to something.

We have to be a part of a bigger picture. We need interaction and to feel that we somehow, somewhere, are valuable. We have the ability to meet this need as well, by shedding light on the truth that they are already accepted in the beloved.

*"To the praise of the glory of his grace, wherein he hath made us accepted in the beloved." Ephesians 1:6*

Do you remember the day that you were overwhelmed by the knowledge that He loved you and accepted you as His own when you didn't deserve it?

I remember the day I was full of darkness, lost in an abyss of sin with no way to help myself out. I remember when Rev. Angley prayed for me, and the darkness had to leave, and His glorious light came inside of me, redeeming me, changing me, owning me. I was free. I found myself in Him again. I realized His love and acceptance that day. God's heart accepted us before we were decent and acceptable. Someone out there is waiting to be accepted.

To be a soul-winner we must give acceptance.

*God's heart accepted us before we were decent and acceptable.*

# I AM A SOUL-WINNER!

## Day 162

3. The third thing that is inherent in man is to be not only provided for, but to provide.

Satan has tried to mess with God's original DNA by taking His people into lack.

Let's go back to Genesis and the fact that love made us in the image of Himself. Love never wants those whom they love to be in lack … Love wants to provide.

Every person has the nature to be a giver. That nature is stolen when others fail to show love and circumstances begin to dictate their belief system instead of the truth of God's word. The world has a system of economics; it is credit, debt, survival.

God (Love) has a system too. It is: Seek Him, seek His righteousness in your life. Be a God magnet.

You have a promise:

*"But thou shalt remember the LORD thy God: for it is he that giveth thee power to get wealth, that he may establish his covenant which he sware unto thy fathers, as it is this day." Deuteronomy 8:18*

Why would God give such a promise?

He is establishing His covenant, but He is establishing it for purpose. He wants you to be blessed, to be a blessing.

**Be a God magnet.**

# I AM A SOUL-WINNER!

## Day 163

We must understand that everyone's real nature is to give. It is not something we have to do, but it is something that we were created to want to do.

That is why Jesus said in Luke 12:33-34

*"Sell what you have and give alms; provide yourselves money bags which do not grow old, a treasure in the heavens that does not fail, where no thief approaches nor moth destroys. For where your treasure is, there your heart will be also."*

Do you like to receive?

Me, too!

Have you given and found out it was even more fun?

Do you know why?

You are re-identifying with the real you.

Inside of every person is the DNA of God that says you are above, not beneath. You are a lender, not a borrower. You have everything it takes to make a difference.

That is why Satan is so busy at twisting it, perverting it, and stealing from people. Then they will forget who they are. They will forget they were made to help others. They were made to meet the needs of the needy.

You have something because you are something. You are created in God's image and in His likeness.

When you realize that giving is a part of who you are, you will go out with an intention!

*You are above, not beneath.*

# I AM A SOUL-WINNER!

## Day 164

"Listen! Behold, a sower went out to sow."

When you understand the principle of sowing and reaping, your mindset will be "not what the Kingdom can do for me, but what can I do for the Kingdom?"

Jesus was talking to the Pharisees one day, and He was trying to explain this principle. He was trying to get them to understand how things work for you as you work for God.

He was trying to get them to see that GOD had invested IN them and they were to draw from that which was within and give to those who did not have.

He was trying to get them away from wanting to be the "big shots" to walking in the love of God to the point they would, out of His nature, be doers and givers. He was also trying to show them how they could always be prosperous.

By giving you receive treasure in heaven that will not be exhausted. You're building up your heavenly account so that when you need it here on earth, you can make a withdrawal.

To be a soul-winner we must give to the needy. The ones who are poor in any way, are in need of you today!

If we do the will of God, if we are good and do good, good things are coming our way!

Stop talking about what you could've, should've, or would've and start DOING what's in your heart to do today.

***By giving you receive treasure in heaven that will not be exhausted.***

# BE A BLESSING

Day 165

We are blessed to be a blessing. Today I want to tell you about a cute little old lady who was standing in front of me in a line at the pharmacy. Her name was Ella. She looked sad and bewildered. I listened in as she asked them to check again to see if they had her medicine in generic. The answer was the same the second time, "no." The cost of her prescription was just around $100. I said, "It is hard these days with the price of medication." She said, "It is so bad, but I have to have it, it is for high blood pressure and I don't want to have a stroke." I said, "Well my church gave an offering to bless you," and I handed her a $100 bill. She said, "Oh no, I can't." I said, "Oh yes, we really want you to have it." With tears swelling in her eyes, she thanked me, hugged me and said, "Tomorrow is my 80th birthday." I said, "Well Jesus loves you very much. Happy Birthday." She said, "Oh yes, I know He does, I wouldn't be here without Him." Yes, indeed :)

Let me tell you something, when you know that God loves you, when you know that God has accepted you, when you know that God has blessed you – it will cause you to look at life from a totally different prospective.

### DECLARE:

*"I am coming into the realization that I am really accepted by God. Therefore, everything in my life will be alright. Today I want to sow my seed to you Father, and thank You for the way that You love me. I thank You that I don't have to seek blessings because You've already blessed me with all spiritual blessings.*

*When I call upon You, Your ears are open to my cry; when I begin to reach out You've already been reaching out towards me. When I ask You for something You've already provided what I have asked for. As I live my life for You today let the windows of heaven open and let me see with Your eyes the blessings that are being manifest for my life as I realize I am accepted by You, and loved by You today. In the Name of the Lord Jesus Christ, AMEN."*

### *It will cause you to look at life from a totally different prospective.*

# The Floodgates Are Opening

## Day 166

Today's Kingdom Guide is an excerpt from a recent prophetic word from the Lord over our church. Your Action Step for the day is to read the following prophecy once and when you finish start right back at the top... But this time speak it aloud over your personal life and allow the Holy Spirit to touch and minister to you with these words.

"This Church is crying out for its future and it's coming closer. I am matching them spiritually with My purposes. (Everyone is finding their groove) They will realize the importance of the foundation that I have laid in them for such a time as this. My church is realizing the importance of their training; they are realizing the importance because it is time they begin reigning as I rain upon the earth and they can because of their desperations for more of Me and My desires to come to pass on My earth. Spiritual diligence is happening.

Floodgates are opening: the floodgates of evaluation, the floodgates of evaluating your own life, the floodgates of knowing who you are, and evaluating what your own needs are.

*Today, evaluate the level of your desperation, evaluate how much, how much, how much, how much are you aware that you and your gifts are needed.*

<u>The Lord is asking you today...</u>

<u>How much, how much do you love me?</u>

<u>How much are you tapping in to what is going on in the spiritual realm?</u>

<u>How much are you desperate for what I am doing on the earth?"</u>

*Spiritual diligence is happening.*

# The Floodgates Are Opening

**Day 167**

Today's Kingdom Guide is an excerpt from a recent prophetic word from the Lord over our church. Your Action Step for the day is to read the following prophecy once and when you finish start right back at the top... But this time speak it aloud over your personal life and allow the Holy Spirit to touch and minister to you with these words.

"My floodgates are opening for magnification: the magnification of Me, the magnification of My whole self, the magnification of Who I am on the earth, the magnification of the declaration of Who I am, that will come out of your mouth, the magnification of the reality of Who I am, the magnification of what I have provided. Realize I haven't stopped my hand of giving. I haven't stopped my faithfulness, I have not stopped those things that My people have need of. They just need to come into the rain. Come under the cloud. Come into the place where it is raining now.

For I am raining, I am raining, I am raining.

The floodgates are opening of realization of Who I am - to who they are. Realization of who they are to the world, and realization of My purposes that need to reign in their hearts. They are taking hard places, they are saturating them with My presence. They are making a way for others and they are making a way for themselves. Because now they are a unit. They are unifying things by the Spirit. There is a spiritual attachment to others around the world in the spirit right here, right now. The same heart, the same spirit, the same desperation, desperate to desperate. To those who are desperately waiting for Me, to those that are desperately waiting for more, and they are touching those who are desperately waiting for someone to come to them with answers. The Sons of Issachar discerned the times to make David King, now the Sons are discerning the times for THE KING, for the KING to rule and reign again. Your praises are putting Me in proper position, your praises are putting Me on the throne. Your praises are putting Me in a place where I can have full engagement with you, full engagement with you, and on the earth.

*I REQUIRE THE FULL ENGAGEMENT, I REQUIRE THE FULL ENGAGEMENT.*"

*The same heart, the same spirit, the same desperation*

# Displaying God's Love

**Day 168**

We are on a journey. God told us that we are conquerors.

There is much we must understand if we are to conquer all that God has given us to conquer.

God is requiring us to stay in the river of unity.

To do that we are going to have to agree on the same goals, and we must go to the things that God has revealed to us about our identity as a church, if we are to move forward into all that He has for us. Specifically, "Embracing, Displaying, and Sharing God's Love". It's what drives our church. However, it's not just for our church, it's God's heart, so its really for everyone, especially those who say they are Christian. Over the next series we are going to delve into this declaration and mission of Displaying God's Love. It is my prayer that we will come to a greater understanding of our purpose, destiny, and strategy to fulfill the call on our lives.

So, I am going over some of the things He has said to describe us. Those of you that have been here for many years; and those of you that are now a part of this family, need to know that Liberty's foundation is based on Isaiah 61.

*"The Spirit of the Lord GOD is upon Me, Because the LORD has anointed Me To preach good tidings to the poor; He has sent Me to heal the brokenhearted, To proclaim liberty to the captives, And the opening of the prison to those who are bound; To comfort all who mourn, To console those who mourn in Zion, To give them beauty for ashes, The oil of joy for mourning, The garment of praise for the spirit of heaviness; That they may be called trees of righteousness, The planting of the LORD, that He may be glorified."  And they shall rebuild the old ruins, They shall raise up the former desolations, And they shall repair the ruined cities, The desolations of many generations.*

*Isaiah 61:1-4*

***God is requiring us to stay in the river of unity.***

## Displaying God's Love

### Day 169

He said to me a few weeks ago, I am the one who named you Liberty. That was my mandate on you and the church. It is a big name to live up to. But you are called to bring freedom. To do that, you and your people will walk in a new level of freedom.

If you look further at those scriptures, we are not just to bring freedom to the captives, but we are to reproduce trees of righteousness.

That means we must first walk in the fullness of that. We must first be planted ourselves.

Planted on the Word; with the Word going down deep on the inside of us. Planted on the dreams God has given us as a church and as individuals.

Planted in our purpose: To love, to bring healing and wholeness, and then we are called to rebuild old ruins and former desolations.

That means INDIVIDUALS and CITIES. For it goes on to say we will rebuild ruined cities and generations that were desolated.

I have now been able to attend two Encounter weekends, and I see the effectiveness of that; people coming together for the purpose of experiencing God on a one-to-one encounter with Him. In the midst of others, there is still one-on-one with HIM. But there is a mass amount of work from the people that are behind it. They are making an investment in the generations that have been left desolate by the attack of the enemy.

It is time for us to understand that the call of God is not going to just happen by some kind of "magic" but by us coming together as a people that understand our call and our destiny and are reaching out to others.

*Planted in our purpose: To love, to bring healing and wholeness.*

## Displaying God's Love

### Day 170

We have moved more corporately into agreement in prayer. We have continued to grow in our ability to yield to the Holy Spirit to move in our midst. It isn't that we haven't been in these deep waters before. We have. I remember many times we were unable to get up off the floor from prayer or intercession, and I have pictures to prove it! We are moving past the things that the soul dictates and are concentrating together on the more important things.

I was thinking of all the people all over the world that walk in the heat to hear one message and then stand in the sun to receive it and they stand there for hours. Perhaps, God just wants us to relate to those who do not have the advantages that we usually enjoy. To see how desperate we really are. How committed we are to worship Him, to serve Him, and to move forward together. I am so happy about the fire of the Holy Ghost, and that while He is burning within us we can swim in the river of God. Where the enemy is watching from the shore and unable to come near us. We are learning that MORE happens when we press in together as a unit. I believe God is giving us opportunity to go to another level. But I don't want to visit there. I want to stay there. I want to keep pressing higher. I want His glory to be normal among us. I want others to come because He is known for being in our midst. I am so excited that God is igniting our passion with the things that excite Him.

When we praise Him, He comes, when we share our testimonies, it brings Him near. When we utilize the gifts we have, He is filled with joy as He sees us doing something with what He gave us.

---

*We are moving past the things that the soul dictates and are concentrating together on the more important things.*

## Displaying God's Love

**Day 171**

We have also been going over some of the other things God has said to us to help define us. We must continue on this journey together and to do that, we must be secure in our identity that He has given us. I remember the place I was, the moment He said this to me. I was so excited because it just fit with who we are. I was in a conference. In the midst of many, but submerged in Him until it felt like no one was there but Him and me. In the midst of His presence, He spoke to me about Liberty. About His love for us, about our future. He showed me growth and souls.

He talked to me about the draw. It wouldn't be the things you read about in another book. It would be because we had come together in a unified heart and one voice to seek Him, to find Him, to proclaim Him because we were so filled up with Him, that He would flow out of us like a river. He would announce us as we pressed into Him wholeheartedly. He said the formula was embracing, displaying and sharing His freedom.

We talk about embracing Him. And we do, when the musicians are playing and there is a corporate anointing or someone is praying and it is drawing us to Him. But how often do we press past the difficulties at home to press into His presence to receive the embrace we need daily? What will it take for us to remain desperate for His presence? What will you be willing to do to stay in His arms? What if He requires you to pray at HOME an hour a day? What if you have to turn the TV off? What if you have to get up earlier or go to bed later? How can we win against the enemy if we can't press past just being uncomfortable in our everyday life to seek Him with all our heart?

*He showed me growth and souls.*

# Displaying God's Love

## Day 172

We must live to be with Him. To feel His arms of love around us; to be assured that He is good, to be secure that He has a plan for us and He won't ever leave us. He has surrounded us with His songs of deliverance. It is found in His embrace. It is the greatest feeling in the entire world when He is the center of your life.

I went to the Encounter and someone told me about another young man who was in a service where an evangelist was so on fire. He was so excited as he identified with him so very much, and so he approached him and told him he wanted to be just like him. To his surprise, he said he would meet him the next day and share his deepest secret with him about how it could be done. He was so excited. He dressed in his best suit and met him the next day at the address provided. He was surprised to find the evangelist at the water side in his bathing suit. He said, what are we doing here? He said, I am going to show you my secret. He took him in the water. Ankle deep, waist deep and then up to his shoulders. The young man could feel the anointing get stronger as he went into the deep waters. Then the evangelist pushed him under the water and held him there. He came up after a while gasping for breath. He said, what are you doing? He said I am showing the secret of the power of the presence of God. You must gasp for Him as you gasp for every breath, as you did right then. You must fight for your life in Him. God has called us to have a passion to be in His embrace.

It is easy when we are here. But we must go after that embrace daily as we seek His face, His touch, His breath. We must long to feel that warm embrace stronger today than yesterday, because we can't live without it. And as we do, we will find Him waiting to hold us, to love us, to be with us. Then we will begin to move into the rest of His dream for us. Then we will become a display for Him!

*Be secure that He has a plan for us, and He won't ever leave us.*

# Displaying God's Love

## Day 173

He has called us to display His love. Paul was very strategic as he faced down the obstacles in the way that kept those whom God loved in bondage to idols that were lifeless and useless. He had been embraced by the power of his love to go out to conquer the world.

He had been with Jesus, he had the same spirit that raised Christ from the dead awakened on the inside of him. He was so alarmed by the state they were living in. He was looking at lost souls and it provoked him. He got stirred up with truth. He knew the Spirit of the Lord was upon him. There was a real God that was making Himself known to them through someone who was not afraid to proclaim the one He had been with. This God was superior to the gods they had heard about. This God could make a difference for them, and finally answer the cry of their seeking hearts.

Paul addressed them from a place of intimacy. The place no one realized was available to them yet. He would tell them the truth that Christ has made a way for them, and they also had access to the one true God.

He knew that his relationship with God could move others hearts beyond what is natural, into a place where they could let go of their mind and their training and their education and receive the real thing they were missing. You must understand something; our first calling is to love Him.

Every person is called to love Him. There is no place of peace without it. There is no where you can find somethingelse to fill the void. You will find that in the end, all other paths leave you empty.

We must understand that we are a vital link between Him and this troubled, lost world outside.

*WE HAVE TO LOVE HIM, SEEK HIM, BE EMBRACED BY HIM, AND THEN WE WILL BE IN THE PROPER POSITION TO DISPLAY HIM.*

*He had been embraced by the power of His love to go out to conquer the world.*

## Displaying God's Love

### Day 174

We are the church. We are not supposed to display the world or the world's system. We are different. On purpose is different. Our identity is different than other people. God Himself defined it this way:

*And ye shall be unto me a kingdom of priests, and an holy nation. These are the words which thou shalt speak unto the children of Israel. Exodus 19:6*

God is telling Moses that he needs to speak truth into these people. They didn't know who they were, but He was making their identity clearer for them. They were not ordinary. They just wouldn't and shouldn't fit in with other people.

Why? Because they were chosen.

They were part of a different kingdom. God said they were all priests. They must have been a little confused. They thought that was an office that was given to the Levitical tribe only; that there were different levels of priesthood.

Yet God said they were all priests.

The priests were set apart for the service of the tabernacle. To make sure everything was presented properly before the Lord so that everything would be in order when He would show up with His power and His instructions. They were to minister in prayer, praying between porch and altar asking for mercy instead of judgment.

They were to be the ones to lead others into the ways of God and they were to hear from Him so that others would also have ability to know His voice.

The people were also to be different enough that their nation would be holy. Imagine a nation of people who displayed holiness. That was God's intention for His chosen.

We are His chosen. His intentions haven't changed.

*They were to minister in prayer, praying between porch and altar asking for mercy instead of judgment.*

# Displaying God's Love

## Day 175

Peter repeats the words from Exodus and gives even more insight into what we, His chosen people, now should be displaying to others.

*But you are a chosen generation, a royal priesthood, a holy nation, His own special people, that you may proclaim the praises of Him who called you out of darkness into His marvelous light; who once were not a people but are now the people of God, who had not obtained mercy but now have obtained mercy. 1 Peter 2:9-10*

We are to be walking billboards proclaiming His mercy upon our lives and offering that same mercy to others; living before the world in a way that causes them to see Him because we have displayed Him properly. How could that happen?

*Read The Message version: "But you are the ones chosen by God, chosen for the high calling of priestly work, chosen to be a holy people, God's instruments to do his work and speak out for him, to tell others of the night-and-day difference he made for you—from nothing to something, from rejected to accepted. Friends, this world is not your home, so don't make yourselves cozy in it. Don't indulge your ego at the expense of your soul. Live an exemplary life among the natives so that your actions will refute their prejudices. Then they'll be won over to God's side and be there to join in the celebration when he arrives."*

We are beginning to realize that we are chosen as instruments that display the difference between our God and others; between what a sin life looks like, versus a life filled by God's love and light. To display that, there are choices we have to make along the way: Choices to: -- Live differently -- Act differently -- Living, not piously, and not having judgment or prejudice because of our priority status. For we were all once sinners also, undeserving, unrighteous, and nowhere near holy or priestly.

But now, because of His love, His embrace, we can live a life displaying what has affected us to the point that we live our lives gladly choosing different ways to please Him. Because we love Him, because He first loved us, He has become the center of our life. He is the reason we exist and we can't breathe without knowing Him more each day.

*We are to be living before the world in a way that causes them to see Him because we have displayed Him properly.*

# Displaying God's Love

## Day 176

We are living in a wonderful time. It is time to go up. It is time to go higher and there is a reason for it. We are building a tabernacle fit for God to dwell in.

When we dwell with Him we are able to gain what is needed to build a proper place for Him to dwell, and when we glorify Him His glory will fill the tabernacle we have prepared for Him. This is where I believe we are right now.

*Go up to the hill country and bring lumber and rebuild [My] house, and I will take pleasure in it and I will be glorified, says the Lord [by accepting it as done for My glory and by displaying My glory in it]. Haggai 1:8*

First you have to go up, and then you have to be focused.

Your intention must be to build and to glorify Him. When you do it for His glory He will also display something. HIMSELF!

We keep asking for the glory to come down, but now, because of Jesus – His glory dwells inside of us.

We are asking for Him and He is asking for us to just let it out of us. God has deposited something inside of us that is great. With that greatness comes responsibility.

When He gives vision, He also gives grace because He knows there will be obstacles. But we serve a big God and nothing is too hard for Him.

It may seem hard. But if you want to go up, you can and you will. You are not doing it in your own strength. God has provided everything you have need of.

*With that greatness comes responsibility.*

# Displaying God's Love

**Day 177**

We are to build a tabernacle for Him to dwell in. That is YOU. You are the tabernacle now. He wants his glory to shine there. He wants you to be the light to the world. He wants to display His love through you.

*Your God has commanded your strength [your might in His service and impenetrable hardness to temptation]; O God, display Your might and strengthen what You have wrought for us! Psalm 68:28*

He has even provided the hardness you need against the temptation the enemy would bring. To display Him properly, you will need assurance of His acceptance. And you have it.

*Ezekiel 20:41 I will accept you [graciously] as a pleasant odor when I lead you out from the peoples and gather you out of the countries in which you have been scattered, and I will manifest My holiness among you in the sight of the nations [who will seek Me because of My power displayed in you].*

God is doing something right now. He is calling His people together. He is calling us to display Him for a reason. Because as we do we are releasing what is necessary for Him to come and show His holiness. There may be other so called gods that try to steal your worship...

Distractions • Depression • Circumstances • Other relationships

But there is only One that deserves your worship.

And I don't just mean by raising our voices and our hands. I mean living a life that is obedient. For that is the highest form of worship.

People can come and lift hands and voices and even come to the altar, but the difference they will display to the world, will not come from what we do inside these walls. It will come from being passionate to continue to press into His presence, knowing who we are in Him, AND taking action to reach out.

*He wants you to be the light to the world.*

## Displaying God's Love

### Day 178

Paul taught us something else in: 1 Corinthians 2:1 (AMP)
*AS FOR myself, brethren, when I came to you, I did not come proclaiming to you the testimony and evidence or [a]mystery and secret of God [concerning what He has done through Christ for the salvation of men] in lofty words of eloquence or human philosophy and wisdom;*

He is saying, what we experience, as high as we go in HIM may not be the way to win others over. He is not saying he doesn't have lofty words of eloquence, because he was the most educated of all the disciples. He isn't saying he didn't have philosophy or wisdom, he is just saying, that those things are not going to make the difference for a lost and dying world.

*For I resolved to know nothing (to be acquainted with nothing, to make a display of the knowledge of nothing, and to be conscious of nothing) among you except Jesus Christ (the Messiah) and Him crucified. 1 Corinthians 2:2 (AMP)*

He had a resolve. His resolve was not to display all his eloquence and all his wisdom – he was resolved to display Jesus. Nothing else. He was aware of the importance of being authentic.

He couldn't have anything to lean on except his knowledge of Christ and the power of the cross. He knew if he could bring that, lives would be changed forever. We must have the same resolve. WE need to be committed to Christ. Fully committed. How can we display a God we only have read about or heard about?

We must KNOW Him. By His Word, by time with him in prayer. He can't be a God you visit on Sundays and maybe another day of the week. He must be your God. Jesus must be your Saviour. The Holy Spirit must be your companion and your teacher. God knows who you are and who you are to be. But we must fight for the relationship with Him.

We must make Him a priority in our lives.

***WE need to be committed to Christ. Fully committed.***

# Displaying God's Love

## Day 179

While Paul was saying he wanted to share just Christ and Him crucified, he did not mean that we need to water down the power of God. Just the opposite is true.

*For our gospel did not come to you in word only, but also in power, and in the Holy Spirit and in much assurance, as you know what kind of men we were among you for your sake. 1 Thessalonians 1:5*

They walked in power, because they had co-labored with the Holy Spirit. That doesn't mean they just had signs and wonders and miracles all the time. They operated in the gifts of the Holy Spirit when they were needed. But the whole picture of how they lived is that daily, when they needed to know something, they got info from the Holy Spirit. It meant that they let the Holy Spirit lead them to the right places and the right people at the right time.

One day I went to see my grandson Gaven, who was in the hospital for a high fever. I parked at the wrong end of the hospital and had to walk all the way around the building and that hospital is very large. I got about half way around and was wondering if I was even going in the right direction. I ran into a young lady who said she would take me where I wanted to go. She began to walk with me, and suddenly, I knew.

I said, thank you so much for helping me and blessing me, you need me to pray for you, don't you? I told her I was a Pastor and she said, yes, so we stopped on the sidewalk, I laid hands on her and prayed, and prophesied to her and she wept and God began to heal some things. She said it was right on and that I read her mail. She was filled with hope again. Why? Because I was able to display my relationship with God. I could be bold, because I know His voice. I can share the truth, because I am assured it is the truth.

If you know your God, and you are filled with the power of the Holy Spirit, then you will easily display Him to others and you will be enabled to face whatever you need to.

*I could be bold, because I know His voice.*

# Displaying God's Love

## Day 180

*It doesn't mean we won't face anything. No, we will actually, but we have a promise. And you became followers of us and of the Lord, having received the word in much affliction, with joy of the Holy Spirit, receiving the Word in much affliction. 1 Thessalonians 1:6*

For followers then and followers now, It may not be an easy ride. It was a decision that people were making to follow Christ in a time it could cost them their very life. They had to endure something. Affliction. But they could, because they had joy from the Holy Spirit. God was smiling through them.

We sometimes have a hard time smiling through a hang nail. But they were resolved to know Him and to display Him even if it cost them their lives. They could be stoned, crucified or face the lions in the coliseum. But to them, if knowing Him and loving Him, meant they had to face some things, then they would face them; but not alone, together with the Trinity and with each other.

They were examples. They were disciples that others could follow and be secure in their life and in their growth.

*...So that you became examples to all in Macedonia and Achaia who believe. For from you the word of the Lord has sounded forth, not only in Macedonia and Achaia, but also in every place. Your faith toward God has gone out, so that we do not need to say anything. 1 Thessalonians 1:7-8*

Paul says they have brought not just any word, but the Word of the Lord; they were the sound that was needed.

Not just locally, but in every place.

- In the church
- In the business
- In the different cities and regions

### *God was smiling through them.*

# Displaying God's Love

## Day 181

Their faith was decided; determined to show forth the praises of Him.

They had been obedient to the heavenly call. They had embraced the truth of God and the price of His Son, Jesus, and they displayed Him to others because they were not willing to back down, no matter what.

They went out. They stayed in unity; they loved God with all their heart, soul and mind. And it made a difference.

We are here today because of them and others that followed in their footsteps. So we are in a new season. We need to press forward together, but with purpose.

Not just so we can grow deeper in the Spirit, though we most certainly will, but also so we can get filled up with what is necessary for us to be effective in our calling.

The Spirit of the Lord is upon us. Yes He is. So we can preach and proclaim and bring liberty to the captives, and to heal broken-hearted people.

I have seen them. They look like they are OK on the outside, but inside, weeping, hurt and wounded. They needed something more. They need to embrace God, and sometimes through human arms. They need to see Him displayed by determined, passionate people who love Him and demonstrate that love without apology. As they experienced seeing others free, they were able to let go themselves of some things.

*Get filled up with what is necessary for us to be effective in our calling.*

## Displaying God's Love

### Day 182

The importance of Unity.

God has been speaking to us for the last couple of years about staying together, about being a team. It is harder for me today to do things altogether by myself, than to include others. One of my favorite things is to see the gifts of others coming forward.

Unity and celebrating one another is not just something we should do. If we don't do it, we have seen what the enemy has been able to do. The Body of Christ has often been segmented and divided because we've not understood how important it is for us to dwell together in unity.

One of the major things that bring us together in unity is to come together in prayer. If I could agree with you in prayer I probably could walk with you in unity the rest of the way. Look at this following scripture:

*"Again I say to you that if two of you agree on earth concerning anything that they ask, it will be done for them by My Father in heaven. For where two or three are gathered together in My name, I am there in the midst of them." Matthew 18:19-20*

When we can get in unity our prayers become so powerful that God will respond, not some of the time, but every time because we're in unity. Remember: first with God, the trinity. In one place in one accord, with heaven's will and then with each other!

I am so happy we are going to come together in agreement in prayer, and we will see what our God will do.

*In one place in one accord,
with heaven's will and then with each other!*

## Displaying God's Love

### Day 183

Say this after me:

"God is a good God, God loves ME and God wants to bless ME!"

Get that in your mind and in your spirit, and when you wake up in the morning begin to think about how much God really loves you.

He loves you so much; He has already provided you with a blessing. Oh yeah, we are blessed!

*Blessed be the God and Father of our Lord Jesus Christ, who has blessed us with every spiritual blessing in the heavenly places in Christ, Ephesians 1:3*

God is not "going" to bless us; He's "already" blessed us with every spiritual blessing. Get into your spirit and into your mind that once you come to understand that you are accepted by God, everything in your life will be alright!

You know God has accepted you, you know that if God is for you, who can be against you? You find in this scripture today that He's already - He' not going to - it's God's will - to bless you. He's already blessed you with all spiritual blessings, but you have to come into the understanding of how much God loves you so that you can step into that arena where He's blessed you. He's not going to bless you, God has already blessed you.

Now on your job you can be sure that you are on the way to a blessing. We should be looking for the hidden treasures that He speaks to us about. A road of discovery that as we walk holy before Him, all the blessings He has provided for us will manifest in our life and through our lives.

Now find someone today and tell them:

"God is a good God, He loves YOU and wants to bless YOU!

*He's not going to bless you, God has already blessed you.*

## Displaying God's Love

**Day 184**

We are called to preach and bring love and freedom to others. We do have a choice. We can agree, or we can settle into our usual mode of doing things and let the aggressiveness go. But then others may never hear the truth about His love. They may not understand salvation.

We don't know when Jesus will return, but we know He will. We know He is coming soon. We know He is looking for some people to rise up and conquer some things right now, to take back that which the enemy has stolen. We need to fight for the vision of this house. We need to do our part and stay on the same pathway. We must be vibrant, passionate people that want His heart and want to touch the lives of others. If you are a part of Liberty, then you need to become a part of the vision that God has placed upon us. We have many leaders in this church that have their own vision, their own passions. I want you all to reach all your dreams. But you will not if you won't dream Gods dreams with me about this house.

I remember when I had the heart for the nations, but not for this city. God will not take away your dream, but you can stop it from coming to pass by not becoming a part of the corporate vision and call. God believes in you. He knows you and he knows what He can do through you. We have been given a mandate, and God is not retreating from it. We must not either. The devil IS a LIAR. He cannot steal our hope, our dreams, our children, our finances or our destiny… unless we give it to him on a silver platter. So, let's agree again that the dreams of God are worth fighting for.

*<u>We will embrace Him…We will display Him…We will act like kings and priests…We will have power…We will use that power to win the lost…We will go after the things that He has asked us to.</u>*

**We know He is looking for some people to rise up and conquer some things right now.**

# Displaying God's Love

**Day 185**

If you are not coming to church with the intention of growing, don't worry-you won't. If you are not taking notes in service if you are not going over them, if you are not agreeing with someone else, if you are not putting the word in your heart, you will not grow.

What can we do? We can be actively participating in our church home groups and actively inviting someone even if it inconvenient to you. We can realize we have opportunity to invite people to an unusual setting to meet an unusual God and make unusual friends. We can be pursuing Him, and His dreams, corporately, then individually. We can embrace Him every day. WE can display Him every day.

The Spirit of the Lord is upon us to preach good news by living our lives the way it pleases Him.

Let us embrace Him today, not for the sake of making ourselves feel better, but for the purpose of knowing that from the overflow of His presence, life comes to us and through us.

Let us display His love & His freedom as we recognize our call.

### SAY:

*I am a part of a chosen people. A people who are free from the world, and free from sin. I am called to be loved by God. I am called to fellowship with God. I am called to be filled up with his love to the overflow.*

*So I yield now to you Lord. But I yield for purpose. Fill me Lord*

*Fill me with all your intentions. Let me know your affection. And empower me to see who you see that needs it.*

*Let the overflow of my life in you be on display for others to join in the celebration of knowing you.*

---

**The Spirit of the Lord is upon us to preach good news by living our lives the way it pleases Him.**

# Displaying God's Love

## Day 186

Intimacy with God is being confident in your position with Him. This confidence comes from being embraced by Him and knowing the power of His love. You can't become 'godly' by trying; you become 'godly' by training. When you are confident in His love, then YOUR passion and your love for God will drive you to spend time with Him, getting His heart and obeying what He says.

*Love never fails. - I Corinthians 13:8*

You must be compelled by your passion to spend time with Him. Communication is important in any relationship, and that is what prayer is! It involves BOTH listening and speaking. If you are to really embrace His love, then you must transition from knowledge of Him to an intimate relationship with Him.

Don't fall into the trap of knowing what you already know and letting go of these intimate times. Seek Him further for deeper knowledge and a closer bond. Our hearts need to burn within us to know Him better.

God promised Jesus a bride (that's us… the church!). His bride will love Him with all their heart, soul and mind, committed until the end of times. When that occurs the dynamic of heaven and earth will come together.

Declare 1 Corinthians 4-7 over yourself:

*GOD'S LOVE is patient and kind. HIS LOVE is not jealous or boastful or proud or rude. It does not demand its own way. GOD'S LOVE FOR ME is not irritable, and it keeps no record of being wronged. HIS LOVE does not rejoice about injustice but rejoices whenever the truth wins out. GOD'S LOVE FOR ME AND MY FAMILY never gives up, never loses faith, is always hopeful, and endures through every circumstance.*

**Our hearts need to burn within us to know Him better.**

## Displaying God's Love

### Day 187

So many times people say yes to God on Sunday, and then three weeks later they're doing just the opposite of their short-lived commitment. They come up with every excuse in the world. The reality is that you are going to have to learn to stay committed to what God has called you to do. In order to walk in unity, you have to stay committed no matter what situations you face. If you will stay committed to what God tells you to do… no matter what it looks like, feels like, sounds like – you can have the best job you ever had. You can make more money than you have before. Yes, I know they say this is a recession. God is not moved by a recession, He's moved by your commitment to walk in unity in the Body of Christ and if you're willing to dwell in unity God, is willing to command blessings upon your life forevermore!

Be committed to do what God has called you to do, no matter what. If this is your commitment, if you've made up your mind that this is the way you will live your life, get ready, God's about to command something over you that's going to be more than you can contain, it's called the blessing of life! Get involved in what God is doing in worship, celebrate the presence of God, get committed to walking in unity and watch how God is going to do the impossible for you!

### DECLARE:

*"To see God move I must be totally committed to doing what God has called me to, no matter what. I will be committed to where God has placed me. I sow my seed because God has given seed to the sower and on this day, I choose to recognize that which I've sown is flowing back to me from the hand of God. Because as I release what's in my hand, God releases what's in His hand.*

*I will not live in lack because I have the blessing and the promise from God. My family will never be forsaken. I have sown seed and I walk in the blessing of the Kingdom of God. I am in unity; therefore I have certain things that the world cannot alter and that's the blessing of life forevermore, in Jesus' Name, AMEN."*

**Get involved in what God is doing.**

## Displaying God's Love

### Day 188

You see, if I can get you to pray with me and we can honestly get into agreement, everything becomes a possibility and success is not a question, success is a fact. I am believing that God will continue to help us to dwell in UNITY at a higher level, because there we will experience what we can't experience any other way.

So today, we are not going to come into agreement for our needs. Instead I want you to focus on agreeing with the needs of those in your life and around you. I want you to exercise your faith for them even more than you would for your own situation.

We must press forward for each other, and with each other.

#### DECLARE:

*"To walk in unity, I must be around people that I can pray the prayer of agreement with.*

*Father you emphasized the importance of prayer, the importance of agreement, and the importance of sowing a seed together because you knew that in doing that, we would be establishing the power of the Kingdom of God, so that what we say today will come to pass.*

*Therefore, I declare miracles of healing, I declare miracles of deliverance, I declare miracles of salvations upon my friends and family members today. I declare the intervention of God in every situation that concerns those around me, and I declare victory for them in Jesus' Name, AMEN."*

*We must press forward for each other, and with each other.*

## Displaying God's Love

*Day 189*

*Love never fails. But whether there are prophecies, they will fail; whether there are tongues, they will cease; whether there is knowledge, it will vanish away. 1 Corinthians 13:8*

- But the Love of God doesn't make mistakes
- The Love of God doesn't fall down by the wayside
- The Love of God is sustaining
- The Love of God NEVER fails

When you walk in love you're not a failure.

When you walk in the understanding of love, you're not a failure; when you make your choices based upon the Love of the Father, you cannot fail!

If He's designed you to win, then walk in the vehicle that He gave you and that is LOVE.

Because of the Love of God failure is not an option!

Failure shouldn't come into your vocabulary - success is the only option when you walk in Love. The Love of God will never fail!

### Declare:

*"My seed that I give represents my commitment to Your love, Father, and I am expecting a return in the heavens and in the natural.*

*By capturing the revelation of Your love in my life, I will not fail because Your love never fails. I sow my seed and Father I thank you that You've given me the vehicle of LOVE and I will walk in the success that You've called me to.*

*I will be the example that you have mandated me to be.*

*I will be a witness so that others will come to Your Love.*

*My seed represents my commitment to Your love and I am expecting a return in the heavens and in the natural in the Name of Jesus, AMEN."*

**When you walk in love you're not a failure.**

# Displaying God's Love

## Day 190

The Love of God! It's the most powerful thing that a man or woman can ever experience in their life.

So many times people say, "Oh it's being filled with the Holy Spirit..." No, being filled with the Holy Spirit is wonderful; I don't know how I can live without the power of the Holy Spirit in my life. But the reality is that I couldn't have the power of the Holy Spirit if I didn't experience the Love of the Father.

If I'd never accepted the love that He bestowed upon me through giving His Son Jesus, if I never allowed the Love of God to take control of my life and take me out of the depths of sin and place me into a place of acceptance with the Father, if I never meditated and understood the importance of God's Love in my life, then I could never have experienced the power of the Holy Spirit or understood or experienced the blessings of God and what God has done for me.

Love is the key factor.

*Love never fails. But whether there are prophecies, they will fail; whether there are tongues, they will cease; whether there is knowledge, it will vanish away. 1 Corinthians 13:8*

Underline, highlight, circle this in your Bible! You need to get in your spirit that all these other things are good (not saying they are wrong or not real, or beneficial) – people can get into all these other areas and make mistakes.

- **BUT THE LOVE OF GOD DOESN'T MAKE MISTAKES**
- **THE LOVE OF GOD DOESN'T FALL DOWN BY THE WAYSIDE**
- **THE LOVE OF GOD IS SUSTAINING**
- **THE LOVE OF GOD NEVER FAILS**

***The Love of God!***
***It's the most powerful thing that a man or woman***
***can ever experience in their life.***

# God's Ways Set Your Future

## Day 191

Every day we are faced with a choice--do I do what is right or what is easy? Sometimes choosing to walk in integrity is not the easy road, but it will pay in the long run. When you are walking in integrity you are walking in obedience to God. When you are in obedience to God, you are in favor with God and man.

> "Let not mercy and truth forsake you; bind them about thy neck; write them upon the tablet of your heart: So shalt you find favor and good understanding in the sight of God and man. Trust in the Lord with all your heart; and lean not unto your own understanding. In all your ways acknowledge Him and He shall direct your path." Proverbs 3:3-5:

Integrity means "to be truthful, trustworthy, honest, and sincere." To be full of integrity is to choose right over wrong, convictions over convenience, truth over popularity, and to uphold God's high standard over word and deed.

I want to place my trust in the great and mighty God, not in man. When you are trusting God, He lines things up in the natural for your benefit to bring about His perfect will. In Numbers 27, Joshua walked in loyalty, obedience, and in integrity before Moses and God. During that time, Joshua didn't know he would be chosen to take Moses' mantle and lead the Israelites into the Promised Land. Serve God, serve His leaders; and your destiny will be secured by God Himself.

### PRAY:

*Heavenly Father, I thank you for your mercy and grace that is so abundant. I know I have not always been found perfect in integrity but I do know that you have. Lord, I want to be more like you. Let your will be done in everything that I do whether it be at school, home, work, or when I am out with friends. I want to be found trustworthy in your sight. Let your Holy Spirit guide and convict me daily to always do what is right. In Jesus' name, Amen.*

**Serve God, serve His leaders; and your destiny will be secured by God Himself.**

# You and Me Eternally

## Day 192

You and Me Eternally; A prophetic word of the Lord to you...

"Some of you have come to think that there's a cost to come into My presence, but the cost for coming into My presence was paid for by My Son. He is the One that paid the price, not you. Coming into My presence will only take your life and make it better. It will only turn the things around that need to be turned around. It will only make the things that you desire come to pass. And even those who love me and even those that have honored me, satan comes and tries to take you off the course, telling you that it's not worth it all.

But what would you invest in? What is worth the investment of your time? What is worth the investment of your affection? What is worth the attention? Where will you place the value?

There are those that I have already prepared. They're waiting to hear from you. And so many of you want to jump and run and do the things that leave Me out. But I'm inviting you to come and do the things that will join Me to you, that will bring the fun and the life that you've been looking for. I'm the one that never leaves. I'm the one that's always connected. I always know what you have need of, and that's my heart – for you to thrive, not just survive. I'm looking for ways to make your life have joy and satisfaction. I just need you to come along with Me. To agree and walk this life out with Me day by day, minute by minute, together, hand-in-hand, heart-to-heart. I'll drop My thoughts right inside yours. I'll let you see how to prioritize and how to become you wise. You ask of Me and I say yes. You ask for wisdom and I will give it to you. You ask for direction and I'll tell you which way to turn. You ask for more and I'll pour My love out on you like never before, because there's never an end. There's never an end to My love. There's never an end to the flow. There's never an end to how much I will give you. Because My love will never end. My affection for you will never stop."

*I'm looking for ways to make your life have joy and satisfaction. I just need you to come along with Me.*

# You and Me Eternally

**Day 193**

"My commitment to you, it never goes away. I'm committed to you throughout eternity. I would just like you to be the same. I made you in My image. I made you capable of this. I gave you gifts and talents and opportunities. I just wish you'd take them with Me. If only you'll let Me wrap My arms around you tonight. I'll dry your tears. I'll let you see the hope that you've desired. I'll let you know that everything will be okay. Because when I'm involved, everything will be more than okay. I want to be your best friend, not just an acquaintance. I don't want you to just know Me as Lord, but as Savior and King and as the One that loves you forever. I want to draw you right into the place that I've prepared for you. I want to teach you. I want to train you. I want to let you know how it all works out in the end. I want to encourage you and draw pictures for you.

I want to run around with you and let you see the flowers of life that you've been missing. I want you to see the sun the way that I make it every day. I want you to be aware of the beauty, so that you can enjoy My creation. I want you to see the faces that are happy as well as the ones that are sad. I want you to hear the joy and the laughter, as well as the ones that are crying out for help.

I didn't create you for burdens. I created you for answers, but I created life for you to enjoy it. I created a life for you that has all kinds of wonderful things at the end and along the way. I don't want you to wait 'til heaven to see My glory. I don't want you to wait until you're there until you can enjoy life everlasting. Because life everlasting began on the day you asked me in your heart.

So every day there's a treasure hunt for you - something hidden that I'll reveal. Something that I've tucked away, waiting to see if you want it. With expectancy I wait to see if you're going to come and to look for that which is hidden, so that I can see your face as you spin around in grace. So come along with Me and let this life be what it's supposed to be—You and Me eternally."

*I want to let you know how it all works out in the end.*

# Nehemiah's Heavenly Perspective

## Day 194

To have a proper perspective that matches the one that heaven has, we have learned that instead of focusing on our condition, we must start focusing on our position. Our understanding and acknowledgement of our position provided us by Jesus will change our conditions. But if we only look at our conditions, we will never operate in our true position as a son or daughter of Almighty God. Our minds are beginning to change as we begin to understand who we really are in Christ. He has given us significance. We are beginning to understand how much meaning our life really has and how much power and influence has been entrusted to us, as we are His representatives on earth.

God knew what the requests were before you came to Him. He had already provided the answer through Jesus' sacrifice on the cross for our sins and sicknesses. God is much more aware of the whole picture, and your part of it. He is not concerned with the things that appear like such a huge obstacle to you, because He has already prepared whatever miracles may be necessary to get you to the end result of His divine design. When we begin to understand the blessing has already been pronounced upon our life, we boldly approach the mercy seat of God. There we receive His love and mercy whenever we need assurance, because we have entered into a new level of trust with our Father.

Through that close relationship with Him, we begin to take on a new ability to see from a heavenly perspective. We not only begin to operate in the understanding that we have favor because of the blessing upon our life, we begin to see that the things that are important to God, are important to us. There is more to life than just getting by. There is a purpose for us.

Each one of us has an important role to play and that role will help us to discover the hidden gifts and talents God put in us before the foundation of the world, so we could live out our life knowing that we made a difference to others. This heavenly perspective – focusing on eternal things, the things that will make a difference for others, is what really gives us fulfillment and excitement along the way.

*He has given us significance.*

# Nehemiah's Heavenly Perspective

## Day 195

To others, our focus and our lifestyle may appear ridiculous, but eventually our lives will make the very impact that they needed. As we are more in love with God, we move past self-focus and begin to focus on giving Him what His heart desires. We begin to welcome change in our lives, even if it seemingly interrupts the natural flow of life.

When we desire to please Him more than we desire for Him to meet all our demands or desires, we are placing ourselves in position for many miracles to take place in our life.

The people in the world right now are looking for authenticity. They are looking for someone who has proof that they are living under a higher reality. They are longing to belong. That is why they get caught up in the cults, the occult and even gangs. They are living a different life, longing to find the answer that has some meaning to it. That is where we come in, to display that our God is not only alive, but He has provided us a life worth living for. Sure, we have valleys, but we have even more mountain tops! Yes, we have many challenges, but we are intimately acquainted with the One who has all the answers! We face tribulation, but we are with the One who has overcome them all! So why are we not living in a way that always draws people to Him?

Most Christians have the idea that they are insignificant. Especially those who don't seem to have an obvious, prominent place. But God has chosen each of us to live a life of significance. In fact, much is depending on you realizing the power of the influence you have. If you have relationship with God, then you have favor, and favor gives you influence in whatever status of life you have

*"For You, O LORD, will bless the righteous; with favor You will surround him as with a shield. Psalm 5:12*

Today is meant to be significant. It is up to you to realize it and take advantage of it. Ask God to open your eyes to see the opportunities set before you today and to see where your favor is awaiting you.

*Today is meant to be significant.*
*It is up to you to realize it and take advantage of it.*

# Nehemiah's Heavenly Perspective

## Day 196

Let's look at a man who seems to be insignificant until he starts to see things from heaven's perspective.

*"The words of Nehemiah the son of Hachaliah. It came to pass in the month of Chislev, in the twentieth year, as I was in Shushan the citadel, that Hanani one of my brethren came with men from Judah; and I asked them concerning the Jews who had escaped, who had survived the captivity, and concerning Jerusalem. And they said to me, 'The survivors who are left from the captivity in the province are there in great distress and reproach. The wall of Jerusalem is also broken down, and its gates are burned with fire.'" Nehemiah 1:1-3*

This is bad news. Sad news. But to some it would just be news. Unless you had become acquainted with God in a way that you knew what that meant. I believe this man, Nehemiah, saw things from a different perspective. You see, what this meant was there was no place for worshiping Almighty God. There was no temple for the people to learn, to grow in the knowledge of God, to become one with each other and to prove that they were chosen of God. Worst of all, there was no temple, no place for the presence of the Lord to dwell.

*"So it was, when I heard these words, that I sat down and wept, and mourned for many days; I was fasting and praying before the God of heaven." Nehemiah 1:4*

Nehemiah was broken-hearted. He was affected because he was no longer just living a life that was all about him. It is obvious that his relationship with God has affected his life to the point that he was concerned more about God's heart, and the lives of others, that it would cause him to not just hear the news—he would do something about the news. The first thing would be to communicate with God through the power of prayer. He needed to see more than the problem; he was looking to see the answer. He got rid of his logic by fasting. He set aside time to be with his God and to go where he needed to go, to get what he needed to get.

*He needed to see more than the problem;
he was looking to see the answer.*

# Nehemiah's Heavenly Perspective

**Day 197**

Who is this Nehemiah? Is he a king? No  Is he a priest? No... Is he a prophet? No.  As a matter of fact, he looked insignificant in his position in the natural.  He was just an average man, with a very secondary position in life. You see, he was a cupbearer to the king. A cup-bearer was an officer in the royal courts, whose duty it was to serve the drinks at the royal table.

On account of the constant fear of plots and intrigues, this person had to be regarded as thoroughly trustworthy to hold this position. He had to guard against poison being put in the king's cup, and was sometimes required to swallow some of the wine before serving it. This would take courage. He was about to discover that this position had a primary purpose, for he was exactly fitted into God's perfect will in the position he held on earth.  For the Lord had a plan and he was included in the plan ... to turn all things around for good. Nehemiah was an amazing employee. He must have been, because what is about to unfold to us through his life, is quite unusual. *"And it came to pass in the month of Nisan, in the twentieth year of King Artaxerxes, when wine was before him, that I took the wine and gave it to the king. Now I had never been sad in his presence before. Therefore the king said to me, 'Why is your face sad, since you are not sick? This is nothing but sorrow of heart.' 'So I became dreadfully afraid,' and said to the king, 'May the king live forever!'"* Nehemiah 2:1-3

There is a reason for this. Having a sad countenance in front of the king was not allowed.  It could cost you your position ... or your life. This was nothing that Nehemiah was doing to manipulate. He was sad. He just was being transparent. When the king noticed, Nehemiah let him know, and quickly, that this has nothing to do with his respect and honor to the king, but as he was honoring his employer, another honor was arising again in his soul. He thought of his God, and his brethren and he suddenly had a boldness. He transformed in a moment of time, from being afraid to being bold and speaking out of the very depth of his heart's cry: *"Why should my face not be sad, when the city, the place of my fathers' tombs, lies waste, and its gates are burned with fire?"* Nehemiah 2:3

How about you, where you work?  Would you be able to call on your boss for help?  Are regarded as "thoroughly trustworthy"? You may have the courage to ask, but do you have the respect? Or you may have the respect, but do you have the courage and openness of your heart?

*He thought of his God, and his brethren and he suddenly had a boldness.*

# Nehemiah's Heavenly Perspective

## Day 198

Nehemiah could not keep the cry of his heart on the inside; he just had to speak out what he was feeling. He had been in the place of intercession. He had stood in the gap for himself and for the people of God. This was his prayer: *"And I said: 'I pray, LORD God of heaven, O great and awesome God, You who keep Your covenant and mercy with those who love You and observe Your commandments, please let Your ear be attentive and Your eyes open, that You may hear the prayer of Your servant which I pray before You now, day and night, for the children of Israel Your servants, and confess the sins of the children of Israel which we have sinned against You. Both my father's house and I have sinned.'" Nehemiah 1:5-6*

He had humbled himself. He had presented himself before the mercy seat. And now, he would find that he had indeed found help in a time of trouble. He repented for himself. He stood in the gap and he repented for the children of Israel. The atmosphere shifted. Instead of him serving an earthly king, suddenly there was a change of heart, and a change in circumstances, as he recognized that he was serving another King as well. He was a servant in two spheres at one time.

Many times, when we have a position that some count as important, we excuse ourselves from also being the example to others of serving the King of all kings. We are to be great in whatever our "job" is here, but we must also be excellent in the realm of the spirit. We must be the spiritual representatives for the Kingdom of God. Without recognizing the importance of our heavenly call and how it affects earth, we can return to selfishness. Selfishness or self-centeredness is the root of all sin.

Think about it ... all of your sins go back to this root somewhere down the line. Ultimately, it's all about you, what you want, what you desire, what is more convenient for you. If this is a pattern in your life, then you are in need of an identity change. Once you realize your true God-given purpose in life, your focus incurs a shift. As a representative of the Kingdom of God your focus will be on the King and on the needs of the others around you.

*We must be the spiritual representatives for the Kingdom of God.*

# Nehemiah's Heavenly Perspective

Day 199

By pursuing God for help in the matter of those that held a dear place in Nehemiah's heart, he not only began to get revelation from God Himself and insight into what needed to be done, but something else was happening. There was an atmosphere from heaven to earth that began to affect the King. Instead of him being annoyed or angry, he asks a question to this cupbearer: *"Then the king said to me, 'What do you request?'" Nehemiah 2:4*

Now Nehemiah is being asked one of the greatest questions that could be asked, for the king had many possessions. The king had great protective power. The king had authority. He could help in so many ways. So Nehemiah did what every representative of God should do. *"So I prayed to the God of heaven." Nehemiah 2:4*

Wise, wise Nehemiah. He could be a former cupbearer, a memory to the king, or he could be a man who walked in blessing and favor. But you see, while he was in that place of intercession prior to this conversation, I believe he saw some things from a heavenly perspective. He saw those walls in Jerusalem that were broken down. He pictured the plight of God's people. He felt the sadness of the situation, and then he saw something. He saw walls being rebuilt. He saw restoration. He saw people arising and joining as one to fulfill the desires of God's heart. He knew that it was necessary for God to have a dwelling place, and necessary for his people to be able to have access to Him. He must have seen the provision for the vision. He couldn't die yet; his purpose had not been fulfilled. He was carrying a vision on the inside of him. For this is what he said:

*"And I said to the king, 'If it pleases the king, and if your servant has found favor in your sight, I ask that you send me to Judah, to the city of my fathers' tombs, that I may rebuild it.'" Nehemiah 2:5*

What is it that God is calling you to? What is it that is on your heart to do in this world, the thing that stirs excitement, emotion, passion? Have you spent the time in prayer and intercession to the point where you can say that you have seen it? Those who have made the biggest impact for God on this earth have also had the greatest impact on their floor with their face to the ground in unrelenting prayer for God's help and guidance to see it through.

***He couldn't die yet; his purpose had not been fulfilled.***

# Nehemiah's Heavenly Perspective

## Day 200

*"Then the king said to me (the queen also sitting beside him), 'How long will your journey be? And when will you return?' So it pleased the king to send me; and I set him a time." Nehemiah 2:6*

This cupbearer, this person who was probably thought of as insignificant to most, suddenly became the architect, the engineer, the general contractor, the boss, the man in charge of a most important project that would affect many lives, a city and a nation. Favor caused the king to ask, how long will you be gone, but he also said, your job is waiting for you. He just wanted to know how long this would take. Obviously, Nehemiah had seen it. He had walked the process through, because he had an answer for the king. He had a clear answer regarding the time frame.

How awesome is HIS God? How impacting do you think this would be? The king had to take note that this man not only had a heart, he had a plan, he had a time frame; he had a purpose that was burning so deeply, it affected the atmosphere. Not only the king, but his wife, came into agreement with this idea. Now Nehemiah unfolds the rest of the equation that he would need.

*"Furthermore I said to the king, 'If it pleases the king, let letters be given to me for the governors of the region beyond the River, that they must permit me to pass through till I come to Judah, and a letter to Asaph the keeper of the king's forest, that he must give me timber to make beams for the gates of the citadel which pertains to the temple, for the city wall, and for the house that I will occupy.'" And the king granted them to me according to the good hand of my God upon me. Nehemiah 2:7-8*

He was asking for the authority of the king to open doors for him along the way. Protection for the vision. Now he was asking for money. Yep, provision for the vision. And the king financed the dream of his cupbearer. Because Nehemiah was willing to put God's desires above his own. This was not about him, this was about God, and about His people. It included him, but it was not selfish. It was generous. He was putting the cause for God and of his people before his own personal comfort. The position he held as cupbearer was the set up of God to have His dreams and the dreams of His people come true.

*This was not about him, this was about God, and about His people.*

# Nehemiah's Heavenly Perspective

**Day 201**

Let us begin to recognize the significance of Nehemiah's life. His work ethics must have impressed the earthly king. His intercession must have impressed the heavenly One. Now God was bringing heaven to earth for him. Because he had proven himself excellent in his natural job, it was easier for him to be excellent in his heavenly assignment.

Yoohoo! Walls rebuilt, temple restored, people happy, right? In a fairy tale, maybe. But in life, when we are on a mission, a commission from God, we will face some opposition. Big deal. It is only as big as you allow it to be in your own imagination. Opposition was immediate. Nehemiah just kept riding towards the dream.

*When Sanballat the Horonite and Tobiah the Ammonite official heard of it, they were deeply disturbed that a man had come to seek the well-being of the children of Israel. So I came to Jerusalem and was there three days. Then I arose in the night, I and a few men with me; I told no one what my God had put in my heart to do at Jerusalem; nor was there any animal with me, except the one on which I rode. And I went out by night through the Valley Gate to the Serpent Well and the Refuse Gate, and viewed the walls of Jerusalem which were broken down and its gates which were burned with fire. Then I went on to the Fountain Gate and to the King's Pool, but there was no room for the animal under me to pass. So I went up in the night by the valley, and viewed the wall; then I turned back and entered by the Valley Gate, and so returned. And the officials did not know where I had gone or what I had done; I had not yet told the Jews, the priests, the nobles, the officials, or the others who did the work. Nehemiah 2:10-16*

Sometimes when you have dreamed the dreams of God, and then you arrive on the scene where destruction has occurred, it is best for you to survey alone. You don't need others telling you the impossibility of the situation, you just need to see what needs to be done and keep your vision intact. There will be a time when others will have to be included. But in this moment, it was important for Nehemiah to be alone with his God. What he saw did not devastate him. Instead he was made more aware of the work that had to be accomplished.

*You just need to see what needs to be done and keep your vision intact.*

# Nehemiah's Heavenly Perspective

## Day 202

Now came the time for Nehemiah to share the dream.

*"Then I said to them, 'You see the distress that we are in, how Jerusalem lies waste, and its gates are burned with fire. Come and let us build the wall of Jerusalem, that we may no longer be a reproach.'" Nehemiah 2:17*

He states the obvious, but then he reveals the plan and the reason for the plan. The plan is to take care of the problem, together. Rebuild. But the reason is that leaving it in its present condition is discrediting to God, and it is disgracing His people.

Disgracing is "the state of being out of favor." It causes the loss of respect. This is the ingredient that is producing the passion in Nehemiah. He must do something about it. He has seen the real deal. He has seen what the enemy has been able to do ... what his agenda really was. Satan's plan was to depict the people of God, and ultimately God Himself, as those who don't have as much power as he did to influence society. The enemy still wants to hold the place of prominence. Nehemiah has seen it, and now he will share the genuine truth. There has been a shift – first in the heavenly realm, and now the natural has begun to line up.

*"And I told them of the hand of my God which had been good upon me, and also of the king's words that he had spoken to me." Nehemiah 2:18*

This natural man is now a man operating in a different realm. He is affecting a nation. He is stirring a people with his passion, for he knows that his dreams are not his alone. God has shown up. He has instilled a strength inside of Nehemiah that comes from the place of the throne. God's grace has infused him with the ability to do what he was called to do and be what He had called him to be.

Now others are beginning to dream the same dream, and not only to come into agreement, but be willing to do something about the situation.

*There has been a shift – first in the heavenly realm, and now the natural has begun to line up.*

# Nehemiah's Heavenly Perspective

## Day 203

*So they said, "Let us rise up and build." Then they set their hands to this good work. But when Sanballat the Horonite, Tobiah the Ammonite official, and Geshem the Arab heard of it, they laughed at us and despised us, and said, "What is this thing that you are doing? Will you rebel against the king?" So I answered them, and said to them, "The God of heaven Himself will prosper us; therefore we His servants will arise and build, but you have no heritage or right or memorial in Jerusalem." Nehemiah 2:18-19 NKJV*

They set their hands to help accomplish it. Immediately opposition appears, mocks, laughs, and accuses them of being disloyal. Just as it appeared that the enemy had hit so hard in Jerusalem, it appeared that the temple and the city where God dwelt was utterly destroyed.

Just as the enemy raises his voice, nothing really has changed in the plan. To God it was just another opportunity to show His power strong from the least expected, a cupbearer by trade, but a son of God in reality, chosen for the great restoration of a dwelling place for God's presence.

This just reiterated to everyone that God's children had the ability to display His favor, His power and His abilities through them. There was a part for them to play. Yes, God put them to work. They didn't just walk into the city and God just "poofed" a new temple into position. No. They had to build. They had to be willing to fight for it. They faced one thing after another, but they knew everything that they faced meant more victory – more blessing. It was the worst of days, and the best of days:

*...chosen for the great restoration
of a dwelling place
for God's presence.*

# Nehemiah's Heavenly Perspective

## Day 204

*But it so happened, when Sanballat heard that we were rebuilding the wall, that he was furious and very indignant, and mocked the Jews. And he spoke before his brethren and the army of Samaria, and said, "What are these feeble Jews doing? Will they fortify themselves? Will they offer sacrifices? Will they complete it in a day? Will they revive the stones from the heaPsalm of rubbish -- stones that are burned?" Now Tobiah the Ammonite was beside him, and he said, "Whatever they build, if even a fox goes up on it, he will break down their stone wall." Nehemiah 4:1-3*

Intimidation comes from the enemy in a last-ditch attempt to get him to see himself as incapable instead of assigned. But all he needed to know was that as he followed God and God's desires, God Himself would take care of his enemies. When the enemy came, Nehemiah prayed again.

*Hear, O our God, for we are despised; turn their reproach on their own heads, and give them as plunder to a land of captivity! So we built the wall, and the entire wall was joined together up to half its height, for the people had a mind to work. Nehemiah 4:4,6*

God would turn the tide against satan and all his minions. In the meantime, what did Nehemiah do? He continued; he and the people that had the same passion now. When they just continued, when they just keep building, despite the opposition, the enemy started to get angry for he knew that God's people were beginning to realize their position.

*Now it happened, when Sanballat, Tobiah, the Arabs, the Ammonites, and the Ashdodites heard that the walls of Jerusalem were being restored and the gaps were beginning to be closed, that they became very angry, and all of them conspired together to come and attack Jerusalem and create confusion. Nevertheless we made our prayer to our God, and because of them we set a watch against them day and night. Nehemiah 4:7-9*

Are you seeing a pattern here?
Pray, get the strategy, and put things in proper place.
Then press on.

***The enemy started to get angry for he knew that God's people were beginning to realize their position.***

# Nehemiah's Heavenly Perspective

**Day 205**

*And our adversaries said, "They will neither know nor see anything, till we come into their midst and kill them and cause the work to cease." Therefore I positioned men behind the lower parts of the wall, at the openings; and I set the people according to their families, with their swords, their spears, and their bows. Nehemiah 4:11,13*

Satan gets so mad, he begins to threaten them with death. What did they do? They stayed in their POSITION.

Then Nehemiah began to remind them of why they were doing what they were doing, and for whom they were doing it.

*And I looked, and arose and said to the nobles, to the leaders, and to the rest of the people, "Do not be afraid of them. Remember the Lord, great and awesome, and fight for your brethren, your sons, your daughters, your wives, and your houses." Nehemiah 4:14*

Their tenacity would bring the enemy's threat to nothing. The enemy is the one who loses ground. It is he who is confounded and confused and disabled, for it has become obvious that God is on their side.

*So the wall was completed on the twenty-fifth of Elul, in fifty-two days. When all our enemies heard about this, all the surrounding nations were afraid and lost their self-confidence, because they realized that this work had been done with the help of our God. Nehemiah 6:15-16 NIV*

***It has become obvious that God is on their side.***

# Nehemiah's Heavenly Perspective

## Day 206

The outside work was done, now it was time to do some inside renovations and realign with God's Word.

*All the people assembled as one man in the square before the Water Gate. They told Ezra the scribe to bring out the Book of the Law of Moses, which the LORD had commanded for Israel. Nehemiah 8:1 NIV*

Time to praise the Lord!

*Ezra praised the LORD, the great God; and all the people lifted their hands and responded, "Amen! Amen!" Then they bowed down and worshiped the LORD with their faces to the ground. Nehemiah 8:6 NIV*

Time to celebrate!

*Then Nehemiah the governor, Ezra the priest and scribe, and the Levites who were instructing the people said to them all, "This day is sacred to the LORD your God. Do not mourn or weep." For all the people had been weeping as they listened to the words of the Law. Nehemiah said, "Go and enjoy choice food and sweet drinks, and send some to those who have nothing prepared. This day is sacred to our Lord. Do not grieve, for the joy of the LORD is your strength." Nehemiah 8:9-10 NIV*

Oh yeah. Walls are being rebuilt. Restoration was taking place of all that would be necessary for others to see the greatness of their God and His strength and power upon His people.

It was time. It was their position. It was a delight to be a part of the restoration process so that their God's name was glorified. When that is the focus of their life … when they were doing the things that delighted His heart, there came a time when there was nothing left but the rejoicing.

*there came a time when there was nothing left but the rejoicing.*

# Nehemiah's Heavenly Perspective

## Day 207

Glory To God but wait, it gets better... Back up. Ezra, the priest and scribe was there. And so was Nehemiah, the cup bearer. But he was no longer called a cup bearer, he was called the governor. A governor is a person charged with the directive of representing a higher power, appointed to govern a providence, a town, or the like.

It began by this cupbearer, bearing more than a cup. He was bearing a burden. But he took the burden before the Lord and he took it to God in intercession.

He took the responsibility of seeing what was necessary in the spiritual realm. He stood in the gap, where he saw the perspective of God and he carried out his restoration process with favor, with provision, and with protection. In other words, the miraculous began to be an active part of his life. And he reproduced a people that was just like him.

*On the twenty-fourth day of the same month, the Israelites gathered together, fasting and wearing sackcloth and having dust on their heads. Nehemiah 9:1 NIV*

They repented.

*Those of Israelite descent had separated themselves from all foreigners. They stood in their places and confessed their sins and the wickedness of their fathers. Nehemiah 9:2 NIV*

They got God's word on the matter and then they worshipped Him.

*They stood where they were and read from the Book of the Law of the LORD their God for a quarter of the day, and spent another quarter in confession and in worshiping the LORD their God. Nehemiah 9:3 NIV*

From one man's obedience, out of the rubble not only came a city and a temple, but a people who thought differently and acted differently and returned to the things of real importance.

*He took the responsibility of seeing what was necessary in the spiritual realm.*

# Nehemiah's Heavenly Perspective

## Day 208

*When the priests and Levites had purified themselves ceremonially, they purified the people, the gates and the wall. Nehemiah 12:30 NIV*

When we do our job as priests and kings, when we purify our lives, and make a way for others, things begin to shake. We get our priorities in order. We begin to want to be pure before our God. As we do, we make a way for others to have the same desires, and to be willing to live a life of purity and holiness as well. Things begin to change...

*And on that day they offered great sacrifices, rejoicing because God had given them great joy. The women and children also rejoiced. The sound of rejoicing in Jerusalem could be heard far away. Nehemiah 12:43 NIV*

There is a sound that is beginning to come. It is a sound of accomplishment. It is a sound of victory. It is a sound that will cause others to come into awareness of the awesomeness of our God.

You are significant. You are His people who can go to the throne and hear His voice, a people who can see what He sees and who can do the impossible.

It is time for us to pray. To be gap standers.
It is time for us to get the strategies of God.
It is time for us to be bold.
- To expect the provision for the vision.
- To stand firm against the tactics of the enemy.
- To arise and put our hands to preparing a place where the presence of God can reside.
- To be the people that even the enemy will have to acknowledge that our God is with us.
- To accomplish all the things that God has pre-designed in this time frame of history.

And then, we will be known as He always saw us. Governors. We may look like we just have a job, but in reality we have a ruling position on this earth. Can you see it?
Can you see from heaven's perspective?

**Be willing to live a life of purity and holiness.**

# Nehemiah's Heavenly Perspective

**Day 209**

Are you a part of the last great awakening?

Then let us begin by being earnest in prayer for those who have lost their way. For those who have not heard or those who do not understand that they were fashioned for the habitation of our God. The time is now; the time to make a difference in the face of adversity is our privilege.

God has positioned us. He is changing our perspective. He is opening doors of favor for us. He is causing the body of Christ to arise into proper position. We have been given an earthly assignment from a heavenly perspective.

Even if it looks like what you are doing has nothing to do with the spiritual sense, it doesn't matter. God sees things different.

Unless you are living in direct disobedience to Him, He has a reason for you to be where you are right now at this present time.

We are the outward manifestation for others to see our lives as different from theirs, if they do not yet know the Lord as Savior. Your relationship with God is an assignment itself to make a difference to others.

What are we supposed to be doing? We are here to build enough relationship with God, our Father, that we begin to think differently, see things differently and respond differently than those who don't know Him.

We are to be the light. We are to be the salt—making them thirsty for the well we drink from. It all begins by what we are seeing. If we are just looking at the obvious, we will miss reality. It is time for us to hear what the Spirit of God is saying.

We are blessed. We are favored. We have access to the throne of God. We go boldly and then when we have entered, we see what is not seen in the natural.

*Your relationship with God is an assignment itself to make a difference to others.*

# Nehemiah's Heavenly Perspective

## Day 210

We are going beyond loving God to being in love with Him. Completely. As we do, He changes our hearts' desires. Selfish motives fall off as we become more aware of the things that are on His heart and what the true condition of His people are. We are able to see through His eyes that the walls of Christianity are being broken down. There has been destruction. Some of it has been because Christians have done it themselves through disobedience and sinful acts, or complacency. Some destruction has come from satan's tactics to infiltrate the seven mountains of influence and to destroy the confidence of God's people by circumstantial evidence and false accusation. The enemy asks "What is this thing you are doing? Building a place for God to dwell? Whose God? Your God? How do you think you are capable of rebuilding that which is in ruins already? What is this place? This territory? Why do you think you could change anything?

But our resolve and the cry of our heart must be like that of this significant individual who has changed his perspective. He doesn't care what others see, he knows what he has already seen. This is where your perception needs to change. You must understand God's people are now the temple that His presence dwells in. We must hear what the Spirit is revealing. The church's walls are broken down in many areas. We have seen promiscuity, abortion and divorce become almost as prevalent in the Church as in the world. There are broken places that must be rebuilt. There are mindsets that must be changed.

There is a great need to be able to hear the truth, to evaluate the damage and then cry out with intercession for the intervention of God and for WHAT our part is in rebuilding the place where God can have a position of authority and habitation again. When we get God's heart, then we get God's provision.

When we have His attention, we also have His affection and His intervention. Our enemies are put to shame and put out. When our eyes are fixed on our destination, we are immune to their attacks because our hearts are fixed on the sight we have seen in the heavens. It is vitally important to look ahead to what God has for us and put all our efforts and energy into fulfilling His purpose for our lives.

*Your relationship with God is an assignment itself to make a difference to others.*

# Nehemiah's Heavenly Perspective

## Day 211

God wants us to pursue the miraculous – to believe for greater works from Him. He wants to show the world what He is capable of and needs us to believe for more – not just for ourselves, but to display His power to the lost. The world is becoming increasingly more cynical about the things of God, and we are the ones that are to turn it around.

Many see the increased wickedness of the world we live in and say, "Yep, this is just the way it's gonna be. We can't stop it. The world gets darker every day." Too hard, you say? That's why He wants us to expect more from Him. But this isn't the first time that darkness has increased. If you look at history you see in many societies darkness has increased and tried to destroy the works of God.

We must fight for God's power in our own personal lives, the Church and also the world. When we line up with God and we operate from what we know after spending time with Him, they will see it and recognize He is the one true God. God desires to pour out His Spirit in a mighty way – to demonstrate to masses of people just how powerful He truly is. Without a demonstration of His power, those who have been led astray by the anti-Christ spirit prevalent in today's society may not have a chance to choose Him. This is simply because they have not been given the opportunity to know Him as He truly is.

Do they know He is a God who loves, heals and delivers? God wants them to know His power and who He is. We must step out in faith and reveal His power to the world.

It may look like the church is broken and poor and desperate, but if you will go to God and see what He sees, you will understand you have been assigned to do your part for the rebuilding of that which is broken.

You are going to pour out the oil of gladness over those who mourn. You are going to rebuild the waste places.

***We must step out in faith and reveal His power to the world.***

# Nehemiah's Heavenly Perspective

## Day 212

We, the Church, should be preparing ourselves and all of God's people for another great awakening. When we hear the bad news, instead of being discouraged, we need to arise as warriors to fight for the souls of men – those who have sinned to be restored. We must be the ones who will stand in the gap and bring the thoughts of God from heaven to earth. We then can expect victory through every place of opposition.

God is not done yet. He is sending His Spirit once again to call upon those that He has placed strategically in different places so that they can pray. They can penetrate the darkness and rescue those who will believe in Him.

We have to prepare for it. We have to expect it. We must align our hearts with His in order to rebuild that which is necessary for His Spirit to dwell again in His people ... for the demonstration that is about to be seen by those that are called, and prepared for victory. If we do not see from His perspective, we can get discouraged and disinterested. We can begin to buy into our part being insignificant.

But if we expect God to act, we will posture ourselves in the proper position so that we will be the proper vessels for His glory to shine through. And we will be the ones who will build a place for others to come and experience our great God.

We must ride through the land, and see the devastation. But when we have seen the answer before us, when we follow Him closely and trust Him completely, we will have the ability to walk over every lie, overcome ever obstacle, and build that which has eternal value. We need to shake off passivity and BELIEVE He needs us – each one of us.

We are not destined to just sit in a pew – no one is. We are called of God first to embrace Him, to prepare the atmosphere that provides His people opportunity to display His power and love. Now is the time to get ready – we do not have much time left.

*He is sending His Spirit once again to call upon those that He has placed strategically in different places so that they can pray.*

# Nehemiah's Heavenly Perspective

**Day 213**

We must focus, train and build, for His Kingdom is coming to this generation and we must stay vigilant – not doubting – but expecting. For God wants to reveal His power as He did in the days of Nehemiah. When we just continue, when we just keep building, despite the opposition, the enemy will start to get angry, for he knows we are indeed realizing our position.

What do we need to do? Stay in our POSITION. And recall why we are doing what we are doing, and for whom we are doing it.

The enemy is the one who loses ground. It is he who is confounded and confused and disabled, for it has become obvious that God is on our side. God's grace has infused us with the ability to do what He has called us to do and be what He has called us to be.

Now others will begin to dream the same dream, and to not only come into agreement, but be willing to do something about the situation. We must be the ones who will mount up and ride with Him through the devastated places with the planned purpose of restoration.

- Assess
- Intercede
- See
- Arise
- Build
- Accomplish
- Praise
- Repeat

It is time. It is our position. It is our delight to be a part of the restoration process so that our God's name will be glorified.

When that is the focus of our life, when we are doing the things that delight His heart, there comes a time when there is nothing left but the rejoicing. Glory to God!

*God's grace has infused us with the ability to do what He has called us to do and be what He has called us to be.*

# GREATNESS

**Day 214**

The following two Kingdom guides are excerpts from a prophetic word for the Body of Christ that I call "Greatness."

The fires have begun. You will be a part of the great awakening of the soul-mindedness of the saints. They have gone from the reality of the flames of hell, looking for the flames to heal their own lives. It must happen, for My Bride must be whole to bring about the whole that I have planned for the end. I will continue to blow my wind, and breathe into the lungs of those who will give me room to breathe through them.

There is a fight going on for the territories that I have preserved. The fight is part of what you feel. The seducing spirits are running and looking and trying to hook those that can be taken out of the harvesting. The world will try to focus on them; you must keep your eyes on me and train others to do the same. If you begin to look for those that have complete integrity, they will disappoint you. Do not allow the frailty of others to bring you to their level. You know there is a level in Me that I have brought you to. Do not try to understand it, and above all do not try to defend it or explain it. Just walk in it. I will do the rest.

The things will follow you just as you have said. Now they will begin to be a reality. You will see that they will continue as long as you continue with me. There will be no lack or sorrow as you are fixed --fixed on Me, fixed by Me, fixed with Me. And you will bring a "fix" for others. The world says they must have the next "fix," but the fix I bring is permanent and eternal. I have placed My hand and My call on you for such a time as this.

*There will be no lack or sorrow as you are fixed*
*--fixed on Me, fixed by Me, fixed with Me.*

# GREATNESS

### Day 215

Do not be frustrated in the processing. For it is not just you that I am processing. I am bringing together those of like mind and like spirit who have a mind to work for the Kingdom. They will bring the vision together and work with you and build and establish. I am bringing those who have the same passion and the ability to stay focused without regret or complaint. Those who want to grumble and complain will soon be lost in the greatness of those that surround them. The ones that have my greatness on the inside will be able to bring it to the outside and they will begin to soar and bring a new elevation. The weariness of the work will subside as eagles take their place and begin to fly with their portion, tirelessly, because I have brought them on the wind of My Spirit. Look for the greatness, not just the willing. They will be compelled to complete, not just partake, what I have invested in you. Not the blood suckers, but the blood-infused. My heartbeat beating through their chest. My thoughts in their mind. My capabilities being unleashed to bring about the end result that is necessary for the fulfillment.

The weeping will continue. Not for sorrow, but for those things to be brought forth in the Spirit and for the divine connections to continue. Walk wisely. Listen intently. I will bring the alignment. I am in charge.

Do not allow comparison to be in your midst. You must not allow it in any of the ranks. Guard. Watch. Pray. Be aware, but rise above. Do not take yourself down to the place of trying to convince anyone of what I am doing. Do not doubt the greatness I have aligned with you and in you. Yes, greatness. Study it out. You will see. Identify with it. You have been entrusted with my greatness, with goodness and mercy and truth. Together they will bring about that which you have longed for. The changed lives, the saved souls, the places of training and fulfillment are nigh at hand. I will supply.

*Walk wisely.*
*Listen intently.*
*I will bring the alignment.*
*I am in charge.*

## Prophetic Ministry

### Day 216

We can operate in a dimension of releasing the power of the Kingdom of God. We can operate in a dimension where we do not tolerate circumstantial situations. We can operate in the dimension where we can see things the way God sees them and operate in His power, in His Kingdom and His promises. We can be a people of success and not failure, a people of victory and not a people who lose battles. We can be above and not below, the head and not the tail. But we must first have insight regarding the power of the Holy Spirit in the believer, how the third person of the Godhead operates in our lives, how we can depend upon Him, the person or personality of the Holy Spirit, to be manifested in the life of the believer:

*However, when He, the Spirit of truth, has come, He will guide you into all truth; for He will not speak on His own authority, but whatever He hears He will speak; and He will tell you things to come. John 16:13*

He will guide YOU into all truth, and He will tell YOU things to come! That's why it's important that you develop an intimacy with the Holy Spirit. He is the comforter, He is your friend, He is your teacher, He is the one who will show you the truth and what is to come, so you are not held captive by the circumstance.

Let the Holy Spirit be your guide; let Him be your friend. Develop an intimacy with the Holy Spirit and allow Him to take you to a place where you can see the truth and you can see what is going to take place in your future. When the Holy Spirit becomes an intimate friend, you will walk in a totally different dimension of life.

*Declare: I will give first place to the Holy Spirit, not to the spirit of this world. The Holy Spirit is my Guide. I welcome the power of the Holy Spirit in my life. Holy Spirit, I welcome You; speak to me, guide me, teach me, correct me and direct me so that I may walk in the truth of God's Word and that I might walk in the reality of seeing, not what the world sees, but seeing what God sees, in the Name of Jesus, AMEN.*

### He will guide YOU into all truth, and He will tell YOU things to come!

# Prophetic Ministry

**Day 217**

What really happens from the power of the gift of prophecy?

A. Salvation will occur

*But if all prophesy, and there come in one that believeth not, or one unlearned, he is convinced of all, he is judged of all: And thus are the secrets of his heart made manifest; and so falling down on his face he will worship God, and report that God is in you of a truth.*
*1 Corinthians 14:24-25 KJV*

There is such a powerful connection between God and the individual that is receiving the word from Him because he or she is aware that there are things that only God knew, and now He is saying it to them. All people have dreams and passions because God made us that way. When God addresses their heart's cry, they find His love, and how personal He is. They can no longer deny His existence or His interest in them in a personal way, and their hearts melt into accepting Him as Lord.

B. Truth and Destiny are revealed

*This charge I commit unto thee, son Timothy, according to the prophecies which went before on thee, that thou by them mightest war a good warfare... 1 Timothy 1:18 KJV*

When God speaks to an individual, He speaks to their potential over a period of a lifetime. However, He will reveal things and begin painting a picture for the individual. When He speaks to the potential, it will be up to the individual to respond by adding faith to the word and warring with that word (declaring it, putting into effect any directives given in it, and trusting God to do His part as they do their part).

*When God addresses their heart's cry,*
*they find His love,*
*and how personal He is.*

# PROPHETIC MINISTRY

## Day 218

C. The Church is strengthened

*But he that prophesieth speaketh unto men to edification, and exhortation, and comfort. He that speaketh in an unknown tongue edifieth himself; but he that prophesieth edifieth the church.*
1 Corinthians 14:3-4 KJV

*How is it then, brethren? When ye come together, every one of you hath a psalm, hath a doctrine, hath a tongue, hath a revelation, hath an interpretation. Let all things be done unto edifying.*
1 Corinthians 14:26 KJV

The power of prophecy in a church will bring: Strength, Insight, Compassion, Strategies, Diversity, Joy, and Peace

D. You are able to discern strongholds and bring prayer strategies for the corporate vision or for nations

Satan is afraid of sons of God because they bring in holiness and light, and holiness is stronger than sin and light is stronger than darkness.

His system will fall as the Church rises into their own position and begin to live righteously and stand in their positions of influence in the earth. As we do what is right, as we proclaim truth, as we invade dark places with His life and His light, satan will lose his ability to hold people in his deception.

Prophecy is a speaking forth of what God is saying. He knows the moment of time we are living in and he knows the "now" word that will shake nations and bring people to their knees or to their place of safety or to their place of war.

*Prophecy is a speaking forth what God is saying.*

# Prophetic Ministry

E. It gives you and others direction, instruction and encouragement

*For ye may all prophesy one by one, that all may learn, and all may be comforted. 1 Corinthians 14:31 KJV*

When the prophetic is in operation, there are spiritual insights that are flowing out of individuals. As it flows, not only is the vessel that is being used learning, but all in the room can hear and learn from every word that proceeds from the mouth of God.

When we hear the voice of the Lord, it will bring whatever is needed at the time and that always is what brings us comfort.

F. It brings protection for you and your family.

*And they shall take of the blood, and strike it on the two side posts and on the upper door post of the houses, wherein they shall eat it. Exodus 12:7 KJV*

*And the blood shall be to you for a token upon the houses where ye are: and when I see the blood, I will pass over you, and the plague shall not be upon you to destroy you, when I smite the land of Egypt. Exodus 12:13 KJV*

This was a direct instruction from the Lord, to Moses to the people. When Moses gave this directive and they followed it, it saved a nation from destruction and saved their children and their households.

The word of the Lord is still coming. It will save you from destruction no matter what is going on in the world around you. No matter what disobedience brings to other households, when you obey the word of the Lord, God's protection is on you and on your household and preserves your future generations and your future destination.

*When we hear the voice of the Lord, it will bring whatever is needed at the time and that always is what brings us comfort.*

# Prophetic Ministry

**Day 220**

G. It lifts up Jesus and draws us closer to Him.

*And I fell at his feet to worship him. And he said unto me, See thou do it not: I am thy fellow servant, and of thy brethren that have the testimony of Jesus: worship God: for the testimony of Jesus is the spirit of prophecy. Revelation 19:10 KJV*

I love this one maybe the most. Since the testimony of Jesus IS the spirit of prophecy, He is behind the word. He is making it real and making Himself real through it. When Jesus is speaking, it is like a flood that consumes your soul and ignites your spirit. You fall in love with Him more than you knew you were capable of. He becomes so close to you, He is able to define things for you and refine things in you. His love becomes tangible and it draws love out of you. It leaves a deposit that cannot be destroyed. That is why satan hates it so much. It portrays and displays Jesus Himself. Hallelujah!

H. It benefits EVERY man.

*But the manifestation of the Spirit is given to every man to profit withal. For to one is given by the Spirit the word of wisdom; to another the word of knowledge by the same Spirit; 9 To another faith by the same Spirit; to another the gifts of healing by the same Spirit; To another the working of miracles; to another prophecy; to another discerning of spirits; to another divers kinds of tongues; to another the interpretation of tongues: 11 But all these worketh that one and the selfsame Spirit, dividing to every man severally as he will. 1 Corinthians 12:7-11 KJV*

What is the best gift? The one needed the most at the time. The Holy Spirit is in charge of the dispersing, but we are assured that it will be beneficial to all. The Holy Spirit works through the diversity of the gifts and the diversity of our deliveries to bring about the desired end result of God.

He will display His power on this earth. If we are willing to yield and do our part, then we can be a vessel He can use to help all profit.

*What is the best gift?*
*The one needed the most at the time.*

# Prophetic Ministry

## Day 221

II. Prophetic Ministry is our responsibility.

A. We must exercise in order to come to full age.

*But strong meat belongeth to them that are of full age, even those who by reason of use have their senses exercised to discern both good and evil. Hebrews 5:14 KJV*

How do you exercise the senses of the spirit? Reason of use! Of what? Reason of USE! So we must stay stirred up by writing, declaring, and praying prophetically, and by practicing in "safe" environments and then releasing it under proper authority to have the full benefit of it utilized.

B. We must realize how much potential we really have residing within us.

*What is it then? I will pray with the spirit, and I will pray with the understanding also: I will sing with the spirit, and I will sing with the understanding also. 1 Corinthians 14:15 KJV*

If we would truly tap into what God has said we can do, we would not only hear His voice, but we would cooperate with it and then understand it.

Does that mean we will understand every word in our own language?

It could. But it could also mean that we would understand what He was doing, where we were in the spirit realm and the reason why. We would understand His heart. We would understand the needs we were praying for, and the answers we were singing out.

Limitations are being removed and we can know what they are.

WHEN?

NOW! We must realize that this is the time of the Kingdom to affect people in every walk of life.

*If we would truly tap into what God has said we can do...*

# Prophetic Ministry

## Day 222

The Book of Acts provides a historical narrative of the phenomenal growth of the church, which directly related to the mighty power of the Spirit, who released signs and wonders through obedient people.

In the Book of Acts, we see that each time people were filled with the Holy Spirit, they became powerful, miracle-working, fruitful people for the Kingdom of God.

Utilizing the power from within they were able to keep:

- Impacting
- Increasing
- Engaging

Now is the time, we are the people.

Why is it important for us to desire to be used in these ways?

This is clearly laid out for us in Isaiah. There is a reason the Spirit of the Lord is upon you. Let's break it down.

*The Spirit of the Lord GOD is upon me; because the LORD hath anointed me to preach good tidings unto the meek; he hath sent me to bind up the brokenhearted, to proclaim liberty to the captives, and the opening of the prison to them that are bound; To proclaim the acceptable year of the LORD, and the day of vengeance of our God; to comfort all that mourn; To appoint unto them that mourn in Zion, to give unto them beauty for ashes, the oil of joy for mourning, the garment of praise for the spirit of heaviness; that they might be called trees of righteousness, the planting of the LORD, that he might be glorified. And they shall build the old wastes, they shall raise up the former desolations, and they shall repair the waste cities, the desolations of many generations.*

Isaiah 61:1-4 KJV

*The Holy Spirit helps us become powerful, miracle-working, fruitful people for the Kingdom of God.*

## Prophetic Ministry

### Day 223

No man, no movement is greater than the prayer that goes before it. There has never been a revival birthed without true intercession. We are a vital link between Him and this troubled, lost world outside. When we pray and seek Him for who He is, He will embrace us with His love. When we are secure with Him, His glory will fill the temple and people will come because they are hungry for truth. And it only comes through brokenness, it comes through honesty. Our help comes from the Lord. And the only way is in submission and brokenness. We must be honest and admit that we've failed and seek again the place of prayer, and the place of cleansing, and the place of anointing.

*We need to pray this way: Lord, I don't have the vision I used to have. I don't have the passion I used to have. I don't have the concern I used to have, not for this world, or for lost souls. I need to return to You and allow You to make Yourself known to me again. I don't want to remember You as a God I used to be close to. I don't want to think of You as one of the many things I desire. I want You to be the deepest desire of my heart. I want seeking You to be like Paul, who said "This - one - thing - I - do."*

He lived God. He thought God. He prayed God. That's all. You can lash him, but you couldn't whip it out of him. He can float on a piece of wood in the Mediterranean a night and a day - thirty six hours, but you couldn't wash it out of him. They tried to starve him, but they couldn't starve it out of him. Because he had a relationship with a KNOWN God. He had embraced the Savior of the cross. He had passion for more of Him. He believed in resurrection power, for he had been resurrected himself.

Let us continue in our pursuit to embrace His love, then His love will be seen, known and declared throughout the world. Come Lord Jesus Come.

May His glory shine forth again as He makes Himself known, to us, to them, as we embrace His love.

**No man, no movement is greater than the prayer that goes before it.**

# VISION – GIVING UP THE FLESH

**Day 224**

The following two devotions are from a powerful vision that the Holy Spirit gave to one of the people in our church. Read it and meditate on it. God gives dreams and visions not just for fun but always for a purpose. Listen to what the Spirit is trying to convey to you through this vision...

"I saw hundreds of individuals sort of scattered over a vast distance. It seemed to go on forever, and each one was surrounded with things of the world – spirits so to speak – things that attacked each person (spirit of fear, spirit of deception, etc.). Each person had sort of a "sphere" around them and over them, like a clear sheet just blanketed over them to shield them from the enemy that surrounded them. On the top of the "sphere" was a smear of the blood of Jesus, similar to the blood of the lamb they painted over their door post when the spirit of death was passing through. They were under the covering of the blood of Jesus to protect them from the influences of the world and the flesh. Each person was crying out to God for Him to roar on their behalf. They were calling on the name of the Lord of Hosts, Lord Sabbaoth – the God who will fight their battle and destroy the enemy that surrounded them.

Some of the people were running to get under the covering of the blood of Jesus. These were the newly saved people that had just learned of the saving and delivering power of Jesus and His blood. Others, sadly, were stepping out from and coming out from under the covering of the blood of Jesus.

They had turned their eyes off of the blood of Jesus and looked to the things on the outside. They were trading in their covering to entertain the things outside of the sphere – the flesh, the world, the "easy way."

*Each person was crying out to God for Him to roar on their behalf*

# Vision – Giving up the Flesh

## Day 225

"As the people cried out to God to roar, they braced themselves for He was about to roar. They put their arms over their heads as if something was going to fall on top of them. The Lord of Hosts looked down and opened His mouth to begin to roar and destroy the enemy. You could see the fierceness in His eyes. He was not playing games. There was no time to mess around. You were either covered by the blood of Jesus, or not. If you were not for Him, then you were against Him. He only saw you as one of the enemies He was about to destroy. Those that were running to be under the covering were saved. Those that were already under the covering were saved. Those that had stepped out of the covering were destroyed along with the enemy when God roared. It was like a wind that came through from the sky - like fire, but clear. It was His breath, His voice, His roar and the ground shook. It blew away the enemy that surrounded the people, turning them to dust. Unfortunately, those that were not under the covering of the blood of Jesus, were blown away with the enemy.

It was a sad and very serious feeling I got. I was gripped with a heartbreaking feeling over those who had CHOSEN to trade in their covering, their blessing, their anointing, their gifts and callings for the things of the world, the things of the flesh. They were only seen as the enemy of God when it came time for Him to roar. However, there was also a sense of urgency to grab hold of those people who were trying to find the covering. There was an urgency for those who were searching for the truth, the life, the saving knowledge of Jesus and His blood, as well as those who had stepped out to have restored salvation and understanding of God's forgiveness. There was an urgency to make sure they understood that time was short, that they had to get under the "sphere," the "blanket" of the blood of Jesus.

Luke 9:60-62, says, "Your duty is to go and preach the coming of the Kingdom of God. Some said, Yes, Lord, I will follow you, but first let me say good-bye to my family. Jesus told them – anyone who puts a hand to the plow (follows Me) and then turns to look back is not fit for the Kingdom." He's very serious about being fully committed and surrendered to Him. We don't have time to be playing games or entertaining the things of the world. He's about to roar to destroy our enemies."

*He's very serious about being fully committed and surrendered to Him.*

# Fertilizing Your Seed

## Day 226

Our priorities are going to be adjusted because we must look at things according to the importance that God has put on them.

Seedtime and harvest was instituted by God and the principle of the Kingdom was introduced in Genesis and carried throughout the Bible.

Seeds will reproduce after their own kind.

The world's system is to look at a situation of apparent lack or impossible circumstances as a problem, but Kingdom mentality sees those situations not as a problem, but an opportunity. It is an opportunity for displaying the attitude of Kingdom, and the power of a seed released.

We can now realize that for every need, there is a seed.

As we give our seed to God in faith, with expectancy, we remove it from natural restraints and bring it into the Kingdom realm where it is blessed and multiplied by the King for our use.

We now understand that every seed has exponential potential for a hundred-fold return, but not all realize the hundred-fold return.

To reach the full potential of the seeds sown:
- We must have the correct attitude toward God.
- We must settle it in our hearts that it is God's will for us to prosper.
- We need to release our seed with faith and see ourselves walking in His abundant provision.
- We need to be committed and purposeful in our sowing.

Tell me in one word how much God is committed to seed, time and harvest?

### J E S U S !

That's right! "Jesus" is the most important seed ever sown!

*We now understand that every seed has exponential potential for a hundred-fold return, but not all realize the hundred-fold return.*

# Fertilizing Your Seed

**Day 227**

God is so committed to the system He put in place, He gave seed. Not just any seed. The most precious seed that He had. He gave His only Son! We must understand that we are a part of that seed and that we are to be seen, to make a difference in the world in which we live. We can do that by realizing the opportunities we have in front of us today, and take advantage of them.

He created mankind, man and woman, in His likeness. Then God blessed them, empowered them with favor, success, and told them to operate in authority. You can't be in His likeness without authority. Jesus reflected God as He spoke with authority, not a religious system. Jesus operated in the authority of His Father and impacted people, regions and systems.

God will empower you with the ability to operate in the authority you were created for, in the way His Kingdom operates. He has spoken His word into you. It is a seed of truth, a seed of vision, a seed of destiny. Your destiny will always include certain steps:

1. Seed – the DNA of God
2. You being a part of a system of relationship – with God, with His people
3. An action that will include you seeding, fertilizing your seed by acting on it and having faith until the harvest
4. Enjoying and sharing the harvest
5. Repeat

We talked about a farmer sowing, and that he has to release the seed and scatter it on the ground. Why do you do that? To produce a harvest.

Why? It's in your DNA to do so.

*God will empower you with the ability to operate in the authority you were created for, in the way His Kingdom operates.*

# Fertilizing Your Seed

## Day 228

God has given us a mandate. It requires dominion and reproduction. I can give you a set of keys and if you never put the key in the door, you can stand outside of what is available to you, longing to be inside, but not taking advantage of the keys in your hand.

"Keys of authority" in the Kingdom represent:
a. Seed being recognized (they are in your hand, in your mouth, in your testimony, and in your talents)
b. Seed then being sown
c. Seed then being fertilized
d. Seed then being realized

When we discover the modes of operating in authority that God has set in place then we will be able to operate in them accordingly. We know, according to Genesis 8:22, while earth remains, so does seedtime and harvest. Why? Because God wants us to operate in the authority that He designed for us to experience victory in.

Unless we are bearing fruit of some kind, we aren't walking in the full authority that was given to us by virtue of precious seed. We have the ability to operate in full authority when we sow seeds and operate in Kingdom principles.

The key of authority is found in a seed. You hold the keys. They are called seeds. Now you must place them in the door to be able to walk into the places God has prepared for you. God wants us to live in abundance in every dynamic of our life. Abundance of life is the overflow of the presence of God.

Do you value the seed of salvation and what it did for your life? Then, if what you received is so wonderful, why wouldn't you want to share it?

*We have been given a mandate to hear the voice of God and see beyond the natural to the unlimited blessings of the Lord.*

# Fertilizing Your Seed

**Day 229**

The majority of Christians are not leading others to Christ, or the world would be closer to being won. In other words, the seed is sown for you to be fruitful, multiply and replenish. But how are you actively participating with the seed to bring about the full harvest? Today I want to concentrate on fertilizing our seed. We are to be fruitful in our gifts and talents to bring forth something lasting.

*But as it is written:"Eye has not seen, nor ear heard, Nor have entered into the heart of man The things which God has prepared for those who love Him." But God has revealed them to us through His Spirit. For the Spirit searches all things, yes, the deep things of God. 1 Corinthians 2:9-11*

Seed – God has something prepared for you, but you have to walk in the understanding of the authority you have, by revelation of the Spirit, and take back from the enemy what he has stolen.

It starts with a seed. A seed of truth, a seed of love that was sown in you first by God's spoken word, and then by an action of love – the seed of His Son. It was a seed sown for this purpose: The harvest of sons.

Why?
He was restoring man to the place of dominion and authority.

He was manifested to set us free from the works of the devil. Jesus was incorruptible seed. God loosed us from the hold of the enemy based upon the seed that He sowed.

*Having been begotten again, not of corruptible seed, but of incorruptible, through the word of God, which liveth and abideth. 1 Peter 1:23 ASV*

God sowed the seed of Jesus to us and if we will walk in the realization of what that means to us, we will understand that He has provided us a seed of authority and dominion that renders the enemy inoperative in our lives.

*We are to be fruitful in our gifts and talents to bring forth something lasting.*

# Fertilizing Your Seed

## Day 230

God has provided the seed necessary to loose the power of His Kingdom for the purpose of productivity and multiplication.
- We must recognize the Sower has sown the word to us, made it available for us.
- He has sown seeds of power, authority and destiny into us.
- We must receive it and fertilize it by reiteration to make sure we have gotten the revelation of the truth of it.
- We must take action by doing something that agrees with it.
- We must be sowing ourselves into the Kingdom, into others, with whatever seed we have been given personally and corporately.

It is up to us to take advantage of the seed sown. If you do not, it can become unfruitful and the desires of other things trip you up. Or the distractions of other things trip you up. Or the distress of other things trips you up.

That is why it is important for you to hear and hear the word. That is the purpose of providing you the avenue of Community Life Groups (Home Groups). You will hear and hear and you will develop lasting fruit. You can have an experience on Sunday morning, but the life-changing sermon isn't life changing for long without the necessary fertilizer. That is, the reiteration of the Word, the revelation that God brings through others that will stick with you in a different way that is not of my experience, but of theirs. It is an opportunity for lasting fruit. It is an opportunity to fertilize your seed. It is an opportunity to receive more seed.

Sunday's life-changing sermons can be life changing when shared, and fertilized with your own stories and talents and gifting.

*It is up to us to take advantage of the seed sown.*

# Fertilizing Your Seed

**Day 231**

Seed represents authority. The possessor of a seed has the authority and ability to produce. Authority comes not by just looking at the seed, but as you are looking at it, realizing you are also looking at the harvest. Don't faint, don't get weary. Realize that you are dictating your future with the seed you sow today. It represents life and purpose. It will produce reaping seasons in your life.

Sowing seed brings vision that is in your heart out to good ground, because it is representing fruit. It is representing your belief in the power it has to bring forth transformation. If you are willing to sow seed, you are revealing your thoughts. "As a man thinks in his heart, so is he," and "Out of the abundance of a man's heart, the mouth speaketh."

If you don't believe in seed, time and harvest, you won't speak it, you won't engage in it and you won't take advantage of what has been sown for you. When you sow seed you are showing what your desires are.

You see, your seed reveals:
- Your compassion
- Your character
- Your future

You operate in sowing because you choose to obey God in being fruitful. You are demonstrating how powerful God's seed of love is in your life.

He gave, so you are a giver.

You will demonstrate being a giver.

You will desire to be the one with the ability to meet others' needs that you encounter.

*The possessor of a seed has the authority and ability to produce.*

# Fertilizing Your Seed

## Day 232

When you sow, your motive should be that you want to sow to be a blessing to someone else. What you make happen for others will happen for you. Seed establishes the fact that you are acting in an authority given to you that goes beyond natural thinking. Giving seed requires you to walk by faith and not by sight. You can't see seed operating, but you believe it is.

*Give, and [gifts] will be given to you; good measure, pressed down, shaken together, and running over, will they pour into [the pouch formed by] the bosom [of your robe and used as a bag]. For with the measure you deal out [with the measure you use when you confer benefits on others], it will be measured back to you. Luke 6:38 AMP*

It's the "upside-down" kingdom. Receiving comes from giving. If you are one of those people who waits to give in certain situations, your harvest is left in the field. You see, a person can give once, or maybe give a few times when they are moved by emotion, and occasionally by compassion.

But a person who begins to understand this principle of the Kingdom will become a giver. A giver gives all the time. It's not determined by whether they have a lot to give. They will find a way to give. It's not about economy. It's not about their feelings. It is about the fact that they have become a partaker of the gospel of Jesus, in the revelation of the kingdom of seed time and harvest. They have settled things in their heart. They have settled the bottom line, and the word of faith in the seed bringing their harvest is a decision they will never be wondering about again.

A giver is seeking for the prosperity and well being of all those around them. Givers want to bless. Takers want to take from you and make you feel obligated to give to them. Givers are living according to the principles of the kingdom.

*A giver is seeking for the prosperity and well being of all those around them.*

# FERTILIZING YOUR SEED

**Day 233**

Seeds must be sown and they must be fertilized ... by prayer, by practice, and by action.

What harvest are you looking at now from seeds you have sown in past? How are you activating your faith?

What harvest are you expecting from the seeds you sow today?

There are opportunities presented before you today to not only hear, but be a doer of the word, and in so doing, become a giver, a sower and a receiver.

Recognize the seed today that you have been given.
Fertilize your seed by participating in the mandate.

- Open your heart - ask God for the vision to be implanted in your heart
- Open your eyes - look for someone who has a need
- Open your mouth - to invite or share your testimony or build relationship with someone.
- Open your minds - to the truth of living a lifestyle of seed, time and harvest
- Open your gifts and your talents to others
- Open your homes, your giving, your food

Everybody has a story, and you have incorruptible seed on the inside of you. It is time to scatter, it is time to fertilize our own seeds with actions; it is time to prepare for the harvest promised.

*Everybody has a story.*

# What's the Truth?

## Day 234

It's time to get real.

Real means "of or relating to fixed, permanent, or immovable things."

Christians are to face their battles from a godly perspective, not a worldly one. How we behave in a crisis makes us different from non-believers. We are to be fixed, having a permanent mindset, not a temporary one. We need to be immovable on what He has provided and promised us.

We need to recall the things God has told us, both personally and corporately. Do you remember? Have you focused on the prophetic word we received last December? Part of our responsibility is to be 'real' about how we are doing in the faith realm. Can you say you have been immovable in trusting Him lately?

Satan's #1 tactic is FEAR. Fear will move in where faith has moved out. If Satan can shake our faith in God and His word, then we fall into fear and unbelief. Get real.

If Satan can get us to let go of our faith and confidence in God, he has the ability to breach the citadels of our heart. This is when doubt and unbelief begin to take up residence. If we don't hold on to our faith, we begin to sense a loss of purpose and our reason for existence is attacked.

Don't allow Satan to eat your lunch. Go back to the basics and His promises to you. Build yourself up in your most holy faith and fight the good fight.

The truth is you are victorious in ALL your ways!

Is there any area that you have failed to recognize that you have been infiltrated with fear, doubt or disappointment? Take this time to examine yourself and be real.

*We need to be immovable on what He has provided and promised us.*

# You and God vs: _____

## Day 235

*Behold, I give you the authority to trample on serpents and scorpions, and over all the enemy, and nothing shall by any means hurt you. Luke 10:19*

Is this a limited promise or all-inclusive? We have power over ALL the enemy. Satan would like you to forget that you have the authority and he is really powerless against you. The only power he has is the one you give him. Satan's power comes through fear, doubt and disappointment. If he can get you into negative thinking, you will forget to meditate on the positive and what God has said about your situation.

*"I have never seen the righteous forsaken or their children begging for bread." Psalm 37:25*

Satan knows that if you fail to keep your eyes on who God is and His faithfulness to His promises, he can take away your ability to move forward and be victorious. We are winners through Christ! Don't give away the authority God has given you. Use it to defeat the enemy. Are you speaking words out of fear, disappointment, gossip, or self pity? That is what is becoming stronger and louder in your life. Are you looking for people to agree with you? You are strengthening the negative thoughts behind your words and that is what is becoming real to you.

Speaking negatively empowers Satan to operate in your life. Stop coming into agreement with him. You attract the attention of the forces of hell or the forces of heaven by the sounds that emanate from you. Speak positive, faith-filled words and the angels will gather around you to bring them to pass. Stop inviting the demons to your pity party. If you refuse to let go of the words God has spoken to you, then you can move into a new dimension of prosperity and abundance.

### Action Step

*A good man leaves an inheritance for his children's children, but a sinner's wealth is stored up for the righteous. Proverbs 13:22*
Meditate on this Scripture and believe that nothing is impossible for God.

**Speak positive, faith-filled words and the angels will gather around you to bring them to pass.**

# God's Plan – Our Purpose

## Day 236

God has a purpose or plan in regard to all of us and for all the world. God's plan will not be altered. He had power enough that would secure His plan. His plans were, and always will be accomplished.

It would be costly for Him, but it would be free to us.

If in fact, God's plans were not accomplished, there would be reason for doubt and dismay.

But there is no power that can defeat the purposes of God.

God has formed a plan that includes meeting every need that we have. Everything that occurs in our life will ultimately point to the plan He has set out before us.

Jesus' life was a plan. His death was a plan.

*Yet it was the LORD's will to crush him and cause him to suffer, and though the LORD makes his life a guilt offering, he will see his offspring and prolong his days, and the will of the LORD will prosper in his hand. After the suffering of his soul, he will see the light [of life] and be satisfied; by his knowledge my righteous servant will justify many, and he will bear their iniquities. Therefore I will give him a portion among the great, and he will divide the spoils with the strong, because he poured out his life unto death, and was numbered with the transgressors. For he bore the sin of many, and made intercession for the transgressors.     Isaiah 53:10-12 NIV*

<u>PRAYER</u>:
*Lord, I thank you for all that you have destined me for, all of the greatness that you have created me for, and for forgiving me for all of my wrong decisions. I ask you to reveal to me Your plan for my life. Reveal to me today Your freedom, Your abundance, and Your love that I might grow closer to You which is the greatest gift that I could receive. Amen.*

*There is no power that can defeat the purposes of God.*

# God's Plan – Our Purpose

**Day 237**

What keeps us from understanding God's purpose in our life?

Stones, like the one that stood in front of the entrance of the grave where Jesus was laid. Stones that have blocked our way; stones that can include:

- Lies that we have heard
- Hurts that have determined our thinking
- Unhealthy environments
- False conclusions
- Tiredness

Though it may feel like there is no hope…
While it may seem that God has failed you…
While it may appear that He is dead to you…
While it is true that He came, He lived, and He died…
You must realize that was just the end of the beginning.
You see, He left heaven.
He walked the earth and touched it forever, with love.
He was nailed to a cross.
He shed real blood and cried real tears.
He bore our sins.
He breathed His last breath…

But the story didn't stop there.

He came to life, three days later. And on that day, Mary Magdalene, and you and me, were able to be called by His name. We would be able to know Him in a different way.

He would no longer just be Master,

He would be Savior, Redeemer and Friend.

Today, there is an abundant life to be lived for a risen Savior.

Let us celebrate...

He is alive!

*Today, there is an abundant life to be lived for a risen Savior*

# God's Plan - Our Purpose

## Day 238

Jesus is still looking for seekers of truth. The power to change lives is still as real today as when He walked on the earth. He is looking for those who are willing to come into a different system. It is a system of unconditional love, where you are no longer alone, and the enemy cannot keep you, for His nail-scarred hand holds yours and you walk through life together.

Anyone who is willing to look at themselves will have to admit, there have been times of sin in their lives. Everyone must come to the place that they realize they can't make the wisest decisions on their own. They come to the place that they know they need help. And help is available. God has positioned people around us to hear the truth that is offered to every seeker of truth. They could be beside you on an airplane, or even sitting beside you today.

YES! He is alive, and looking for those who are seeking truth today. The same Jesus who called Mary's name and opened her eyes to who stood before her, is standing before you now, inviting you to new life. Welcome to your new life. Now, we must all live our lives according to the full response to the empty tomb. The stone is rolled away, the stones of life that kept us bound, have been removed. It is time for us to enter in.

His death wasn't the end but the beginning of life that's completed in you. Don't you see, He did all this for you ... He came, He lived, and He died, but that was the end of the beginning.

### *Action Step:*

*Behold He makes all things new. Today is a NEW day! If you are holding on to yesterday, it's time to let go and move forward towards God. Today, make an effort to be aware of anything you are holding on to that is keeping you from experiencing the NEW life. Ask God to show it to you and then ... let go!*

**God has positioned people around us to hear the truth that is offered to every seeker of truth.**

# He Is The Risen Lord Indeed!

**Day 239**

Here is the scene… Jesus has been crucified. The disciples felt their dreams were crushed. Feelings of hopelessness and despair must have overtaken them. But there was a compulsion still within the hearts of those whose lives He had touched to do something to honor Him, to care for Him, to serve Him in the best way they knew how.

*Now when the Sabbath was past, Mary Magdalene, Mary the mother of James, and Salome bought spices, that they might come and anoint Him. Very early in the morning, on the first day of the week, they came to the tomb when the sun had risen. And they said among themselves, "Who will roll away the stone from the door of the tomb for us?" Mark 16:1-3*

Please note that though there was a huge obstacle in their way, they kept pressing forward, they didn't know how they were going to do it. They didn't know who would help them. They just knew they had to show their heart of love for the One who had shown the greatest love they had ever known. They took what they had, the knowledge of how to show their honor and love to Him, and the huge rock stone was not as important to them, as just getting to Jesus.

*But when they looked up, they saw that the stone had been rolled away — for it was very large. Mark 16:4*

When you are determined to worship Him, no matter what the obstacle appears to be that seems to keep you away from Him, God will roll away the obstacle, for He has prepared a way for your heart's cry to be met.

*And entering the tomb, they saw a young man clothed in a long white robe sitting on the right side; and they were alarmed. Mark 16:5*

You may not understand the intervention, even in the moment. But God was turning the page for them in the pages of history. Heaven and earth had collided and things would be forever changed.

**He has prepared a way for your heart's cry to be met.**

# He Is The Risen Lord Indeed!

## Day 240

The apostles didn't believe the women's report that Jesus was alive. They were responding to the circumstances of the day, the way it appeared. If you keep staring at what seems to be, you will never be able to see from the heavenly perspective. They did not realize that God was still in control. In the midst of confusion and turmoil, in the midst of the darkest days of their lives, there was still a light on. And it was going to shine until the whole world would know that He is alive.

*Now behold, two of them were traveling that same day to a village called Emmaus, which was seven miles from Jerusalem. And they talked together of all these things which had happened. So it was, while they conversed and reasoned, that Jesus Himself drew near and went with them. But their eyes were restrained, so that they did not know Him. Luke 24:13-16*

In the midst of your confusion, there is One standing beside you, One walking with you, One who has what you need.

*And He said to them, "What kind of conversation is this that you have with one another as you walk and are sad?" Then the one whose name was Cleopas answered and said to Him, "Are You the only stranger in Jerusalem, and have You not known the things which happened there in these days?" And He said to them, "What things?" So they said to Him, "The things concerning Jesus of Nazareth, who was a Prophet mighty in deed and word before God and all the people, and how the chief priests and our rulers delivered Him to be condemned to death, and crucified Him. But we were hoping that it was He who was going to redeem Israel. Indeed, besides all this, today is the third day since these things happened. Luke 24:17-21*

Look at what had happened. They had let the present, apparent circumstance take away their knowledge that Jesus was the Christ, the Son of the living God. They had reduced Him to a prophet that they had hoped would redeem them. But all the doubt in the world, all the adverse circumstances that seem to scream that He hasn't rescued you, doesn't change the fact that He is alive, and He is actively bringing things together for your good. Whether you still believe in Him fully or not, He fully believes in you, and He is working behind the scenes in ways you may not be aware of yet.

*In the midst of your confusion, there is One standing beside you...*

# He Is The Risen Lord Indeed!

**Day 241**

He is trying to send us a message, as He tried that day.

*... And certain women of our company, who arrived at the tomb early, astonished us. When they did not find His body, they came saying that they had also seen a vision of angels who said He was alive. And certain of those who were with us went to the tomb and found it just as the women had said; but Him they did not see." Luke 24:22-24*

Now, the Lord would take the time to give them more revelation. He knew them even if they didn't know Him.

*Then He said to them, "O foolish ones, and slow of heart to believe in all that the prophets have spoken! Ought not the Christ to have suffered these things and to enter into His glory?" And beginning at Moses and all the Prophets, He expounded to them in all the Scriptures the things concerning Himself. Luke 24:25-27*

They were good at believing the glory and the greatness of the kingdom that would make them great, but they would not believe prophecies of the humility and sufferings of their Redeemer.

Imagine having the revelation that Jesus' suffering foretold by the prophets was so that all would know His suffering was pre planned. It was buying back our reconciliation, it was buying back our healing, it was taking us back to peace, and covering all our sin. What a Savior.

*Then they drew near to the village where they were going, and He indicated that He would have gone farther. But they constrained Him, saying, "Abide with us, for it is toward evening, and the day is far spent." And He went in to stay with them. Luke 24:28-29*

He had spoken to them of the truth of the written word, and it had stirred them enough that they wanted to spend more time with Him. Jesus is doing that for us. He is letting us in on revelation of who He is as the scriptures come alive before us and it is compelling us to spend more time with Him. We are wanting to pray, to commune, to have more time with Him. It is with Him that things are changing within us, just as it would be for these two.

*He is letting us in on revelation of who He is.*

# HE IS THE RISEN LORD INDEED!

**Day 242**

*Now it came to pass, as He sat at the table with them, that He took bread, blessed and broke it, and gave it to them. Then their eyes were opened and they knew Him; and He vanished from their sight. Luke 24:30-31*

Now, He would take the elements that He had used with His disciples with the command that they would do it often, in remembrance of Him. When they remembered Him, their eyes were open and they knew Him.

What do you remember? I remember when...
He saved me.
He healed me.
He healed my children.
He stopped a stroke in a restaurant with my Dad.
My children prayed the prayer of salvation.
My granddaughter prayed in the spirit over granddad at 4 years old.
Jesus forgave me and gave me a second chance.
He told me He would never leave me or forsake me.
He told me He loved me, and my heart burned from the truth of the statement taking residence inside of me.

They could also recall the fact that there was always something different about being with Him. There was no one who could awaken their hearts like He could.

*And they said to one another, "Did not our heart burn within us while He talked with us on the road, and while He opened the Scriptures to us?" Luke 24:32*

When you come to the realization of who you are with, who is talking to you, who is giving you fresh revelation, who is tying the past with present, who is merging heaven and earth, it brings a difference to you.

*When they remembered Him,
their eyes were open and they knew Him.*

# He Is The Risen Lord Indeed!

**Day 243**

They had to tell someone. They had to proclaim the truth.

*So they rose up that very hour and returned to Jerusalem, and found the eleven and those who were with them gathered together, saying, "The Lord is risen indeed, and has appeared to Simon!" Luke 24:33-34*

Note: Jesus was no longer just a prophet they had hoped would help them, He was THE RISEN LORD INDEED..

*And they told about the things that had happened on the road, and how He was known to them in the breaking of bread. Luke 24:35*

Though the circumstances had caused them to doubt Him, He wasn't looking at their doubt; He was looking at their struggle. He was looking at their sadness, and He went to them. He found them before they knew who He was. They were talking to the Son of God and yet their eyes were kept from seeing Him, until… He broke bread with them. It was upon the remembrance of Him, upon the remembering of what He had done for them, that got them out of their mind and into the spirit place where they could see clearly and hear clearly who He was. And their eyes were open and they knew Him. Then they realized He was burning things in their hearts all along the way.

It wasn't until there was a remembrance of the past, of all He had said and done in their midst. It wasn't until they recalled all the things He had done to rescue them. It wasn't until they pondered the price that was paid, for them, for the world, that the picture came together that He was there all along. His promises were true all along even if they saw it, or they didn't, even if they knew it or they didn't.

What was the result?
Then they rose up the same hour. I challenge you to take communion today, remember Him, remember all that He has done for you and see if it doesn't cause you to rise up!

**He found them before they knew who He was.**

## HE IS THE RISEN LORD INDEED!

**Day 244**

What seems like a time when dreams have been crushed, when it feels all hope is gone, Jesus is there. He is walking with you.

The Messiah is sharing with you in your suffering and about the necessity of His sufferings. He is sharing why the prophets said what they said. He wanted us to know the power of His suffering, in the midst of not knowing where He is. There are times when He has seemingly left us, but in reality He has always been right near us. We can find Him again, walking with us, and talking with us but sometimes ours eyes do not behold Him because of unbelief. Yet when we sit with Him, when we break bread with Him, when we allow Him to speak to us, the things that seem impossible, become visible.

The understanding of how it all fits together suddenly makes sense, and you will know Him and His resurrection power. You will know about His sufferings and why. You will know that He is risen and that there is a story to be told. You will be compelled to rise up that same hour and proclaim the truth. He is alive and He is in our midst. A new day had begun, and it is the dawning of a new day for us as well.

*"Though thy beginning was small, yet thy latter end should greatly increase." Job 8:7*

Your future will be greater than your past!
The rest of your life will be the best of your life!
The rest of your giving…is going to be the best of your giving.
The rest of your witness…is going to be the best of your witness.
The rest of your prayer life…is going to be the best of your prayer life.
The rest of your praise…is going to be the best of your praise.
The rest of your shout…is going to be the best of your shout.
The rest of your faith…is going to be the best of your faith.

*Your future will be greater than your past!*

# HE IS THE RISEN LORD INDEED!

**Day 245**

Jesus is dispensing His blessings and His truths. His promises are becoming a reality to a band of people who are still looking for a voice of truth in the midst of their sadness. When the disciples remembered Him, their eyes were open and they knew Him.

What do you remember? Do you remember when He saved you? When He healed you or your children or someone you love? Do you remember the first time He revealed His love for you and you responded to Him? Maybe you have faced things you never thought you would face. Maybe your circumstances have clouded who you think He is. Today may be your day for a second chance.

The times have changed, but He has remained the same. He is here today and He wants to recall to you all the times He made Himself real to you. He wants to walk with you and reveal Himself to you. He wants to be the Lord of your life, not just another memory of a prophet that may have made a difference. He is the risen Savior indeed. If your heart is burning within you, then He is speaking to you. His focus is on you. The one He loves, the one He longs to reveal Himself to.

He is already talking to your heart. He is already stirring up things in your spirit, and He is ready to commune with you today and show you that He has been with you all along.

*[He planned] for the maturity of the times and the climax of the ages to unify all things and head them up and consummate them in Christ, [both] things in heaven and things on the earth. Ephesians 1:10 AMP*

Become one with Him today, and allow heaven and earth to collide on the inside of you once again.

*Today may be your day for a second chance.*

# DIVINE DESIGN

**Day 246**

The following Kingdom Guide Series is taken from a prophetic word of "Divine Design." You see, God has a plan (design) for the earth, for His church, and for you and your family. Allow the Holy Spirit to minister this to you as you read this prophecy.

A Sovereign Time of Divine Design

He's releasing His sovereignty, Lordship, rulership. He is releasing the patterns and the understanding of the patterns. A divine design that we will now understand. It will fit into the release from heaven. It will contain strategies.

To see how He has laid it out on the earth. He causes us as the Body to begin to recognize and follow and fit into His pre-designed pattern. As the church arises, individuals can then sink themselves down into it. Then they become partakers of completely understanding God's presence in their life, His kingdom purposes. They will enjoy unity and oneness as they become aware and become fluid with Him. We've come from the 5 senses to the 6th, to the 7th senses. They are literally pulling heaven to earth by standing in the gap, as intercessors, as a person on the earth set to do it.

Establishing A Release of the Seasons …

We've been in different seasons and we are entering into the final season.

It is the season of the church arising. The church is going to have the revelation of who they are called to be. It's the final season of grace. The line is being drawn. Last opportunities are being given to people. They are going to be able to hear it for the last time. That's why it's going to be so dark. When they choose for the very last time, and then they give themselves over completely to evil.

*They are literally pulling heaven to earth*

# Divine Design

**Day 247**

It will be intense. God has been after them. Darkness will be so evident. The same way we're preparing the way for the Lord, they are preparing the way for the Antichrist, the path for wickedness. They don't recognize it; they are not necessarily Satanists, they just don't know what they are doing. Like Oprah, it makes sense. It's the humanistic mindset -- all about self. The selfishness that prevails is making the way; that's why it's so prevalent. Selfishness is the way the Antichrist gains his entrance. He's going to proclaim that he is the answer.

It will be embraced because they get to be selfish.

The catastrophic events will cause people to have to make decisions and that is why God said these things would occur. It's those events that will cause people to run to Him or accuse Him. So they either raise their hands in adoration or they raise their fists. And that's how the separation is occurring.

Fierceness will come on both sides. The people who are coming under the evil regime will be fierce, will justify it, portray it, and not apologize for it. Those on the sides of righteousness – those who know their God will have to know Him, they can't pretend to know Him anymore. No pretense allowed. No pretending to know Him. You either know Him or you won't survive.

Satan is preparing a people for his day of glory. He's masked himself. He's going to have his day of glory, but God is going to rip the mask off. Satan will defile the temple. He doesn't realize it; it's even written and he doesn't realize it. That's how a nation will be saved in a day. In that same moment they will recognize Jesus as Messiah. Simultaneously. Once they see it, their understanding will be complete. The purity of Christ will be revealed and they will realize the Servant of all is the King. The other one will just want it all for him. Jesus came to serve and save the lost. Then they'll know and they'll know why they missed Him – they thought He was going to be on some throne. They'll recognize their need for a Savior and they will know who it was. It won't matter to the Jews if they die – they won't care because they were always willing to die, if they know that it's for God. The fact that so many are slain won't matter because they will finally be giving to their God.

> *They'll recognize their need for a Savior and they will know who it was.*

# DIVINE DESIGN

## Day 248

The last season …Jesus is the reason for the season.

His name has to be lifted up right now.

The church will be persecuted, but victorious. The whole thing happening in the economic realm will strengthen and fortify the church. It has to do with the transference of wealth. It started with the faith-based organizations. They've recognized to a certain extent that those who have faith have been successful because they integrated truth and that's why they've gotten results. God has been releasing the teachings on the seven mountains. People are already positioned and the governments of the world don't know what to do. It's the church, already in place, who has the answers. The wealth will then be transferred because they know what to do. They have the patterns.

God is releasing more strategies and more patterns because he has to. It's not just within the church. It's the structure of the way things are supposed to be handled corporately, and then the individual becomes prosperous. It can't be done in the world's system anymore. I will keep falling. They can't even come up with answers anymore. They are turning to those who have truth because they have no answers themselves.

Prayer in schools, in Washington, everywhere. It will be absolutely necessary. He's doing it on the local level already, starting at the grass roots – green, new. They don't even know that is why they are positioned where they are. It's one of those shafts of light – God has the right people with the right heart, though they don't have the knowledge yet. But He's going to drop it in them. They're going to think they became brilliant overnight. They will be brilliant because of the glory of God. They are having sovereign moments, divine interventions, radical happenings with God.

*They are turning to those who have truth because they have no answers themselves.*

# Divine Design

## Day 249

Satan is fortifying. God is fortifying. The young lions … when the lion roars, part of it is calling his pack, or pride, to himself. That's what God is doing. The Lion of Judah is roaring and the ones listening are the young lions. That's why He's had us so focused on the roar. As we take our positions and release the sound, we're calling the others to us. It's reproduction. He is reproducing Himself through us calling them to Himself, out of the darkness. These are the sounds of heaven that we've been hearing and can't describe. It is the release of the lion. They don't know what they are hearing. He's going to call to them out in the streets – more in the spirit than in the natural. It's like when the charismatic movement came and He poured out his spirit – and the people didn't know what they had – He's bringing them into the atmosphere of heaven. They will have a mindset change. The revivals were bringing things back scripturally. This will be a redemptive revelation also.

They'll come and they'll have authority. Rulership.

It ends up being like the end of the war, the breath of God,. It goes back to Genesis when he breathed on them and they became living souls. God is breathing into the dry bones. The trumpets – the prophets - are blowing and His breath is being released. In one breath, one blast of His nostril, they're changed so that they can absorb and begin to think like He thinks. It's more than an impartation; it's a radical change from the inside out. It's actually understanding finally how we are transferred out of the darkness into His light – redemption reality. More than just the salvation, the awareness of life of God on the inside – the total overtaking of God in the abundance of His presence. There will be no denying it. Believing in your heart, saying it with your mouth that Jesus brings salvation and you shall be saved, be made whole, shall prosper, be complete. It's not just a prayer – it's a happening. They'll be aware in the spirit and in the physical. They'll actually feel it.

My redemption draweth nigh, my redemption draweth nigh.

*He is calling them to Himself, out of the darkness.*

# Divine Design

## Day 250

There is a seven-year period, starting with 2009 and ending in 2016. It is a "Clearing house," a corporation established by an exchange in order to facilitate the execution of trades by transferring funds, assigning deliveries, and guaranteeing the performance of all obligations.

It's like clearing the house in the spiritual – in families, in the church, clearing the debris, the infiltration, even the tabernacle, the habitation of us that He dwells in. The Stock exchange – all of these things are changing in the natural. It's what we put our stock in that's going to change. There's an exchanging going on.

Investments for the future … people have relied on their 401k's and retirement, but the investment for the future is the investment God has made. The young adults – and investments made in those who will train them. It's the real plan – the real investments for the future.

In actuality the retirement plan of God is that when we do our job and we fulfill that which He has called us to do, the quicker we reproduce ourselves, get into direct obedience, the faster He will accomplish His will on the earth. We can actually speed it up. God is the only one who looks into the hearts to see when events will occur. He knows who's going to obey when. The religious leaders of the day are going to be the worst. They're going to seize the opportunity. They will see that the world is going to look to them for answers and they're going to try to seize it for themselves. The real shepherds, the authentic ones, the ones with the right heart, who feed the sheep, protect them, and provide for them, and they'll have it to do so. They'll have it.

There's a landslide! It means territories are being transferred. You'll be given your own land. A lot of people have land, but it's no good to them anymore. They're going to give it away into the hands of the righteous. That's the turn-around – the wealth transference. They'd rather give it away than lose it.

*All of these things are changing in the natural.*

# HEAVENLY PERSPECTIVE

**Day 251**

In order for us to experience the fullness of the blessing, that God has given us… In order for us to accomplish all that He has assigned to us… In order for us to continue to move forward in a season that can be so very challenging at times, we must change our mind and change our perspective.

We must stop looking at things the way we always have because that is the way we have always done it. We have to let the Holy Spirit renew our minds. We have to search the word and let new revelation invade us.

Then we have to be willing to allow the new into the old. It's not going to be easy, especially since we are more comfortable when things just stay, well, comfortable.

But these are challenging times and we must be challenged in every way. I want to talk to you in this Kingdom Guide series about changing your perspective concerning significance and insignificance.

God said: "Do not agree with the enemy that says that you are insignificant. For you are significant to Me. You are significant on this earth, and you are significant for the end times. You are significant for eternity."

There is a spirit being unleashed against many to make you feel insignificant, when the plan of God is just the opposite.

Significant means having or likely to have influence or effect : IMPORTANT

Insignificant means lacking meaning or importance

*change your perspective concerning significance & insignificance.*

# Heavenly Perspective

## Day 252

I had a dream recently. I was lying down, and I had pain in my neck. It was really hurting and someone from the church was there with me. I said, no it's real. You really need to pray.

When I looked up the meaning of it, I found that dreaming that your neck is injured or sore indicates a separation between your heart and mind. There is a literal disconnect between how you feel and what you think. You are feeling conflicted. I realized also that the pain was in the jugular vein. If you have injury to that vein, you can die very quickly due to loss of blood. I am telling you this because God is trying to reveal what is going on so that we can overcome the enemy at his own game.

When you are being attacked by a mind-blinding spirit, you can't see things the way you should. Your perception is off. You can't see from the heavenly perspective. It is like you are just stuck in your natural thoughts with no life line to the spiritual. Satan likes to say things like, "You aren't making a difference and you never will, so you may as well quit trying" "See, they never listen to you." "Just the opposite of what you desire, is what you are getting. All that faith stuff doesn't work anyway." "It won't matter if I go to church or not go to church." "It doesn't make a difference because I don't make a difference, no one acknowledges my x.y.z because there really isn't anything I have to offer."

Of course, when I say them, we see how ridiculous those thoughts and false accusations are. But when you are the one hearing them, you may have a hard time recognizing how much of a plot it is against you. If we are to see this from a heavenly perspective, we will have to look at it from a spiritual sense.

First of all, this is a spiritual battle and you have to fight back in the spirit. You can't win if you handle it in the natural.

*This is a spiritual battle and you have to fight back in the spirit.*

# HEAVENLY PERSPECTIVE

## Day 253

We should work harder than ever before.

We should pursue His love and His ways more than we thought possible. We must surrender totally to Him.

For in the days of destruction we must survey the damage, and we must bring hope again to the hopeless.

We must take that which has been broken down, and we must rebuild. Not just for us but for future generations.

The lie of the enemy is that what we are doing now is just laborious. Not successful. Not significant. But when you are in the place with Him and with His directions on your life, you are not only significant but you are causing others to know that they are too. Your life counts now. What you are doing counts now. In fact, whatever you do for the Lord, you must do now, because your time for being significant on this earth is short.

Why do we look to your past instead of looking to your future? Everything you do will either bring you reward or regret. We have all bought things we regret. Think about your time and how you spent it. Will you be so glad you watched 4,000 movies? So live your life, invest your life so that when you cross this finish line, you can face God with joy.

Don't spend your life down here, looking and investing in the temporal, when that is just what it is, to enjoy right now, not even knowing if you have tomorrow.

It is tempting, but what about the millions of years after?

*Your life counts now. What you are doing counts now.*

# Heavenly Perspective

## Day 254

Paul said he kept his eyes on the finish line. He stretched forward for the trophy. Why? Because he had failed to understand the significance that he had on the earth, until the day, he heard his voice, "Saul, Saul, why do you persecute me?"

On that day, he had an eternal interaction that caused him to rise up. It caused him to begin to govern his life differently. It opened his eyes, and he saw Jesus. And he knew, He saw him too. And he would never be the same again.

Today, have you bought into the lie that what you do is not making a difference? Could you admit that God seems to be dead in certain areas of your life? Do you need to have your dreams and hopes resurrected today?

Today, Jesus is near you, He knows your name, He knows what you need. He knows how to roll your stones away. He knows how to cause you to believe in him again, and to believe in your own significance again. We must survey where the walls are broken down; we must look at what satan has done to destroy our temple and we must give God permission to rule and reign in our lives today.

As we do that, we will begin to understand that though we may have made mistakes, He who is the great redeemer can redeem them for the kingdom's sake. After all, we are only here for a short period of time. Together, with each other and with Him, we can make the difference.

Today, If you seek Him, He will find you. He will call your name, and the power of the resurrection will come upon you and you never have to be the same again.

*Together, with each other and with Him, we can make the difference.*

# Your God-Given Authority

## Day 255

Your God-given Authority - Use it, give it away, or lose it!

God has given us back the authority that He originally gave to Adam in Eve, to rule and reign and take dominion over the earth. That gives us great ability as well as great responsibility. If we don't utilize our voice to stand against evil, we surrender our authority because silence is agreement. If we don't raise the standard, there will be the standard of the world for others to see and to abide by.

If we don't take charge of the kingdoms of this world, by living in righteousness and influencing others by what they see from the favor of God on your life, then we forfeit our God-given right to make the kingdoms of this world the kingdoms of our God.

It is time for the Church to arise. It is time for us to take our places, under authority, with God-given authority, on purpose! It is time for the people of God to take authority in the seven mountains of culture:

Arts/Entertainment | Government | Business

Education | Family | Media | Religion

Are you being influenced by the world's system or are you influencing the world?

When the righteous are in authority, the people rejoice.

Make a difference today.

*When the righteous are in authority, the people rejoice.*

## A Lifestyle of Offering

### Day 256

How necessary it is to develop a lifestyle where you are constantly pursuing the things of God. You have to be persistent in what God is saying to you; not just listening to it but acting upon it. You are called to be doers of the word and not hearers only. You are to be involved participators in God's plan, and not spectators.

You hide the Word of God in your heart so you might not sin against Him but you also hide the Word of God in your heart so that you can discover purpose and destiny and then you can pursue that. You develop that type of a lifestyle of pursuing by seeking God and continuing to knock at heaven's door and asking for more of Him.

Everyone is looking for answers. Everyone is looking for a path to life and to fulfillment. Then you should love this part of God's word:

*You will show me the path of life; in Your presence is fullness of joy; at Your right hand are pleasures forevermore. Psalm 16: 11*

God will show you the path of life because in His presence you will find joy and at His right hand you will find pleasure. You will find that which satisfies you; you will find that which puts a gladness in your spirit and in your mind so that when you pursue God and get into His presence you will find joy and pleasure.

I want you to know that God wants you to have those elements in your life. You can be restored, edified and secure in the freedom God gives you.

*God will show you the path of life.*

# A Lifestyle of Offering

**Day 257**

I want to challenge you today to be persistent after God. Pursue Him with all of your heart, with all of your might and when you get into His presence you will find out that the journey has been worth everything that it has taken for you to get there.

One more time: your persistence is going to declare the type of future you will have; not just your future but the TYPE of future you will have.

You can go through this world just singing "que sera, sera" whatever will be will be," or you can pursue the things of God with all your heart and you will find in His presence joy and you will find pleasure!

Declare:

With my eyes fixed on Jesus, the Author and the Finisher of my faith, I persevere into His Presence where I am restored, edified and secured of my freedom.

Today as I sow my seed, Father, I make a declaration of faith that when I sow the seed the windows of heaven will open and I will experience your heavenly perspective.

I put myself in position that I'm in Your presence and I can hear Your voice and You can show me what I've never seen before.

Father, in Your presence I can find joy and I can find pleasure – that which satisfies my soul.

I thank You today with this seed so that I can enter into this place that I know that I will be made happy, and every need shall be met in the Name of Jesus, AMEN.

*Your persistence is going to declare the type of future you will have.*

# The Voice Of God

## Day 258

David is one of my favorite Old Testament people. I know he was a mess, but he was also mentioned in Hebrews 11 as a man in the Hall of Faith, and he is also called by God "a man after His own heart." God wanted someone - someone after God's own heart who would rule His people differently. We all still benefit from the many things we learn about David's love for God. In the Psalms he wrote about his King.

*Many, O Lord my God, are the wonderful works which You have done, and Your thoughts toward us; no one can compare with You! If I should declare and speak of them, they are too many to be numbered. delight to do Your will, O my God; yes, Your law is within my heart. Psalm 40:5, 8 (AMP)*

This is just a small example of all the wonderful things that David discovered and proclaimed about his God. For him to know Him in this way, he would learn from many things, and hear from many voices, which we will see in this study.

God always has a plan and He has people in place to help you understand God's plan for your life. However, things may need to be adjusted and aligned before things begin to roll out for you in the natural. In David's case, the first voice would be a voice that would influence and impact his life forever.

Let's use his life as our example today, for he had opportunity to hear many voices. In today's scripture we find the first and most important voice. A voice that brings directives that will help all of us. We can learn many things from God's voice as He spoke to Samuel. God has set David apart for ruling His kingdom. In 1 Samuel 16, God is speaking to the prophet concerning David, and concerning Samuel's own mindsets and actions, so that he would be in proper order to bring about the whole will of God properly.

In the following days of your Kingdom Guide we will break the scripture down to see how well this example applies to each of our lives today.

*God always has a plan and He has people in place to help you understand God's plan for your life.*

# The Voice Of God

**Day 259**

The first thing the Lord says to Samuel is, "How long will you mourn for Saul?" This brings us to our first point in this series...

1. Let go of the past

Samuel had anointed Saul to be king. He loved Saul. He longed for the days when Saul was the Saul he knew in the past, when Saul obeyed the Lord and the people had an uncompromised person leading them. I don't know if Samuel was holding on because he had helped birth him into that place, but I do know he was holding on to the hope of restoration of Saul. At that time, prophets were the rulers God put in place to govern the nation. In other words, before the kings, the prophets were in charge. When kings were put in place, the prophets still spoke into their lives and helped to guide and govern the nation. Samuel had held with determination that Saul's position would be returned to him. It made sense to Samuel. So, he longed for the past. But God said directly, "I have rejected Saul from reigning over Israel." That was it. God knew Saul's heart. He knew what opportunities He had given Saul to repent. He knew his position in the Kingdom had changed. God's love hadn't changed. But Saul would never have the same position to God's people as he had before. It was time for Samuel to let go of what was, so he could embrace the new.

You know this voice. It is the voice that urges you forward, to let go of the past. The voice that you try to resist because you care so much for a person, or for a time that no longer exists. I think it may be one of the hardest things for us to do. But the voice of God, is well, the VOICE of GOD. He alone knows what is best for all involved and He is not trying to take something from you, but to get something TO you! Understand that moving on when God tells you to isn't giving up, it is simply allowing God to be God and placing yourself in a position of going to another level to be used even greater for the Kingdom and for your benefit as well.

*He is not trying to take something from you, but to get something TO you!*

# The Voice Of God

Day 260

The second thing we learn from God's voice speaking to Samuel is this. "Fill your horn with oil." In other words…

2. Get ready with what I have given you.

Samuel was the prophet. He was anointed to anoint and to appoint. He was to fill his horn with oil and get ready to do what he had been destined to do. Anoint and appoint others for their position in the Kingdom, and then help them along the way. It is still the job of the five-fold ministers today. Who are the five fold ministers today?

*And He Himself gave some to be apostles, some prophets, some evangelists, and some pastors and teachers,*

For what are they given?

*for the equipping of the saints for the work of ministry, for the edifying of the body of Christ. Ephesians 4:11-12*

Samuel is an example of the pattern that continues today. Like Samuel, we must continue to fill our horn with oil. We must be filled with the Spirit so that when we hear God's voice, we are ready to move in the anointing and the call on our life. I don't know how long it took for Samuel to be willing to obey the voice of the Lord in this manner. I just know his oil could have run out if he had continued to mourn instead of being prepared for the change that was taking place.

God's voice had shown up to Samuel and it will show up to us also to prompt us to move forward, and utilize the anointing that He has entrusted to us individually and corporately. God is good, and He has a plan that will far exceed anything that we could ever muster up on our own.

It is our responsibility, however, to keep our oil ready and to be obedient to go where He calls us to go and do what He asks us to do.

*We must be filled with the Spirit so that when we hear God's voice, we are ready to move in the anointing and the call on our life.*

# The Voice Of God

## Day 261

Then God's voice said:

"I am sending you to Jesse the Bethlehemite. For I have provided Myself a king among his sons." 1 Samuel 16:1

3. Go

He was to go according to God's directive. He was to go to Jesse and from his sons would come the next King.

If God gives you a directive, He will reveal the where and the when. In this case, it was now and it was specifically to a person. We must live our lives in expectancy of God to call us to go somewhere and make a difference. It could be a neighbor. It could be a store, a park, somewhere close or somewhere far away.

Let's be honest and ask ourselves, are we so caught up in what we are doing, or what we prefer to do that we are not taking the time to listen for the instructions of the Lord as to what He would like us to do?

We should wake up, and say, "Good morning Jesus, where do you want me to go today with my anointing oil?"

*We must live our lives in expectancy of God to call us to go somewhere and make a difference.*

# The Voice Of God

## Day 262

Then God's voice gave Samuel this instruction:

*But the LORD said to Samuel, "Do not look at his appearance or at his physical stature, because I have refused him. For the LORD does not see as man sees; for man looks at the outward appearance, but the LORD looks at the heart." 1 Samuel 16:7*

4. Don't look at the obvious or the natural. See others through God's perspective.

God continued to reveal things to this prophet that would be immediately put to use and also be tested. Samuel would have to go against the obvious, to do the will of the Lord. There was going to be some obvious things that were going to occur that day. Part of it was that Jesse had some robust, tall sons that would seem to fit the bill as KING of Israel.

Saul looked like a king, but this next king would not be selected so much from outside appearances. He was good looking, but young, inexperienced in war, and not a large person. Samuel was instructed that He was not to look at them from the natural state of mind. He was to look past the natural and look at the heart and the potential of God's chosen man.

Samuel would learn that day that although people can appear to be exactly what you are looking for on the outside, they have none, or not enough of, the necessary qualities that would be needed to complete a particular job they were chosen for.

Positions in the Kingdom are chosen by the Spirit: God is always looking at hearts, not resumes. Not outwardly, but inwardly.

Not gifting alone, but character and longevity in obedience and loving God wholeheartedly no matter what comes your way.

We must learn and apply this principle also.

*God continued to reveal things to this prophet that would be immediately put to use and also be tested*

# The Voice Of God

## Day 263

David would make mistakes, but his tender heart of worship would always bring him back to center.

*Thus Jesse made seven of his sons pass before Samuel. And Samuel said to Jesse, "The LORD has not chosen these." And Samuel said to Jesse, "Are all the young men here?" Then he said, "There remains yet the youngest, and there he is, keeping the sheep." And Samuel said to Jesse, "Send and bring him. For we will not sit down till he comes here." So he sent and brought him in. Now he was ruddy, with bright eyes, and good-looking. And the LORD said, "Arise, anoint him; for this is the one!" Then Samuel took the horn of oil and anointed him in the midst of his brothers; and the Spirit of the LORD came upon David from that day forward. So Samuel arose and went to Ramah. 1 Samuel 16:10-13*

So now the new King was given a crown and a scepter and an announcement? No, he was sent back to keep the sheep. He had no idea that keeping sheep would help train him for Kingship. The voice of the prophet spoke to his potential, but there is training, there is a place of being willing to obey in the process.

This was not as much of a challenge, perhaps for David. You see he had been listening to a voice. His Father's voice. The voice of authority over his life. He was used to doing what his father told him to do at the time. David's obedience to his natural father was preparing him to obey his Heavenly Father's voice as well. He would hold on to the truth of what the prophet had spoken, but he would still be willing to allow God's timing to be revealed as he was in the midst of submission and obedience to those put over his life. He would take those frustrating sheep and all of their needs and train him to be diligent, protective, and to nourish and love them.

The very first thing you should settle in your life, is to work diligently at whatever you are doing right now, and listen to the voice of authority that God has placed over you. God will utilize all the things that seem to be natural circumstances of life, and use them to train you in your present, for your future. David had no idea the importance of his time on the hill with the stinky sheep. He just did what he was asked to do, and he did it with a right heart. It was on those hills that he had alone time with God. The anointing was on him from that day forward. He ruled over the sheep. He led them, he fed them, he guided them, and he protected them. And he kept at it without demanding a better position because of his anointing.

### *work diligently at whatever you are doing right now*

# The Voice Of God

## Day 264

There are two things that can occur in the process of maturing in God's call. Many miss it because they are not happy being in the position they are in. They have had prophetic words. They know that God has anointed them and they think that what they are doing right now is not really making a difference. Some people start backing up; even stop being diligent at anything. However, God blesses obedience and things "in motion."

The challenge is to continue to stay in the fields, on the hills, doing whatever has been delegated to you with the right heart. Don't get frustrated or mad or throw a temper tantrum with God. Never insist on making things happen in your timing. It never works out for your benefit that way.

Stay faithful and diligent to the small things and God will work out the timing and the details. You are being tested in your diligence and trained for your call, even if you can't understand it right now. God will call you to that which will fulfill the innermost desire of your own heart. He put those desires in you from the start.

Then there is the other side of it.

You may not be fully aware of your anointing or your call right now. You may not feel like you can ever accomplish it. Moses didn't. Abraham couldn't see it. David was a shepherd boy, not a King. But all were willing and all were working when God began to open their ears to hear His goals and plans for their life. From the time of hearing God's voice and walking in the fullness of your destiny, there will be requirements of walking it out, continuing to listen to God's voice and obey Him, and keeping your heart right in the midst of it all. Understand, seed, time and harvest is always going to be in motion.

*Understand that seed, time and harvest is always going to be in motion.*

# The Voice Of God

**Day 265**

Saul was going to be replaced. David was going to be King, but he really didn't know what a King did. God had a plan - a divine way of training. Shepherding would be his "college" to prepare him. There the anointing would come upon him to protect what was entrusted to his care. It's where he would be willing to risk his life, to lose sleep, to rely on God and to sing praises to God no matter where he was.

It seemed like a place of isolation, but it was a place of insulation and training. This is the place where God's voice would become more real to him as he heard from him and began to discover the attributes of God in a personal way. Christianity is unique among religions, for it alone offers a personal relationship with the Creator, beginning here and now, and lasting throughout eternity. Jesus declared,

*And this is eternal life, that they may know You, the only true God, and Jesus Christ whom You have sent. John 17:3*

Unfortunately, many in the Church miss the great blessing of fellowship with our Lord because we have lost the ability to recognize His voice within us. Though we have the promise that "My sheep hear My voice," too many believers are starved for that intimate relationship that alone can satisfy the desire of their hearts. We have to continue to go to the fields, to the hills, to a quiet place and get to the place of stillness where we can go beyond our own thoughts and emotions.

*Let be and be still, and know (recognize and understand) that I am God. I will be exalted among the nations! I will be exalted in the earth! Psalm 46:10 (AMP)*

Note that it says, "Let be." Forget the way you think things should be. Just let it be. And be still and know 'give Him the recognition He deserves as God'. Then you are in a position for Him to use you, to allow Him to be exalted to the nations, on the earth, through YOU. There is a deep inner knowing (spontaneous flow) in our spirits that each of us can experience when we quiet our flesh and our minds. If we are not still, we will sense only our own thoughts. We must focus on what has eternal value, and learn from the voices that are in our life that God has placed there.

As it was for David, it is for you. Your life is influenced also as God speaks through others placed over you for your own good.

*Forget the way you think things should be.*
*Just let it be.*
*And be still and know .*

## THE PURITY OF DEVOTION

**Day 266**

Take time today and tomorrow to meditate on this prophetic word that the Lord once spoke to me on "the purity of devotion:"

When they brought the lions into the arena, they brought the Christians in and thought that by devouring them that there would be a victory won for the enemy's side. But instead of it being a victory for the enemy, it was a victory for Me. For they saw a people that were willing to give their lives and lay it down so that they could be a light to others and show the purity of their devotion.

And so it is even in these last days that though it looks like you've been thrown to the lions, and though you may feel like they're devouring you, you are the victors, for you have been willing to lay your lives down. And now you will live to see it resurrected. You will live to see your dreams resurrected. You will live to see those things that I've put on the inside of you come to life again. And you will be a light and an example of those who have devotion like no other. For there is no other God under heaven where people are willing to give their life wholly and fully and righteously back to the Creator, back to the one who gave them life.

And so it shall be, and so I will invade every arena of life with the light that exudes from you as you spark forth with My glory from being in My presence. As you become the beacons of light, of shining because you have been with Me and My glory has now been embedded inside of you and now it must find its way out. And out of you it will come with words of wisdom and words of life. With love it will be felt and seen through your eyes and your hands. And they will know Me because you have known Me. And to the same level that you love and surrender to Me, you will have the ability to reach out and resurrect those things that are dead on the inside of them and bring them back to life.

*You will live to see those things that I've put on the inside of you come to life again.*

## The Purity Of Devotion

**Day 267**

Don't you understand that it is in giving that you shall receive? So as you take Me in and you give Me out, you will receive back all that you've been asking Me for. So bask in My presence and let My glory fill you up to overflowing. And then My glory will be seen and known and felt. It will be going throughout the land proclaiming the truth that I Am alive, that I Am love, and I Am still raising people from the dead.

Prayer:

Jesus, we thank You. We thank You. We love You. We are devoted to You as You are devoted to us. Indescribable. Indescribable. There is nothing like Your glory, nothing like Your presence, there is nothing like Your love. Thank You for sharing. Thank You for caring and giving the ability to shine through us. It's sacred. It's holy. And we are grateful.

*Don't you understand that it is in giving that you shall receive?*

# Cry of the Lost (A Vision)

**Day 268**

The "Cry of the Lost" is a powerful and sobering vision that one of our Worship Leaders received in the Spirit.

How do you use natural human language to describe and express a spiritual/supernatural experience? You do the best you can … My experience began as a "third person" vision. It felt like I was watching something take place, but no one could see me. I saw a thick, clear glass wall, which stood at least 50 feet tall. On either side of this wall were the church and the lost. As I tuned in to what was happening, I heard some from the church crying out to the lost on the other side, "Come in! You need what we have! You've got to get over here to this side!"

Some of those on the other side began crying out, "Help us! We're trapped! We're hurting! We're starving! Rescue us! Rescue us! We want to get in but we don't know how!" The church cried back, "We want to, but we're afraid! We really want you to be over here with us. We want to rescue you but we're not sure we'll be able to. I'm sorry…" And so the crying out went back and forth, the church crying for the lost to save themselves and come in, and the lost crying for the church to rescue them and show them how to get in… It was one of the most heart-breaking and pathetic scenes I have ever seen.

He then took me to another place. Here the Lord showed me myself. I saw myself with my eyes tightly shut and my fingers plugging my ears. I immediately knew that I had been shutting out the sight and sound of the cry of the lost and dying. Whether knowingly or subconsciously, I was the one preventing their cries and pleadings from reaching my eyes and ears. Jesus then gently removed my fingers from my ears. At first I didn't hear anything. I asked what I was supposed to be hearing. He simply answered in a very deep and sobering tone, "Go down lower…" I bent down to my knees, almost reluctantly. With my eyes still closed, I began to hear crying, weeping, moaning, groaning, shrieking cries for help. Among them were teenagers, young adults all the way through elderly men and women. I felt my heart beginning to crush. My first reaction was to try to get up and tune it out again.

Again, the Lord instructed me, "Go down lower…" At this, I finally laid completely down on the ground and put my ear to the ground, as low as I could get it. What started as only a few cries, began to escalate until I heard what sounded like hundreds, then thousands, tens of thousands, hundreds of thousands, until finally I heard seemingly millions!

*Some of those on the other side began crying out, "Help us! We're trapped!*

# Cry of the Lost (A Vision)

**Day 269**

Amidst the crying and weeping, I would hear ear-piercing, shrieking cries, desperate cries like I've never heard or felt before. It seemed to get louder and louder, until it became almost unbearable. I literally began asking Him to stop it. I said, "I can't take any more! I'm sorry! I'm sorry!" Without speaking, I felt Him saying, "I've opened your ears to hear their cries for a moment in time. These are the cries that are ever before me. I have not stopped their cries from reaching my ears. Day and night, they cry out…"

He then bent down and opened my eyes. I saw them. Wretched, torn, bleeding. Their clothing was ripped and shredded. Their faces were hopeless, lost, full of pain. Some were actually blind and calling out for anyone to help them, to lift them up. Some were stuck in what looked like pits, some were swallowed up in what looked like quicksand. Others were wounded, dragging themselves along the filthy ground, groaning in pain. One in particular was looking right at me as he dragged himself with his hands on the ground. He was crying as he was reaching for me, begging me, pleading me to do something. I then began to smell the rotting stench. I smelled what seemed to be burning flesh. I smelled the filth of the land. I heard, saw, and smelled their true condition.

The Lord then touched me and I felt a sense of something shared between them and me. I can't fully explain it, but I felt like they were my family, my very brothers and sisters! I actually began to see my real brother's and sister's faces on the lost. I then saw dark figures, torturing, tormenting, pushing, kicking, and spitting on these lost ones with my family's faces. He gave me a glimpse of how purely evil, wicked, twisted, hateful, cruel and tormenting the enemy really is. It is unrelenting, merciless evil. The Lord then spoke to me, "Until you hear their cries, you can't answer them … Until you are fully broken, you won't reach them…"

After this experience, I kept hearing Him tell me over and over, "My words are in your mouth. My words are in your mouth." I was reminded of the scripture that says, "…the word is nigh thee, even in thy mouth, and in thy heart…" I later found the full verse in Romans 10:8. "Salvation that comes from trusting Christ - which is the message we preach - is already within easy reach. In fact, the Scriptures say, 'The message is close at hand; it is on your lips and in your heart.'"

May I never forget what I witnessed and experienced tonight.

*The message is close at hand; it is on your lips and in your heart.*

## Prophetic Evangelism

### Day 270

Prophetic evangelism does not rely on natural abilities or tools to persuade people. Instead, it is a reliance on the Holy Spirit's ability to reveal the key to reach each individual.

We don't have to beg; we need to catch the initiatives of heaven and do them. We can because we are no longer restrained to operating in the natural mind.

*For "who has known the mind of the LORD that he may instruct Him?" But we have the mind of Christ. 1 Corinthians 2:16*

The first thing is to recognize we are all called to accomplish God's will on the earth. So we must be convinced of God's will. And, we must be convinced of our part in His will. If God wants us to accomplish His will on the earth, then what is His will?

*The Lord is not slack concerning his promise, as some men count slackness; but is long-suffering to us-ward, not willing that any should perish, but that all should come to repentance. 2 Peter 3:9 KJV*

We must also conclude that He has supplied us with whatever we need. Souls being saved were worth Christ suffering and death to the Godhead. The priority must be in your heart to minister His love to others. To do that, you must understand how much He loves you Himself. It comes from the overflow of His love being poured into you to overflow outward to others. Until you have been enveloped in His love, you are less equipped to share that love.

*We are no longer restrained to operating in the natural mind.*

# Prophetic Evangelism

## Day 271

What does God's voice sound like?

Indeed, He sends out His voice, a mighty voice. It sounds mighty.

*And behold, the glory of the God of Israel came from the way of the east. His voice was like the sound of many waters; and the earth shone with His glory. Ezekiel 43:2*

It's like a sound of many waters. It's loud, yet silent. It floods your soul with the reality of who He is and how He feels about you, about His people. He overwhelms you with His presence until you are in a flood with Him, and He is encasing you with His presence and His majesty. His power is tangible. Terrible, yet gentle. His voice is so very personal, yet corporate. It draws you, it fills you. It excites the depth of what is in you and you begin to see yourself as He sees you.

You feel some things you have never felt before, and it leads you into loving Him, and loving those that are in His heart. And you begin to know Him in a way that goes beyond how any natural language can express it.

*But he who enters by the door is the shepherd of the sheep. To him the doorkeeper opens, and the sheep hear his voice; and he calls his own sheep by name and leads them out. And when he brings out his own sheep, he goes before them; and the sheep follow him, for they know his voice. John 10:2-5*

It causes you to be willing to lay down your life for Him. To follow Him through the valleys and up the mountains. His love causes you to drop whatever used to be a priority, to follow Him to the secret place over and over again, for He is the priority.

*His love causes you to drop whatever used to be a priority, to follow Him... for He is the priority.*

## Prophetic Evangelism

### Day 272

You are drenched in His love and it opens chambers of your heart that you never knew existed. He opens them, and fills them with His thoughts, His feelings and His expressions. Then He enables you to pour them out on others as you see them as the lost sheep in need of this wonderful Shepherd.

You remember how it felt when you didn't know Him in this way. You are aware of how different you feel and how different you have become. Then you yearn for them to know Him like you do. You cannot stand that they would miss this beautiful place of peace, of love, of belonging.

It is here you have found acceptance. You have found the place you belong. You have found the secret place that was hidden and yet now it is so evident, you wonder how you could have missed it before. And then you find yourself looking through different eyes, seeing people beyond the obvious and looking into the needs of their longing, desperate hearts.

Your heart begins to pound for them. You know there is hope, there is life, there is light that will invade their darkness and show them that same unconditional love that you have found.

You reach for them with the depth of your soul, and you ask God for the key that will unlock their ability to receive this profound love that has changed your life.

You trust it will break through the difficulties of their lives, their mindsets and bring them into His marvelous presence also.

You feel as though you cannot live another day, you can't take another breath until you have shared this love with someone.

You must see another one rescued from the land of the enemy. From the place that once was your dwelling place.

*You know there is hope, there is life, there is light that will invade their darkness and show them that same unconditional love that you have found.*

## Prophetic Evangelism

### Day 273

They must know Him as you do. They must feel what true freedom feels like. And you weep until your eyes have no more tears to shed. You have reached them with your prayers. You have prepared the way by allowing your heart to be filled with His compassion. And now you must go. You must seize the moments—the time of opportunity—for this is the day of salvation for someone.

Someone that has been waiting on your obedience.

You know your words must be gentle, like His, as He spoke to you in the time of your need. You understand the need to deliver the purity of His love, for nothing else could have changed your life but His purity touching your uncleanness and bringing you to the pure river where you were able to drink Him in.

When you did, those majestic waters flooded you and took away the debris that had held you in captivity. Now you must share those feelings; you must reach them with the same love that you have experienced.

Nothing can stop you. They are waiting. The assignment is real and their destiny has now joined with yours waiting to intersect in the moment of time that God has pre-designed.

And you understand the solemnness of this moment.

Decisions must be made. You must yield completely, giving your ways over to His ways, so that they too, will feel and respond to the impact of His power.

Now you know why you were born. To be with Him. To know Him, To experience His passion for you. And for you to share it with them.

---

*Decisions must be made. You must yield completely, giving your ways over to His ways, so that they too, will feel and respond to the impact of His power.*

# Prophetic Evangelism

## Day 274

You are being made ready. You see their faces, you feel their struggles, you see their captivity. You want to feel their pain, because you know you are a carrier of their answer.

Today is the day of salvation. He is rescuing you, over and over again as you rescue them.

And His voice is still thundering. Still gentle, and loving and kind. It's irresistible. He is here, to fill you to overflowing. The overflow is for them. Receive it, be healed, made whole and filled up to go to them.

Who is ready for His heart to flow through yours?

Who is ready to identify with His sufferings? For He suffers for His children who are lost. He suffers when He sees their need, and His children seem deaf to their cries. He suffers when He is so aware of the price that has been paid, and yet, no one has reached them with what they hold in their mouth - the power to set them free.

The power to set them free! The truth that eradicates the darkness and brings them into His marvelous light.

Who is willing to be the mouthpiece of the Lord?

Who is willing to be His hands that touch them?

Who is willing to be His love that reaches them in the place of their need?

*Receive it, be healed, made whole and filled up to go to them.*

# Prophetic Evangelism

**Day 275**

Now you are ready to understand the promise of the empowerment that resides on the inside of you.

*And Jesus came and spake unto them, saying, "All power is given unto me in heaven and in earth. Go ye therefore, and teach all nations, baptizing them in the name of the Father, and of the Son, and of the Holy Ghost: Teaching them to observe all things whatsoever I have commanded you: and, lo, I am with you alway, even unto the end of the world." Amen. Matthew 28:18 – 20*

Jesus has all authority. He has given us all authority. It cost Him everything, but He gave it to us freely. However, the gifting of God has to be disciplined by acts of our will lining up with His or it can be dormant or lost. "Go therefore" was not a suggestion. But with the command, we have this promise: HE is with YOU always.

So if He is with us, we can hear Him.

If it is His will to reach them, then we can move past the things that people think they believe, past what they want to hear, and go deeper into the spirit, discerning their real need.

How did you receive salvation? *For by grace are ye saved through faith; and that not of yourselves: it is the gift of God: Ephesians 2:8 KJV*

You see, even faith for your salvation was a gift. Salvation was free. *For we are his workmanship, created in Christ Jesus unto good works, which God hath before ordained that we should walk in them. Ephesians 2:10 KJV*

Faith to receive it was placed inside of us by God.

The works God has called us to do, He has empowered us to do.

Say: "I can reach the lost. In fact, they are waiting on me."

**Jesus has all authority. He has given us all authority.**

# Prophetic Evangelism

## Day 276

Faith arose in your heart when you heard the truth.

But someone had to tell you. Someone has to tell them.

*How then shall they call on him in whom they have not believed? and how shall they believe in him of whom they have not heard? and how shall they hear without a preacher? Romans 10:14 KJV*

We are called to reach them with divine truth. That is the prophetic part. That is when we realize we are called to be a public crier of the truth.

So then, what is different in prophetic evangelism versus just evangelism, as we have been taught it, by simply presenting truth, inviting them to pray?

Without the prophetic, our evangelism programs suffer for the lack of strength to impact them in the same way. Because the prophetic is a gushing forth of God's words, not learned in the natural, but by practicing hearing from God, it enables us to reach them spirit to spirit. We can speak under the inspiration of the Holy Spirit. Then anything can and will happen. God's design is to involve redeemed humanity in speaking life into deadness. The Holy Spirit will charge us with fresh boldness and vision.

We can learn to live by divine inside information that will touch people's hearts and open them to a relationship with God.

*But if all prophesy, and an unbeliever or an uninformed person comes in, he is convinced by all, he is convicted by all. And thus the secrets of his heart are revealed; and so, falling down on his face, he will worship God and report that God is truly among you. 1 Corinthians 14:24-25*

*Someone has to tell them.*

# Prophetic Evangelism

## Day 277

The result of prophetic evangelism is:

1. God will give us revelation into the person's heart.

2. The prophetic anointing will cause us to be inspired and we will be able to release fresh inspiration to them.

3. The prophetic gives us the strategy to unlock strongholds and set the people free.

4. The spoken word is powerful. It brings about change—change in the atmosphere, as well as the individuals.

Unfortunately, what we are facing is that too many fear stepping out into a new opportunity more than they fear missing a new opportunity. Of course, we recognize that fear is a tactic of the enemy.

Fears to deal with:
- Fear that it may not work. Understand that when you do what God says and He is responsible for the results.
- Fear of how to minister each time. We like a system, but the system of the Kingdom is spontaneous obedience. It is for anyone who believes.

We must overcome the fear that holds us back from reaching out. If we are to operate in the prophetic, we must do it by faith, trusting that we will hear from God and it will make a difference.

Because the opposite of faith is really a lack of trusting God and in reality we are giving in to a spirit of fear.

*We must overcome the fear that holds us back from reaching out.*

## Prophetic Evangelism

### Day 278

If he can keep us silent, then he can keep the world from hearing the truth that will set them free. In order for us to beat him at his own game, we must face the fear down. So how do we do that?

1. Expectation - We must have a sense of expectation. I'm expecting something to happen today. God is going to do something. He will do it through me for His will to be done. When I move in the prophecy, I am believing that God will speak into the situation in each person's life. Lord, anoint my eyes, ears and mouth.

2. Love - Operate in love. Perfect love casts out fear—fear in you, fear in them. To operate in love you must come from a place of burden for the individuals. He has them in His heart. Ask Him to give you the same love He has that overcomes any apparent resistance. If they don't respond properly it won't affect you. You gave from a heart of love. All people need to know that God loves them on a personal level. Prophecy enables us to offer that love to them in a personal way that tells them He cares.

3. Trust Him - Operate in ease as you trust Him. He wants to see this person, blessed, healed and restored. Ask Him, "Father, how do you want to do this?"

4. Comparison - Don't compare yourself to others; be yourself in God's expression. Fear that you will not do as well as another is fruitless. God made you the way He wanted you to be so that you could reach the ones assigned to respond to how He made YOU. The key is to be the best YOU He made you to be.

5. Release – Give, releasing from your heart, so that every result ultimately comes from the Lord.

*Prophecy enables us to offer that love to them in a personal way that tells them He cares.*

# PROPHETIC EVANGELISM

**Day 279**

We can hear and obey and evangelize through words of knowledge, knowing by the Spirit, not natural knowledge or observation. We can operate in the Holy Spirit's power.

Healing is a great calling card to know the Lord. If one has an infirmity, then the word of knowledge comes into play letting you know what the affliction is, if it isn't obvious to the natural eye.

Ask the Spirit to reveal to you:
- Do they need a healing for themselves?
- For a family member or someone close to them?
- Are you impressing healing to me because they are going to be used in the gifts of healing in a special way?

Then we must believe that the same Spirit that has given us the knowledge will bring the presence of God into the situation where the impossible becomes possible.

We can move in the gifts of the Spirit the same way we operate in faith to hear the word of the Lord. When we are operating by the Spirit, then we can aim the word for them in the right direction. We must exercise our mind and heart ... and practice.

Ask God for insight regarding their:
- Financial concern
- Employment difficulties
- Relationship problems
- Peace needed

Prophetic evangelism is:

Seeing everything through God's eyes and hearing what He tells you to do. Be willing to join Him in bringing about the end result He desires. You need to pray, be silent, look, listen and act according to His instructions. Exercise your faith. And GO, make disciples.

*You need to pray, be silent, look, listen and act according to His instructions.*

# Preparing the Way of the Lord

## Day 280

Most of us are aware that John the Baptist, the prophet, prepared the way of the Lord. Let's read this passage from The Message version of the Bible.

*The good news of Jesus Christ—the Message!—begins here, following to the letter the scroll of the prophet Isaiah. Watch closely: I'm sending my preacher ahead of you; He'll make the road smooth for you. Thunder in the desert! Prepare for God's arrival! Make the road smooth and straight!*

*John the Baptizer appeared in the wild, preaching a baptism of life-change that leads to forgiveness of sins. People thronged to him from Judea and Jerusalem and, as they confessed their sins, were baptized by him in the Jordan River into a changed life. John wore a camel-hair habit, tied at the waist with a leather belt. He ate locusts and wild field honey.*

*As he preached he said, "The real action comes next: The star in this drama, to whom I'm a mere stagehand, will change your life. I'm baptizing you here in the river, turning your old life in for a Kingdom life. His baptism—a holy baptism by the Holy Spirit—will change you from the inside out." (How will He change us? From the inside out!)*

*At this time, Jesus came from Nazareth in Galilee and was baptized by John in the Jordan. The moment he came out of the water, he saw the sky split open and God's Spirit, looking like a dove, come down on him. Along with the Spirit, a voice: "You are my Son, chosen and marked by my love, pride of my life." -Mark 1:1-11 The Message*

God's Kingdom Is Here

If we are the people of God, walking in Kingdom authority, preparing the way of the Lord, we must learn from these scriptures. We are to impact the world by:

1. Shifting mindsets from the religious ways of our day or the old ways to the now way God is doing things. Until that is accomplished, the world will not be able to receive what Jesus will bring.

2. Changing the atmosphere from religion to Kingdom. The Kingdom of Christ will not be as the world's system. It operates above the world's system from heaven's perspective.

3. Invading tradition and introducing new Kingdom principles.

Part of the new Kingdom principles will be proper governmental order.

*Prepare for God's arrival!*

## Preparing the Way of the Lord

**Day 281**

The tactics of the enemy never change. He only has so much in his weapon bag. He just uses them through different people. Paul warned the Thessalonians on this, and the warning continues to us.

*Now, brethren, concerning the coming of our Lord Jesus Christ and our gathering together to Him, we ask you, not to be soon shaken in mind or troubled, either by spirit or by word or by letter, as if from us, as though the day of Christ had come. Let no one deceive you by any means; for that Day will not come unless the falling away comes first, and the man of sin is revealed, the son of perdition, who opposes and exalts himself above all that is called God or that is worshiped, so that he sits as God in the temple of God, showing himself that he is God. 2 Thessalonians 2:1-4*

We are living in the last days. It can be challenging since things may be shaking. But we were warned, as was the early church, not to be shaken.

Our faith is in God--so it isn't supposed to shake.

Our commitment is to the King--so it isn't supposed to shake.

Our relationship with God is not supposed to shake.

Our trust isn't supposed to shake.

Our revelation of Him is not supposed to shake!

But come on, we would have to admit, most of us, have had a hard time not shaking with the shaking. Sometimes, we just need to hear something from the Master that settles things for us. I heard Joel Osteen explain that on many occasions, Jesus went to those who had doubts, such as John the Baptist, to settle their doubt. He said to Doubting Thomas, "Come touch My hands." Jesus said, "Go tell the disciples, but especially Peter."

The reason He went out of the way to give them assurance is because He knew what they could believe, even if it was not necessarily what they were believing at the time. But one word from Him could settle things. After John heard the word from Jesus that the systems of this world were no longer able to stop the impossible from being possible, he believed that lives were touched, healed, delivered and changed. The dead were being raised and the wretched of the world were hearing that God was on their side. John was secure again.

*The systems of this world were no longer able to stop the impossible from being possible.*

## Preparing the Way of the Lord

### Day 282

We are living in present truth revelation. What I mean by that is that when our identity is found in our relationship with Him, we can move to a higher level. In that place with Him, His voice speaks to us and we receive the revelation necessary for us to accomplish what we are called to do.

I believe we are living in a time when God is going to ask us to do some things the previous generations haven't.

Deep is calling to deep.

There are some churches called to raise up sons and daughters for greatness. Liberty is one of them. In our 2010 prophetic word, God said there would be a mandatory sending. "There will be a sending that is mandatory–and you won't feel like you're able to; that's why you're ready." The trip to Belize was planned with me being a part of it, but instead it was mandatory that I send a team. But not a thrown together team who is not aware of who they are in Him, or what their positions were or their importance to the Kingdom. It was a team that took tools, Kingdom message, Kingdom power, Kingdom authority and left Kingdom impact. It was a team that could preach, teach, train and prophecy the word of the Lord. This team could be flexible, and flow with God and with the needs of the Pastor.

Yeah, Liberty is bringing change. We are able to bring change because hungry people got the training necessary to bring change to themselves first, and then to others. If we are to see change, we must be hungry and teachable. We must be desperate for God and for His will to be done on earth as it is in heaven and then we must train others to be able to stand into whatever position is necessary when the circumstances demand it.

I believe in relational leadership. It's how I am. I love you. I want you to succeed. I want you to walk in Kingdom power, Kingdom authority, and Kingdom insights. More than that, so does Jesus.

*The team took tools, Kingdom message, Kingdom power, Kingdom authority and left Kingdom impact.*

## Preparing the Way of the Lord

### Day 283

We must think past our present revelation and continue to believe that Jesus is here. He is among us. He is in covenant with us and He has all we need to be who He made us to be to influence the world. If you are feeling discontent, it is because God is calling you up to something higher. We are in serious times and every church has a purpose. We must engage in a higher level and we must listen to the spirit over the natural. Jesus kept trying to get it across.

*For a long time now people have tried to force themselves into God's Kingdom. But if you read the books of the Prophets and God's Law closely, you will see them culminate in John, teaming up with him in preparing the way for the Messiah of the Kingdom. Matthew 11:14 MSG*

The Messiah of what? The Kingdom. It wasn't against the law and the prophets. It just culminated there. It came together. The system was taken over by a system that was higher. Look at in this way: John was the "Elijah" they were all expecting to arrive and introduce the Messiah. And now here He was, the Messiah. Were they getting it? Some were and some weren't.

*"Are you listening to me? Really listening? "How can I account for this generation? The people have been like spoiled children whining to their parents, 'We wanted to skip rope, and you were always too tired; we wanted to talk, but you were always too busy.' John came fasting and they called him crazy. I came feasting and they called me a lush, a friend of the riffraff. Opinion polls don't count for much, do they? The proof of the pudding is in the eating." Matthew 11:15-19 MSG*

Jesus was the proof. He was the proof by evidence that some still couldn't see. But now, there is a generation rising in the earth today that is hungry to see the demonstrations of the Kingdom of God fully evidenced. However, a true movement won't occur until there is true revelation. You need a revelation of who you are in Him. A revelation that you can do what He has called you to do. A revelation that circumstances are not the dictator of your life. A revelation that your relationship with Him and what He says concerning YOU is true! This will occur and be embraced through an explosion of an outpouring of the Person and Presence of the Holy Spirit of God.

*We must engage in a higher level and we must listen to the spirit over the natural.*

# Preparing the Way of the Lord

## Day 284

John knew, then he didn't, then he did again. How did he finally come to terms with his roller coaster emotions? Conversing with truth. In a world that is spinning, we can stay focused on what is going to make the difference by one thing.

*He who dwells in the secret place of the Most High shall remain stable and fixed under the shadow of the Almighty [Whose power no foe can withstand]. Psalm 91:1 AMP*

In this place, the answers we need come to us because we are surrounded by the angelic. We hear God's voice. We hear the future being revealed, and we hear the present being resolved. Every enemy of ours is crushed before us. Hell itself cannot live or exist in the Light of the Glory of the Presence of God. Those who find the Secret Place of God's Presence find the reality of the Lord Jesus Christ.

In this place, God Himself "delivers us from our adversaries" and causes us to ride on the high places with Him far above all our enemies because we have found the intimate place with Him and have a personal knowledge and friendship with Him.

We can have days, times, and hours where we have doubts. It's OK. But that is when God wants you to look to Him to settle it once again.

Someone has to prepare the way.

Someone has to rise up.

Someone has to be the voice of truth again.

Someone has to lay hands on the sick.

Someone has to raise the dead.

Someone has to influence the world by demonstrating love and commitment.

*We hear the future being revealed, and we hear the present being resolved.*

## Preparing the Way of the Lord

### Day 285

We have been told the least in the Church are greater than John. We, the Church, are to demonstrate the miraculous, the unusual, the bringing of heaven to earth as normal, commonplace things in our every day life as sons and daughters of the Most High God. We represent Somebody.

When people inquire what makes the difference in our lives, when they want to know if the Messiah is Jesus, we should have the same report Jesus had for John. The blind see, the lame walk, lepers are cleansed, the deaf hear, the dead are raised, the wretched of the earth learn that God is on their side. Yes, us!

*"Most assuredly, I say to you, he who believes in Me, the works that I do he will do also; and greater works than these he will do, because I go to My Father. And whatever you ask in My name, that I will do, that the Father may be glorified in the Son. If you ask anything in My name, I will do it. John 14:12-14*

We are to demonstrate the Kingdom of God on earth, where the supernatural is natural and the ordinary is becoming extraordinary! We are going to see a global awakening and a fresh release of the Holy Spirit in power coming forth.

The world is waiting for the body of Christ to come alive with their lives proving the endless flow of the Holy Spirit, with a bold witness to preach the Word with signs following that confirm His Word.

*And He said to them, "Go into all the world and preach the gospel to every creature. He who believes and is baptized will be saved; but he who does not believe will be condemned. And these signs will follow those who believe: In My name they will cast out demons; they will speak with new tongues; they will take up serpents; and if they drink anything deadly, it will by no means hurt them; they will lay hands on the sick, and they will recover." Mark 16:15-18*

The Great Commission comes with an awesome permission.

You can do it!

We can be Kingdom thinkers.
We can change. And once we are immersed in the truth that comes from heaven, we can change the world.

***The blind see, the lame walk, lepers are cleansed, the deaf hear, the dead are raised, the wretched of the earth learn that God is on their side.***

# We Can!

## Day 286

We must gain insight regarding the power of the Holy Spirit in the believer. We must understand how the third person of the Godhead is to operate in our lives, how we can depend upon Him, the person or personality of the Holy Spirit is to be manifested in the life of the believer.

*However, when He, the Spirit of truth, has come, He will guide you into all truth; for He will not speak on His own authority, but whatever He hears He will speak; and He will tell you things to come. John 16: 13*

He will guide YOU into all truth, and He will tell YOU things to come! That's why it's important that you develop an intimacy with the Holy Spirit. He is the Comforter; He is your Friend; He is your Teacher. He is the one who will show you the truth and what is to come, so you are not held captive by the circumstance.

You already can see what God wants to do in that situation. The Holy Spirit is your guide. I'm not going to tell you it's a sin to watch the news, I'm telling you it's a sin to believe the news. I'm not telling you it's a sin to know what's going on in the world but it is a sin to allow what's going on in the world to dictate what's going on in your life.

Let the Holy Spirit be your guide; let Him be your friend. Develop an intimacy with the Holy Spirit and allow Him to take you to a place that you can see the truth and that you can see what is going to take place in your future. When the Holy Spirit becomes an intimate friend, you will walk in a totally different dimension of life.

<u>DECLARE</u>: *I will give first place to the Holy Spirit, not to the spirit of this world. The Holy Spirit is my Guide. Today as I sow my seed, Father, I welcome the power of the Holy Spirit in my life. Holy Spirit I welcome You; speak to me, guide me, teach me, correct me and direct me so that I may walk in the truth of God's Word and that I might walk in the reality of seeing, not what the world sees, but seeing what God sees, in the Name of Jesus, AMEN.*

*Let the Holy Spirit be your guide; let Him be your friend.*

# God's Love Language

**Day 287**

Singing psalms and giving thanks to God is a LOVE LANGUAGE to God. When you learn to develop a lifestyle with this love language of entering every day into His gates with thanksgiving and His courts with praise, and everyday celebrating the goodness of the Lord, every day walking in obedience to the Word of God, it lets Him know that you love Him more than anything.

It shows that your love is now toward His Kingdom. God says if your love is toward His Kingdom He will release His love back into you and you will not fail. If God be for you who can be against you?

Do you want to operate in this love language?

Operate in the Word of God!

Declare:

Today I declare that I love the Lord my God and put Him first today in praising Him, thanking Him, and acknowledging Him in all my ways.

Today, as I sow seed, I activate the power of love in my life. I also activate this seed's ability to give me power to gather wealth. In the act of obedience of sowing, I posture myself to release my love language to You Father.

I give to you daily as a part of my life, and I receive your abundant life back. I anticipate Your love coming back to me through the harvest promised to me in your word.

It is good measure, pressed down, shaken together, and running over today, in Jesus' Name, AMEN.

*Entering every day into His gates with thanksgiving and His courts with praise.*

# The High-Way of Holiness

## Day 288

It is very clear in the Bible that every person who says he is a Christian is to live a holy life. You are able to do this by your realization of who He really was and that God that raised Him up from the dead. That revelation causes you to give Him glory by accepting Him and all that He's done for you. When you did, your hope was turned to God - "THE HIGHWAY TO HOLINESS." If there's a timeless truth that we need to learn in these last days it is that in these last days and tough times, God expects us to be holy. As a matter of fact, the only way we're going to get through these days is to live holy lives.

Now, when you talk about holiness, people get a little nervous. I mean, uh, we don't mind being saved; we're just not all that keen on holiness. We're interested in heaven, not holiness. We're interested in health, not holiness. We're interested in happiness, not holiness. We may even be interested in helpfulness, but how many of us are interested in holiness? How many of us say, "Lord Jesus, I long to be perfectly holy?" God did not save you primarily to make you happy, nor for you to go to Heaven one day. God saved you to be set apart for Him.

*"And you shall be holy to Me, for I the LORD am holy, and have separated you from the peoples, that you should be Mine." Leviticus 20:26*

God saved you for holiness! We read in Hebrews 12:14 that we are to pursue holiness, "without which no one will see the LORD." So what motivates us to be holy? One thing that motivates all of us is if we know it is an obtainable goal. The Bible tells us that it is. WE ACTUALLY CAN BE HOLY. God says, *"For I am the LORD who brings you up out of the land of Egypt, to be your God. You shall therefore be holy, for I am holy." Leviticus 11:45*

It is in this place with Him, that we find the changes that need to be made. We find that the changes we resisted in the past, suddenly become nothing to us, for our desire for Him has drawn us into a higher way of thinking.

That is the HIGH way of holiness I am talking about.

### *WE ACTUALLY CAN BE HOLY.*

# The High-Way of Holiness

**Day 289**

C. S. Lewis said, "How little people know who think that holiness is dull. When one meets the real thing, it is irresistible. If even ten percent of the world's population had it, the holiness of God, would not the whole world be converted and happy before year's end?" The fact is that God is a HOLY BEING, above anything or anyone else in all the earth. God is a HOLY being. He just is HOLY all the way through. There is nothing about Him that is not holy. He is pure. He is sacred. He has strong views on holiness.

In prayer one evening, we were all praying separately, yet we were all in perfect sync as far as what we were praying. Afterwards, when we shared what we were all praying for, we were praying and asking God how we could best meet the needs of the people He loves. There was a theme that ran through every answer. It was to be pure and holy. If we would do that, He would take care of the rest. He told me to not get into the rhetoric. Rhetoric is defined as... •*often disapproving : language that is intended to influence people and that may not be honest or reasonable; marked by the use of impressive-sounding but mostly meaningless words and phrases; it is using words to bring about an emotional response."*

What if when God said "Be holy as I am holy" that what He meant was, "I am holy so you can be holy too?" What if to obtain holiness, it just takes passion to BE with Him? We need to get real. We need to see and understand there is a HIGH way of holiness that is available to us. One night when we were discussing what happened during prayer one of our young adults said he was asking God how to help enlarge the borders of the church— Liberty and the Church, the all encompassing people of God. God said, "Just get more of Me and I will come out of you naturally to bring about the action needed to impact lives." There is no formula. We are such formula people. So, here is the best formula, from what God said, by which we can reach others with the impact of God's love and God's ways: The formula is being with God in a more intimate way than ever before.

You see, Holiness comes from God Himself. His nature gets on you and in you when you hang with Him. Then sanctification occurs as the outward acts result from the inward character that is formed by being with Him.

*sanctification occurs as the outward acts result from the inward character*

# The High-Way of Holiness

## Day 290

Last week, a member of our church recorded this from what he received from the service: "I saw unity at Liberty in the praise and worship, and I believe we were able to go as deep as we did because there was unity in the house from the outset. Secondly, I wrote down one thing that Pastor Dawn said in the sermon, and from my observation, it is exactly what happened after Pastor Dawn had finished giving the message and began praying for people. This is what she said, 'God has your heart, but sometimes He reveals more places of your heart that you must give Him. Satan wants those places.' God was dealing with things we tend to fall into when we take our eyes off of Him for just a moment. I know we were all happy that our God does not condemn but brings freedom into reality."

"God has your heart, but sometimes He reveals more places of your heart to give Him. There is more to give, and as you give it, He gives more to you." He had an encounter with truth. It impacted his life. In reality, it is ultimately encounters with God that will bring us into the places of holiness that will cause the cry of our heart to be like the prophet Isaiah and to go through the same stages of his own encounter:

CONCENTRATION - CONTEMPLATION - CONFRONTATION - SANCTIFICATION - CONSECRATION

*"In the year that King Uzziah died, I saw the Lord sitting on a throne, high and lifted up, and the train of His robe filled the temple." Isaiah 6:1*

The ancient prophet had an encounter with the Lord. At the time of his vision, he was engaged in an act of worship in the Temple, in the sanctuary. He saw the length of God's robe fill the temple. He had a true experience with God, but it involved total, undivided attention to God. "I saw the Lord..." His attention was in CONCENTRATION mode. Concentration means exclusive attention to one thing. Nothing else was allowed to distract him or detract him. He was focused. His attention was on God, on Him alone.

Take 10 minutes and now and practice this life of concentration. Focus in on God and only God. Don't look around, turn the music off, do not plan out your day, do not tell God what you need ... Just HIM ... Give Him all of your attention. It's not as easy as it sounds, but keep practicing. Make it a habit. It will become a part of your life.

*It is ultimately encounters with God that will bring us into the places of holiness.*

# The High-Way of Holiness

## Day 291

*Above it stood seraphim; each one had six wings: with two he covered his face, with two he covered his feet, and with two he flew. And one cried to another and said, "Holy, holy, holy is the LORD of hosts; The whole earth is full of His glory!" Isaiah 6:2-3*

What do you think the prophet was doing then? What would you do if suddenly your focus on God had caused angelic beings to start singing in your midst? He had moved from concentration to the place of CONTEMPLATION, which is thoughtful observation, and deep consideration. He must have been trying to comprehend what was happening and why.

Contemplate the glory that must have been so very evident that day. Then realize an unearthly choir is all around you singing, "Holy, holy, holy is the Lord..." Why did they sing it three times?

Think about the holiness of the Trinity. How can you call God holy without calling Jesus holy and without acknowledging the HOLY Ghost? I believe prophet Isaiah is getting a visual as well as a spiritual awareness of holiness that was tied together by Father, Son and Holy Spirit. Then something else occurred. He was about to be shaken. *And the posts of the door were shaken by the voice of him who cried out, and the house was filled with smoke. Isaiah 6:4*

Who was crying out? It says the voice of him who cried out. I think it was the voice of God. I think He was calling out to Isaiah that day, and that He is also calling out to us. The atmosphere was changing all around Isaiah; he would be changed in the awakening that was occurring.

God is wanting us to contemplate - to realize the atmosphere around us is changing. Something amazing is about to take place on the earth. But it will require you to acknowledge the change and do something that is different. Take time today to purposefully contemplate these things.

*Acknowledge the change and do something that is different.*

## The High-Way of Holiness

### Day 292

Isaiah recognized that something had indeed changed, and it caused an instant response of change within him. Now he was at a place of CONFRONTATION of his own need. He faced his shortcomings.

*So I said, "Woe is me, for I am undone! Because I am a man of unclean lips, And I dwell in the midst of a people of unclean lips; For my eyes have seen the King, The LORD of hosts." Then one of the seraphim flew to me, having in his hand a live coal which he had taken with the tongs from the altar. And he touched my mouth with it, and said: "Behold, this has touched your lips; Your iniquity is taken away, And your sin purged." Isaiah 6:5*

It wasn't that he was condemned as we may think. Suddenly, he was aware of such holiness that he didn't want to stay the same. He desired every part of him to be clean. He wanted all the people to respond to this great God. It was not just any god, but the King, the Lord of Hosts. He saw the Lord, the Lord of Hosts, Lord Sabaoth, and Lord of Hosts that is mighty in battle. He realized that He had come to save him, to rescue him even from himself. Now he is at the place of SANCTIFICATION, to make conductive, for spiritual blessing. God hadn't come to show him what was wrong, but to provide a higher level to him that would bring the blessing.

I believe He must have been communicating with Isaiah. "You have looked past the natural, you have seen who I really am, you have experienced My saving power. Now that You have been in this heavenly atmosphere, are you aware that you are in the very presence of the Lord of Hosts who has warred over you? Do you now understand that the Lord Sabaoth has brought you through the battle that you have had with your own soul? You are at a new place of freedom."

<u>What battles has the Lord brought you through?</u>

<u>What places of freedom has he brought you through?</u>

*God hadn't come to show him what was wrong, but to provide a higher level to him that would bring the blessing.*

# The High-Way of Holiness

**Day 293**

We have been discussing the journey of Isaiah on the Highway of Holiness. Now, from Isaiah's previous encounters we have heard the Lord acknowledge, "You have my heart, and you have experienced a greater place of understanding. You have been touched by the heavenly things and you have received a higher freedom than you have ever known." Now the Lord exclaims, "I will ask, you another question!"

*Also I heard the voice of the Lord, saying: "Whom shall I send, And who will go for Us?" Then I said, "Here am I, send me!" ISAIAH 6:8*

Isaiah was going to the next phase. He said, "Here am I! Send me." His response was coming from his final phase of CONSECRATION, dedication to the service and worship of deity. The need was there all along. God was waiting on Isaiah to come into His presence and be a part of holiness. That dedication and worship would give him access to a higher way of doing things. The High way of holiness would change him, and provide for him an enthusiasm for doing the things assigned to him. He would no longer think of it as costing him, but rather as an opportunity. There is a different response to the needs of others, after you have been with Him. That place of purity, that place of holiness that He desired Isaiah to have, was fulfilled in a moment of time with Him.

Can you honestly say that you have made it this far on the Highway of Holiness? Have you made it to the point of CONSECRATION – the place of total dedication to the service and worship of God? I think there are few of us that honestly could say yes. Nonetheless, it is an actual place that we can reach; it is the location where we will recognize our greatest purpose.

God is waiting for you there. He is crying out even now, "Whom shall I send, and who will go for Us?" All you have to do is answer, "Here am I! Send me."

*"Here am I! Send me."*

# The High-Way of Holiness

## Day 294

In that one interaction, Isaiah went through these stages:
CONCENTRATION - CONTEMPLATION - CONFRONTATION - SANCTIFICATION - CONSECRATION

You see, holiness is an indescribable quality that originates in God Himself. You must understand people are holy only in the degree of their closeness to God. That is why so many Christians have failed. People say, "And they called themselves Christians, then how could they x, y, z?" They could because they didn't stay close to their God. We are trying so hard to figure out how to change ourselves, our desires, how to be more effective. All the while, when God knows we are ready to change, He provides the way.

*And when he had consulted with the people, he appointed those who should sing to the LORD, and who should praise the beauty of holiness, as they went out before the army and were saying: "Praise the LORD, for His mercy endures forever." 2 Chronicles 20:21*

They were singing alright. And they were singing about the beauty of holiness. Yoo-hoo! There is a beauty to His holiness. That magnificence, that splendor, that glory becomes a tangible thing when we honor Him.

*Now when they began to sing and to praise, the LORD set ambushes against the people of Ammon, Moab, and Mount Seir, who had come against Judah; and they were defeated. 2 Chronicles 20:22*

The enemy is defeated. God ambushed them. Do you realize that we have God ready to ambush our enemies, when we praise Him and when we sing praises about the beauty of the holiness we find in Him? Lord Sabaoth, Lord of Hosts, mighty in battle, has a way of conquering our enemies. Though we must be ready for battle, it is when we are ready and willing and following His command that the praise He deserves begins to come out of our bellies and out of our mouth and join with the heavenly host. It is the HIGH way.

*That magnificence, that splendor, that glory becomes a tangible thing when we honor Him.*

# The High-Way of Holiness

## Day 295

*Give to the LORD the glory due His name; Bring an offering, and come before Him. Oh, worship the LORD in the beauty of holiness! Tremble before Him, all the earth. The world also is firmly established, it shall not be moved. Let the heavens rejoice, and let the earth be glad; And let them say among the nations, "The LORD reigns." 1 Chronicles 16:29-31*

The heavens are rejoicing with us and the earth will respond to that kind of praise, for heaven is invading the earth. When He is in our midst, our former empty behaviors are being changed by the revelation of Christ, who was slain before the foundation of the world, but is manifest in these last times for you! His Holiness is to be revealed in our character. Basically, a holy person is one who is conscious of God, desiring to be like God and is totally influenced by Him in every way of life. So, are you holy? When you receive Christ as Savior, you rid yourself of the old life. You enter into a new life without the sin you had. Then you are in a place of renewing - renewing your mind, and changing your actions. You are holy, but what does holiness do? It invades you, and when it does, it brings the manifestation of Him to the earth.

*Concerning His Son Jesus Christ our Lord, who was born of the seed of David according to the flesh, and declared to be the Son of God with power according to the Spirit of holiness, by the resurrection from the dead. Through Him we have received grace and apostleship for obedience to the faith among all nations for His name, among whom you also are the called of Jesus Christ. Romans 1:3-6*

So the spirit of Holiness reveals Him to us. Then we are aware of our grace and our apostleship (our commission) for obedience. There is a HIGH way - a way of living that exceeds anything we have lived thus far. God has prepared a HIGHer way for all of us. *Say to those who are fearful-hearted, "Be strong, do not fear! Behold, your God will come with vengeance, with the recompense of God; He will come and save you." Today I am declaring this to you and over your lives! Isaiah 35:4*

And if He is here to SAVE you who can be opposed to you?

*...a place of renewing, renewing your mind, and changing your actions.*

# The High-Way of Holiness

## Day 296

I was ministering to someone the other day, and they just couldn't figure out what was wrong with them, but up out of my spirit came these words: "It doesn't even matter if you can figure it out. Because the truth is, that no matter what weapon it is that is formed against you, it cannot harm you." He has created the destroyer to destroy the destroyer.

*"See, I made the blacksmith. He fans the fire to make it hotter, and he makes the kind of tool he wants. In the same way I have made the destroyer to destroy. So no weapon that is used against you will defeat you. You will show that those who speak against you are wrong. These are the good things my servants receive. Their victory comes from me," says the LORD. Isaiah 54:16-17 (NCV)*

God has made the destroyer that will destroy every attempt of the enemy to stop us from being conquerors this year. Our victory comes from Him. He has made a HIGH way.

*A highway shall be there, and a road, And it shall be called the Highway of Holiness. Isaiah 35:8*

It is a highway called what? Holiness! No wonder the enemy has twisted its meaning and made us to all look silly trying to have an outward look of holiness, when all we needed to do was spend more time with the Holy one.

*No lion shall be there, Nor shall any ravenous beast go up on it; It shall not be found there. But the redeemed shall walk there, and the ransomed of the LORD shall return, And come to Zion with singing, With everlasting joy on their heads. They shall obtain joy and gladness, and sorrow and sighing shall flee away. Isaiah 35:9-10*

This is the time, this is the season; this is the day and here is the way: The highway of holiness.

*He has created the destroyer to destroy the destroyer.*

## The High-Way of Holiness

### Day 297

I dreamed that I was aware that something unusual was occurring in the atmosphere. I was trying to get people to understand that they needed to do something different. I knew that they were just going about their everyday lives the way they always had and yet I knew that there was a difference. It began to snow in Florida, heavy snow but everyone just kept doing what they were used to doing. I saw the snow fall and begin to cover their cars until they were buried in the snow. Soon there was just a mound of snow so thick that there was no distinction of where the cars and the houses used to be.

I was looking from above and Tearsa was there, but she was not frightened. she had a light that was almost surrounding her. I knew it was keeping her safe and warm. I was looking for others to see if anyone else had responded. I knew I shouldn't get too far away from her, because I knew we had to stick together. There was an urgency to find others but there wasn't fear. Then I woke up. As I wrote this dream out, I got an e-mail that said "Forecasters are predicting 12 inches of snow in Florida!" It happened to be an advertisement for a childrens event, but the fact is, God is just fun letting things like that happen when we are in the midst of a revelation

I was looking at 595, a highway, but I don't think God was talking to me about a physical road. I think He was talking about a relationship. This scripture gives us insight into the meaning of the snow.

*"Come now, let us reason together," says the LORD. "Though your sins are like scarlet, they shall be as white as snow; though they are red as crimson, they shall be like wool. Isaiah 1:18 NIV*

We were covered in white. The land was covered. Tearsa is my daughter but I believe she was representing spiritual children. I believe God is trying to do something here. I knew that something different is happening. God is bringing something new our way.

What if God is letting us know that it is time and He is going to be reigning down purity and holiness upon those who will do something about preparing themselves for the down pouring?

*...something different is happening.*
*God is bringing something new our way.*

## The High-Way of Holiness

### Day 298

What causes transformations of individuals, will also cause transformations of cities and nations. A people of desperation who are sitting in the sanctuary for one and only one thing: to enter into that place with Him so that his holiness would invade their very being. There is nothing that God won't do to show Himself strong on the behalf of His holy ones.

God is moving, He is drawing, He is ready to make His personal appearance to many. It will happen in the places of hungry hearts. If you don't know Him today, you can. If you don't know Him in the place of holiness, you can. If you haven't seen the victory in your life yet, you can. If you haven't fulfilled the desires of his heart for your life, you can. You can live different. You can be different.

It is a higher way. But it will be found in the place where you are consumed with Him and He is indwelling you. Then you are filled up to overflowing. I believe God is showing Himself strong to us and He is drawing us nearer to Him because of our passion for wanting to know His heart. God has made a way for everyone to experience the awesome, powerful, and majestic experience of actually being in His presence.

There is a movement that God has started on the earth. It is spontaneous in that it is not orchestrated by man figuring things out and trying to make it happen. There is nothing religious about it. It is not rules and regulations. It is a happening that is occurring because of pure passion for loving God. In that setting, anything from heaven can happen. As we sit at the feet of Jesus, His holiness will saturate us and when we arise, as Isaiah did, we will touch people who will touch people with His love. Because PEOPLE WHO EXPERIENCE THE PRESENCE OF THE LORD ARE NEVER THE SAME.

Let us worship the Lord in the beauty of His holiness.

That is the High way of holiness for us.

*God has made a way for everyone to experience the awesome, powerful, and majestic experience of actually being in His presence.*

# I Am A Supplier!

**Day 299**

*Now may He who supplies seed to the sower, and bread for food, supply and multiply the seed you have sown and increase the fruits of your righteousness while you are enriched in everything for all liberality, which causes thanksgiving through us to God. 2 Corinthians 9:10-11*

He wants you to know that He will give you seed (seed to the sower); He will provide food and take care of you while the seed is producing a harvest, and He will multiply the seed.

Why would He do this? So that you can be liberal ... have liberality in your giving and supply to others. You were designed to be a supplier and God says the only way you can be a supplier is to take the seeds that you sow – sow them so that He has something to multiply back into your life. It's not something that He adds back to your life; not something that He replaces in your life, but something that He can MULTIPLY back into your life.

God wants to use you to bless others. What do we find in the book of Genesis when God spoke to Abraham? "I will bless you to be a blessing." Well if we're in Christ we're of Abraham's seed and heirs according to that promise - then we are blessed to be a blessing. God wants us to be in a position where we can provide for others and that means we have to believe and we have to live and walk in prosperity.

When someone says to you, "I don't believe in prosperity," just look and smile at them and say, - *"the thief comes to steal, kill and destroy but Jesus came that I might have life and have it more abundantly!" John 10:10*

So I will live that life, and I will live it for the glory of God.

### Declare:
*If I am a supplier, I am in position for provision. Today I will sow my seed and I declare that I am who God has designed me to be. I am a person of productivity; I am a person who will walk in the supernatural presence and power of God so that I may be a blessing to others therefore I am a person of prosperity, in the Name of Jesus, AMEN.*

**God wants to use you to bless others.**

# The "If" Only's

## Day 300

There is evidence that God is doing something different in our world and in our midst. Those whose dreams have died are coming alive again. Those that haven't had a dream are beginning to believe they can dream and realize their dream. You see, we must be able to get over the "if only's" into the promises and hope of God. God is still after us to come up higher and to be aware of the tactics of the enemy and destroy his strongholds. The tactic of the enemy to get you to agree with the "if onlys" of life is nothing new. It is all throughout the Word of God. Let's look at one of these today.

*And all the children of Israel complained against Moses and Aaron, and the whole congregation said to them, "If only we had died in the land of Egypt! Or if only we had died in this wilderness! Why has the LORD brought us to this land to fall by the sword, that our wives and children should become victims? Would it not be better for us to return to Egypt?" Numbers 14:2-3*

If only we were dead we would be better off. If we could just die now, we would be better off. If only we had stayed in Egypt. If we could have our old life back. This walking around in faith is too hard. I have heard about this Promised Land one too many times. I want to see it now. I don't even know if it's really real.

If only I could still eat of the substance that the world has to offer and still be a part of the blessing of our inheritance from God. If only I didn't have to face this hardship on the way to the promise. If only I could see what Moses saw, then I could have enough faith to endure.

<u>ACTION STEP:</u> *Take a minute and determine what are the "If only's" that you have allowed into your life. We must recognize these as areas where we do not trust God. If we did fully trust in God we would know that the only "If only" that is true is that "If only" we have faith the size of a mustard seed, all things are possible.*

*...get over the "if only's" into the promises and hope of God.*

# The "If Only's"

Day 301

I don't know about you, but I don't want you to have me in the list of "if only's of God." I want to be in the list of the conquerors that rose in the last days because I realized that the power of the blood is greater than my sin. That His brokenness bought my wholeness. Are you desperate enough today to agree with what He has declared about us? Let us humble ourselves before Him. <u>Let us agree with Him today and let Him rid us of our "if only"</u>.

*I agree with what you say about me Jesus.*

*I am just like you. I am made in your image and in your likeness.*

*I'm alive today, right here, right now by divine design.*

*I can do whatever you said I can do.*

*I agree with what you say about me and you say I am your delight.*

*I belong to You.*

*I have a covenant with You.*

*I look like You.*

*I shine like You in the darkness.*

*I heal like You.*

*I raise the dead like You.*

This is who I am. I have been bought by the blood of the Lamb.

This is who I am

I am powerful, obedient and utilized in things of eternal value.

This is what I can do. This is my identity.

I am done with my past.

My past failures.

My past mindsets.

My past victories. There are new victories to be had today.

### *His brokenness bought my wholeness.*

# The "If Only's"

## Day 302

**Pray:**

Lord, I am seeking a place in You today.
I am seeking Your heart, Your face, Your love, Your willingness, Your greatness, Your wholeness.
I am seeking Your presence, Your arms, Your eyes.
I am seeking You in the fullness of Your grace.
I will hear Your voice. I will feel Your touch.
I am experiencing Your forgiveness.
I am realizing Your presence in my life right here, right now. In the present. I am realizing Your presence in my future.

Your presence in my place of need is healing, delivering, sanctifying, and resurrecting me.

*He raises the poor from the dust*
*And lifts the beggar from the ash heap,*
*To set them among princes*
*And make them inherit the throne of glory.*
*1 Samuel 2:8*

I am determined to be with You, to respond to You, to believe You, to embrace who You are and to serve You wholeheartedly.

There is nothing impossible with You, my Lord, my God, my Savior, my Redeemer, my Provider, my Shepherd, my Creator, the lover of my soul, my bright and morning star, my answer, my love, my maker, my baptizer, my realization. You are never going to leave me or forsake me; this is Your commitment to me. I am never going to leave you or forsake you, that is my commitment to You, for YOU are My designation. SELAH

*You are never going to leave me or forsake me;*
*this is Your commitment to me.*

# Expect

Day 303

God is in the business of multiplying back to you what you sow - your love, your compassion, your faith, your financial giving. In fact, He will multiply back to you your entire spirit of giving. You have evidence for the releasing of your faith. Expect your harvest; expect your multiplication.

CONSIDER YOUR SEED. Something I have realized is that when you give sacrificially, you remember it, to release your faith. Whenever the Lord has required me to give beyond my comfort zone, until I really "feel it", I can tell you, I remember. Every time I remember, I thank God for the harvest on that seed. If you are willing to give sacrificially, your harvest will come, because you let go of that seed!

Remind yourself of what you have sown. See it growing and bringing in the harvest. If Satan reminds you of lack, remind Him of your seed. Then remind God of His promises to you. Expect a miracle. Stay in expectancy.

If I feel fear trying to grip my heart, I start shouting the Word and start reminding myself - out loud - of my seed time and harvest time. I have learned to obey God and then I can expect great things from God.

*Delight yourself also in the Lord, And He shall give you the desires of your heart. Commit your way to the Lord, Trust also in Him, And He shall bring it to pass.- Psalm 37:4-5*

**Expect your harvest; expect your multiplication.**

## Living From the Inside-Out

### Day 304

We talk many times about Kingdom mentality for we know we are continually in a process of getting new revelation about what that really means. We know that the Kingdom of God has been referred to as an upside down Kingdom. The system of the Kingdom of God is in direct opposition to the system of the kingdom of Satan, referred to as the kingdom of the world.

- *In the kingdom of the world: You fight your way to the top*
- *In the Kingdom of God: You go lower to go higher*
- *In the kingdom of the world: You grab, cheat and lie to have monetary gain*
- *In the Kingdom of God: You give to receive*
- *In the kingdom of the world: You are willing to cause others' lives to be adversely affected if it will be to your own life advantage*
- *In the Kingdom of God: You lay down your life to help others have life*
- *In the kingdom of the world: You take vengeance against your enemies*
- *In the Kingdom of God: You forgive your enemies and do good to those that do evil to you*
- *In the kingdom of the world: You forgive if you feel the person has finally paid for it and you feel they finally deserve it*
- *In the Kingdom of God: You forgive not because anyone deserves it, but because it is the right thing to do, because you understand grace. You have freely received, therefore, you freely give.*

I believe there is new revelation to what God is saying to us about expanding our understanding of living as we should in the Kingdom of God. We are not to only live in the upside down Kingdom but to reach that potential is to live from the inside out.

*ACTION STEP: Grab a pen and cross out the above ways that things are done "in the kingdom of the world" considering them no longer acceptable. Now looking at the ways "In the Kingdom of God" which one do you struggle with the most? How can you walk it out today?*

**We are not to only live in the upside-down Kingdom, but to reach that potential is to live from the inside out.**

# Living From the Inside-Out

**Day 305**

To live in the Kingdom of God is to live from the inside out...

Inside out (Dictionary – Mirriam Webster)
- *In such a manner that the inner surface becomes the outer*
- *To a thorough degree <knows the subject inside out>*

Inside out (Dictionary.com)
- *The inner or internal part; interior*
- *A select or inner circle of power, prestige,*
- *Confidential or secret information.*

Jesus is the perfect example of living from the inside out.

*As long as I am in the world, I am the light of the world. John 9:5 KJV*

He was so filled up with the illumination of truth and love on the inside that it was turned inside out for the entire world to be affected by it.

*Then Jesus spoke to them again, saying, "I am the light of the world. He who follows Me shall not walk in darkness, but have the light of life." John 8:12*

We do not have to walk in the darkness of the world's insight or the systems of this world. We can live from the inside out because we follow Him; we have the light of Life itself on the inside of us.

We can have the life of God, the love which illuminates the unknown things that were obscure in darkness of life, and now it is known and it changes us. Things that can't be seen or understood in the natural are seen in the spirit realm as His illumination occurs from within us and brings it to the outside.

Tell yourself today that...

"Today with Christ in me, I will literally be turned inside out so others may see the difference of what I understand and the knowledge I am privileged with."

***We can live from the inside out because we follow Him; we have the light of Life itself on the inside of us.***

# Living From the Inside-Out

## Day 306

If we live from the inside out we will have confidential and secret information. We have knowledge of situations before they happen; therefore, we can help people. There are many TV shows and movies that have been made about these kinds of things. They refer to it differently. But they are just picking up on the atmosphere of heaven that continues to press things to earth and they just don't have the correct interpretations of it. But God has pre-determined things in our lives, and in the lives of His church, and His universe. No man or demon of hell can stop them.

However, those that have inside information and handle it correctly will bring things to light, and others will be amazed at their insight and wisdom and be drawn to the morning star. We are being challenged to live life at a different level. We may see things in the natural that don't seem to line up with the promises of God but they will no longer carry any influence upon us because we have been illuminated to the truth.

*I am come a light into the world, that whosoever believeth on me should not abide in darkness. John 12:46 KJV*

So the people of God should not abide in darkness.

*And He said to them, "You are from beneath; I am from above. You are of this world; I am not of this world." John 8:23*

Jesus was in the world, but He never operated in it. He was more aware of what else was occurring than that which appeared to be occurring in the natural. He was always speaking at a higher level for He had inside information. He was living from the inside out.

<u>ACTION STEP:</u> *Today, make it a point to recognize what is going on in your surroundings in your home, school, or at work. You will probably be able to recognize a lot of darkness... Now your job is to determine how it is that you will shine through it.*

### *We are being challenged to live life at a different level.*

## Living From the Inside-Out

### Day 307

Jesus was in the world but He never operated in it. We should not either. But it is a choice because to do that, there is something we must do... *Then Jesus said to them, "When you lift up the Son of Man, then you will know that I am He, and that I do nothing of Myself; but as My Father taught Me, I speak these things. And He who sent Me is with Me. The Father has not left Me alone, for I always do those things that please Him." John 8:28-29*

We must lift HIM up. We must stop thinking about ourselves and think, ponder, and meditate on Him and His love and be aware of His desires. Jesus was in constant communication with the Father. He spoke accordingly. He acted accordingly. It did not matter what anyone else said or did. He had a higher authority that He was living with inside. He just allowed the illumination to have so much room in Him that the inside of Him was more on the outside of Him.

*Then Jesus said to those Jews who believed Him, "If you abide in My word, you are My disciples indeed. And you shall know the truth, and the truth shall make you free." John 8:31-32*

If you abide - if you hold fast to His teachings and live in accordance with them, then you are His disciple and the truth will set you free – the truth of the Word. His words become a part of you – a reality. More real to you than the circumstances, more real than the darkness that tries to overtake you. It wasn't until death was defeated that we were able to be a part of this life. But death HAS been defeated! It's not going to be defeated. Jesus won over death, hell and the grave and the same Spirit that raised Him from the dead, lives in us. Now we say that. We may be aware of it, sometimes. We may even shout over the revelation of that. But when you receive the pure revelation of what that means to you, that the Spirit of God that lived in Jesus and awakened His senses to pure truth, all knowledge needed in every situation can and will do the same to you.

#### ACTION STEP:
*(Now repeat this paragraph at least two more times and don't stop until you get something deeper than that which is written on this page.)*

### But death HAS been defeated!

## Living From The Inside-Out

### Day 308

The spirit of the living God was breathed into you in the garden. It was here that you received the fullness of it. After the fall, the reality of it was diminished. But man still contained the seed of the fullness of the power of the Spirit. And that power was fully restored when the second Adam took it back. The disciples were the first partakers of the infilling of the power of the Spirit after the resurrection of our Savior.

*Now when the Day of Pentecost had fully come, they were all with one accord in one place. And suddenly there came a sound from heaven, as of a rushing mighty wind, and it filled the whole house where they were sitting. Then there appeared to them divided tongues, as of fire, and one sat upon each of them. And they were all filled with the Holy Spirit and began to speak with other tongues, as the Spirit gave them utterance. "We hear them speaking in our own tongues the wonderful works of God." Acts 2:2-4,11*

The disciples got a dose of the Ghost that day. They got endued with power from on high. That power came because they could hear and experience the truth of the wonderful works of their God. He became so personal to them. The face-to-face interaction they had with Jesus was still in the natural except when the spirit would come upon them to work with them to bring about the desire of God's heart to the world. But on this day, this was the day that the church would become kings and priests in the spirit realm, not just the natural arena. They had an illumination from the Spirit that went beyond natural comprehension. It was the Spirit that had brought the life of God into their beings so they could also live life from the inside out.

- *They were no longer going to be contained to natural knowledge*
- *They would no longer be restricted to natural actions*
- *They would no longer be limited to natural evidence*

<u>Now Declare this over your personal life in the Spirit...</u>
- *I AM no longer going to be contained to natural knowledge!*
- *I AM no longer be restricted to natural actions!*
- *I AM no longer be limited to natural evidence!*

*That power came because they could hear and experience the truth of the wonderful works of their God.*

# Living From the Inside-Out

**Day 309**

*Then Peter said, "Silver and gold I do not have, but what I do have I give you: In the name of Jesus Christ of Nazareth, rise up and walk."*
*Acts 3: 6*

This declaration is amazing. When he said he didn't have any silver or gold he wasn't saying he was too poor to offer him any silver or gold, he was saying, that is not my assignment today. What I have for you today, I will give you. Because He was aware of something higher.

He said, what I HAVE I will give to you. Peter had come to live from the inside out. He was aware of who He was and what he had on the inside of him. He was so aware of the power of God that he had been endued with from on high, that all he needed to know was that this was the day for that which had been stolen from this man to be completely restored.

The church has become crippled by the enemy, who has gotten them to sit in the outer courts because they have been injured, stolen from and have allowed it to cause them to gaze from the gates into the courtyard of the Lord and to be hindered from access to the holy place. But Jesus came and when He paid the ultimate sacrifice for us, the partition was torn from heaven down to give us access to the Holy of Holies. His intention now on the earth is to have us live a life that reflects that access and what that really means to us. He is taking those that have been disabled. The body of Christ that has been under attack so long that they have begun to act as though they are permanently disabled: crippled, injured, incapacitated. And He has prepared a gate, a portal for them to enter in once again. He has called the gate by name. It is Beautiful. When Peter and John became aware of who they were and what they really had access to, the power that really lie deep within them, they could reach right in and they could pull out what was needed to bring the restoration to the disabled in front of them. For it was a season, a timely time; a time of flourishing for this man once again. Do you understand? We are entering into the season when the church will rise out of its disability and begin to operate again from the inside out.

*...what I HAVE I will give to you.*

## Living From the Inside-Out

### Day 310

We are entering into a new time of realization of the revelation of who we are and what we carry on the inside of us. *"Ye are the light of the world. A city that is set on an hill cannot be hid. Neither do men light a candle, and put it under a bushel, but on a candlestick; and it giveth light unto all that are in the house. Let your light so shine before men, that they may see your good works, and glorify your Father which is in heaven."* Matt 5:14-16 KJV

We are the light now. Jesus was the light when He was here, now we are the light and we can no longer be hidden. Our light is shining before men. How? By our good works! What good works? The works that occur when we tap into the God on the inside of us. What kind of works is it when you see a lame man and you speak words of life to him and he runs and leaps and praises God? GOOD WORKS! *"And he took him by the right hand, and lifted him up: and immediately his feet and ankle bones received strength. And he leaping up stood, and walked, and entered with them into the temple, walking, and leaping, and praising God."* Acts 3:7-8

Where did he go? Straight into the temple. The place he had been denied access to before! What did he do? Oh he was filled with gratefulness. He knew his God in a different way. His deliverance had come. And the world and many of God's own people were filled with wonder and amazement.

*"And all the people saw him walking and praising God: And they knew that it was he which sat for alms at the Beautiful gate of the temple: and they were filled with wonder and amazement at that which had happened unto him."* Acts 3: 9-10 KJV

Peter and John had fixed their gaze on the God that lived within them, before they fixed their gaze on the lack, the need, and the disabled. Then they turned that which was on the inside of them outward. Believe it or not, you have this same power! Be determined today to show your good works by taking what is in you and pouring it out!

*Then they turned that which was on the inside of them outward.*

# Living From the Inside-Out

## Day 311

The church has been disabled due to inward gazing at the debris that has been left un-dealt with inside of them. The church has allowed contamination of fear and doubt. They have allowed unclean things to be a part of what was within. The church has become paralyzed. (*To affect with paralysis. To bring to a condition of helpless stoppage, inactivity, or inability to act.*)

However, God told us we were to contend for Heaven in 2011 and I believe we are to fight for what is rightfully ours. It is time for the church to become aware of its power again; its ability, and the wisdom and power of God that is available. And those things that we have allowed to occupy us will be flushed out in the presence of Almighty God.

The glory of God and the momentum of God's activity are coming in a new place of revelation and ability to seize the moments of time as that which is revealed from the inside as it is turned inside out. God's life and light will not be contained any longer. When people are touched in their areas of infirmity, whether it is in body, soul, or spirit, they will rejoice. Their voices will be heard once again. Their voices are calling even now, come Lord Jesus, come! Come to us in this way, come to us and reveal all that has been bought by Your blood to a place of reality to us.

The church has been in a place of desperation. (*Loss of hope; hopelessness. To lose, give up, or be without hope.*) The church has allowed circumstances to dictate to them the obvious, and they have not pressed into heaven's reality. But that is changing. This is the church of the living God, not the church of the broken, dead God.

<u>**Declare this aloud as an act of faith in contending for Heaven:**</u>  *God in all His wonder is still reigning. He is reigning on high and He is longing to see me reign with Him on earth as I re-discover my life in Him. The power He has deposited within me is being resurrected in the Name of Jesus! He reigns on this earth, in my home and in my life!*

***It is the time for the church to become aware of its power again; its ability, and the wisdom and power of God that is available.***

## Living From the Inside-Out

### Day 312

Satan thought He was winning when He called death forward to strike a blow to Jesus. Oh but God smiled, for He knew He had already given the death blow to death. Victory had been won from eternity past. Now it would be realized in eternity present the day that Jesus conquered death, hell and the grave. We are in the timing of God right now that eternity present is joining in eternity future so that God's name will be glorified in the earth. I believe that all the prophetic words that God has given to Liberty Life Center and to you individually are being compressed into this time so that they will explode in the timing of God.

Get ready to go through the gate Beautiful leaping and singing and praising God. We must live from the inside out. We must build our spirit man up. How? Praying in the Holy Ghost; it's the way Peter and John lived, and it will be the way we live.

*Jude 20-21 KJV But ye, beloved, building up yourselves on your most holy faith, praying in the Holy Ghost, Keep yourselves in the love of God, looking for the mercy of our Lord Jesus Christ unto eternal life.*

### Action Step:

Now read this declaration taken and modified to the first person from the Amplified version of how the Spirit works in us, through us and for us.

*I am assured and know that [God being a partner in my labor] all things work together and are [fitting into a plan] for good to and for me because I love God and am called according to [His] design and purpose. As for me whom He foreknew [of whom He was aware and loved beforehand], He also destined from the beginning [foreordaining me] to be molded into the image of His Son [and share inwardly His likeness], that He might become the firstborn among many brethren. And for me whom He thus foreordained, He also called; and as for me whom He called, He also justified (acquitted, made righteous, putting me into right standing with Himself). And as for me whom He justified, He also glorified [raising me to a heavenly dignity and condition or state of being]. Romans 8:28-30 AMP*

**We must build our spirit man up.**

# Living From the Inside-Out

**Day 313**

We are going to live from the inside out and turn the world upside down to join the Kingdom of God. There is nothing on earth that is too hard for God, too hard for His word, too hard for His love or too hard that faith can't overcome. As we get the revelation of His love we can demonstrate that love with compassion and be led by the Spirit to carry out whatever action He leads us to do at the time. The power to invade the natural with the power of the living God flows through vessels that are living from the inside out.

Prayer, fasting and continuing in the word, and most importantly seeking His face in the holy place, makes place for His presence until we are turned inside out and He who lives within us becomes apparent for all to see and to experience.

Let us realize the time and season we are living in. Let us contend for that which He has already provided, for the demonstration of the fullness of the Spirit, to demonstrate once again to the world what power is available to those that are living for God in these last days of the last days.

- We will no longer be contained to natural knowledge!
- We will no longer be restricted to natural actions!
- We will no longer be limited to natural evidence!

Why? Because the evidence of the Holy God, the risen One, and the power of the Spirit will now be experiential to us and for them.

That's living from inside out...

And that's your call to action today...Yes, today... And every day!

*The power to invade the natural with the power of the living God flows through vessels that are living from the inside out.*

# A Turn-Around in The Kingdom of This Land

**Day 314**

A prophetic Word to this generation...

If My people, which are called by My name, will humble themselves and pray and seek My face and turn from their wicked ways, then I will hear from heaven and will forgive their sins and will heal their land. WHEN My people, which are called by My name, humble themselves and pray, and cry out and seek My face, and My face only, and turn from the way they used to do things and turn to righteousness instead of wickedness, then I will hear from heaven, and I will forgive their sins, and I will heal, restore their land.

BECAUSE My people, which are called by My name, are humbling themselves, and they are beginning to pray, and they are beginning to seek My FACE above all things, then I am turning them from their wicked ways, and I am hearing the sounds from heaven and I am entering the atmosphere with My answers, and I am forgiving your and their sins and I am healing this land. And I am healing your land. And I am healing this land. And I am healing their land. And I am healing your land. And I am bringing healing, and I am bringing wholeness, and I am hearing the cries, and I am saying, "Here am I". Here am I in the midst of your cries. Here am I in the midst of your prayer. Here am I in the midst of your sorrow. Here am I in the midst of the mess to blow my My paths of righteousness before you by the wind of My Spirit laying it out for all to see.

For I, the Lord God Almighty, am raising up My name among the nations. My light is shining into the darkness. It is exposing the sin. The separation has begun - the separation between the goats and sheep, between the evil and the wicked and the righteous and the holy. For My name is above all names and I will not share My name with those who want fame for their own glory. But I am bringing up a holy people, a righteous people, who care no longer about their own selves, or their own issues. But they are coming to Me with the issues and the concerns with compassion for those that are lost, for those who can't find their way, for those that are waiting to hear that there is a way out, there is a way up, there is a way of deliverance, there is a way of forgiveness, there is a way of wholeness.

*My name is above all names...*

# A Turn-Around in The Kingdom of This Land

**Day 315**

And so My voice will be heard resounding through the heavens. And it will echo on the earth, bringing forth joy and gladness, deliverance and wholeness; bringing into the land of the people who will cry out completeness in My name. For there is a turn-around that is happening - a turn-around for your good, a turn-around for the nations' good, a turn-around for those that have been so lost to be able to be found, a turn-around inside of minds that will now work according to Kingdom-thinking and dare to believe Me for what I have pre-designed. For the church that I'm raising up is not a begging church. It's not a church that is needy. But it's the righteous, holy, whole, complete, able church. To reach out and meet the needs of those who are in trouble, and those who are lost, and those who have no way. They will lay out before them the paths of righteousness. They will lay out before them the paths of wholeness and healing. They will lay out before them the paths that they can walk upon and in, and declare and become a part of the answer instead of a part of the problem.

For you see, the winds have begun to blow and the voices are beginning to come together just as I have said. And the trumpets are beginning to blow and those that have ears to hear are beginning to hear the voice of the nations calling collectively, the voice of the church arising in a symphony of love to a higher degree than ever before.

The unity shall be unprecedented because they have now begun to understand that it is not about what they wish, but what I wish. And so the tide is turning against the enemy. For the time is short and I will open the ark of safety. And many will come in as you prepare the way. As you arise and build when it looks impossible, as you begin to see the vision and the hope and make a place of safety for others to run in, that when the rain and the tide begins to turn, they will run inside and be saved, they and their family.

*They will lay out before them the paths of righteousness.*

# A Turn-Around in The Kingdom of This Land

## Day 316

For I wish that all men would be saved, and I have made a way. But you must work with Me until the day. You must work alongside Me with a heart to the finish. You must take the tools in your hands that I have provided for you on a personal level and for you on a corporate level. And for you to begin to co-labor with those who have insight, who have ability – even those whom you have discounted because they are still in the world – but don't you understand the way I think is so much higher? If you get them excited about meeting a need, they will come alongside of you, and then the anointing and the presence of Me that lives on the inside of you will overtake them and they will not be able to resist My love. They will not be able to resist that which I have placed on the inside of you because it is catching – it will overwhelm them – and they will say "TRULY this is the God of the earth". They will want to know Me because of the way you have presented Me.

So present Me with purity. Present Me with love. Present Me with compassion. Present Me with giftings and talents and time and tithes and energy and show them what the Kingdom looks like in heaven. Then it will begin to be built from the foundation of the earth up. Those things that I have laid out before you – the words that I have spoken from the beginning – you will take dominion again and multiply, and subdue this earth and present it before your King. For My Kingdom is coming, and My Kingdom is near.

Now let the church of the living God arise into their kingly position and begin to cause the nations to rock and shake and to come apart at the sound of My voice until the Kingdoms of this world have become once again My Kingdom place. For I will rule and I will reign and I will finally have My perfect way. For I will have a people – I will have a people – that will enjoy My fellowship, that will rule and reign with Me, that will celebrate the God they serve - throughout eternity. Make a way. Make a path. Lay it out. Make it sure. Sound the alarm. Pull down. Root out. And build and plant. For you were born for such a time as this.

*For My Kingdom is coming, and My Kingdom is near.*

# SEED OF AUTHORITY

**Day 317**

We have the ability to walk in authority. The key of authority is found in the form of a seed.

- We must recognize the Sower has sown the word to us, made it available for us.

- He has sown seeds of power, of authority, of destiny into us.

- Seed represents authority. The possessor of a seed has the authority and ability to produce.

- Authority comes not by just looking at the seed, but looking at it, realizing you are also looking at the harvest.

God not only has authority in heaven now, but becoming a man gave Him back the full authority that God intended on the earth. He left heaven, but He never left the Kingdom's system. Jesus, as man, showed us that it could be done, and how. Authority: force, delegated influence with jurisdiction; liberty, power, right, strength.

Jesus bought back the authority God had given mankind, but which man misused. As God in the flesh, Jesus now had all authority in heaven and in earth.

*"All authority is given unto me in heaven and in earth." Matthew 28:18*

His authority lives inside of us, as we are a part of His seed. That authority has given us power over how much power of the enemy? All POWER!

So then, we must realize that as a product of His seed and being made in His likeness, we have authority. We have been restored to the place of ruling and having dominion.

*And God raised us up with Christ and seated us with him in the heavenly realms in Christ Jesus. Ephesians 2:6*

***The key of authority is found in the form of a seed.***

## SEED OF AUTHORITY

**Day 318**

The seed of authority has given us the seat of authority. Our seed isn't corrupted anymore, we are of incorruptible seed, and we have God's divine nature within us. God's seed. Restored to dominion and authority. Just as you have to put the key in and open the door, you also have to put the key into the ignition and turn it to operate the power that is within. Here are some keys we need to ignite in order to learn how to walk in our authority:

1. The first ignition starts by being seed of His seed by being a part of God's Kingdom.

If we haven't received Jesus in our heart as Lord and Savior, then we can use His name, but it will be in vain. Nothing with power will back it. So we must understand, true authority from God comes only under His delegated authority. Accepting Jesus as Savior, gives us access to all the authority of heaven.

*"Nor is there salvation in any other, for there is no other name under heaven given among men by which we must be saved." Acts 4:12*

*"And you, who once were alienated and enemies in your mind by wicked works, yet now He has reconciled 22 in the body of His flesh through death, to present you holy, and blameless, and above reproach in His sight." Colossians 1:21-22*

*"Jesus came and spake unto them, saying 'All power is given unto me in heaven and in earth. Go ye therefore, and teach all nations, baptizing them in the name of the Father, and of the Son, and of the Holy Ghost: teaching them to observe all things whatsoever I have commanded you: and lo, I am with you always, even unto the end of the world. Amen.'" Matthew 28:18-20 KJV*

If Jesus is with us always, then the Anointed One's anointing is with us always too! We just need to learn how to operate in our authority according to God's instruction manual.

**We have God's divine nature within us.**

## SEED OF AUTHORITY

**Day 319**

Here is another key we need to ignite in order to learn how to walk in our authority:

2. Our next ignition comes when we give honor and are willing to be under authority.

God has given us some commandments to follow. They weren't suggestions. So what is the command: "To acquire; to enjoin with authority"? When we agree with Him and do things His way, we are enjoined with that authority and it can't be broken. Without relationship with God, we will have no authority. Without understanding His power system, we won't walk in full authority.

*"Obey them that have the rule over you, and submit yourselves: for they watch for your souls, as they that must give account, that they may do it with joy, and not with grief: for that is unprofitable for you." Hebrews 13:17*

*"And he gave some, apostles; and some prophets; and some, evangelists; and some, pastors and teachers; for the perfecting of the saints, for the work of the ministry, for the edifying of the body of Christ." Ephesians 4:11-12*

God's system is clear. Recognize, yield, trust, obey, make assent toward the authorities He has placed over your life if you want to work in the ministry and if you would like to be edified. If you won't be under authority, God won't trust you with authority. So we find we must be under authority. God doesn't bless "lone rangers" or mavericks. There is an anointing that comes with authority. There is an empowerment that is able to be passed on when you submit to it.

When you recognize authority, faith or anointing in others, you can avail yourself of more than just their teaching, you can partake in their anointing if you stay humble and desirous.

---

*When we agree with Him and do things His way,
we are enjoined with that authority and it can't be broken.*

# SEED OF AUTHORITY

Here is another key we need to ignite in order to learn how to walk in our authority:

3. To walk in authority, you have to guard others' authority. Sowing and reaping applies in every area.

The same principles apply to authority available to you by what Jesus has already provided.

You can hear what He said in the word and your mind can wander and wonder. Or you can be a student that understands the access, the power, the principle of seed time and harvest in your relationship with Him.

We must recognize the position Jesus has. We must do whatever needs to be done for the day, and increase our expectancy of what we want to receive from seeding our time with Him, of serving Him. We can have the harvest of our sowing.

We have the authority, but we can discount what we have access to because we have become familiar with Jesus, with His grace, and we don't take advantage of the fullness of His power. Then it will cause us not to walk in the full authority that He has offered.

To walk in the full authority God has for you, you must be under authority. God first, then His delegated authority for your life. Ignite the power by submitting to authority.

*To walk in the full authority God has for you, you must be under authority.*

# SEED OF AUTHORITY

Day 321

4. We must ignite the redemptive purpose of authority given to us for souls to enjoy our authority to the fullest.

Heaven's authority has been restored to us through Jesus, and although it is for your own needs, your own health, your own prosperity, it is also for the purpose of bringing the lost to the wonderful knowledge of salvation.

Remember Peter, how he denied the Lord? But is that what you remember him the most for? Though his mistake is hard to forget, the memory of his weakness is swallowed up in the victories he walked in after he received the power and authority that came with the baptism of the Holy Spirit. This was the moment of Peter's transition. He was infilled with the same power that kept Jesus through every temptation and trial. It was the same power that raised Him from the dead, and now he was overwhelmed with that power. It was filling up all the empty spots, the places of doubt and meekness. Peter was experiencing the transformation that can only come from the inside out. But what a difference it would make.

People from all the different regions were in town and they heard them all speaking in these tongues.

*So they were all amazed and perplexed, saying to one another, "Whatever could this mean?" Others mocking said, "They are full of new wine." Acts 2:12-13*

Peter's first Spirit-filled sermon:

*But Peter, standing up with the eleven, raised his voice and said to them, "Men of Judea and all who dwell in Jerusalem, let this be known to you, and heed my words. For these are not drunk, as you suppose, since it is only the third hour of the day. But this is what was spoken by the prophet Joel. Acts 2:14-16*

This Peter of the denial became Peter the proclaimer. What will you proclaim today?

*We must ignite the redemptive purpose of authority given to us for souls to enjoy our authority to the fullest.*

## Seed of Authority

### Day 322

Peter didn't just know about God at this point. He had the Holy Spirit living within him and He brought him to another place of boldness. He had revelation of that which he had known about before, but now it was his very own experientially.

When Peter stood in that position of authority, he was empowered by the Holy Ghost. Now that same authority that Jesus walked in had come upon Peter. Is this really the same Peter that denied Jesus? No.

Because, suddenly he got a revelation from Almighty God. It was the same type of revelation that he got when he said, "You are the Christ, the Son of the living God!" It was the kind of revelation that only comes from the inside out. He was changed. There was a new boldness, a new awareness of this new-found authority that rose up from within him, and he had a heart change. The first thing he wanted to do was impact these lost people with truth that would change their lives and their eternal destination.

We see that the same anointing and authority that Jesus operated in, that caused men to repent of their sins, was now flowing through Peter. It didn't die. And it is still very much alive! Peter had seen it flow through Jesus. He had seen many come to repentance and he had learned. Now he had a choice and he received the authority and began to command others to come into alignment.

*"And they continued steadfastly in the apostles' doctrine and fellowship and in the breaking of bread and in prayers, and fear came upon every soul." "...And many wonders and signs were done by the apostles." Acts 2:42-43*

We still have the authority, the power of His presence available today to every believer. That includes YOU.

Think about that!

---

*Now he had a choice and he received the authority and began to command others to come into alignment.*

## SEED OF AUTHORITY

**Day 323**

5. Ignite your authority by walking a love walk

*"So now I am giving you a new commandment: Love each other. Just as I have loved you, you should love each other." John 13:34 (NLT)*

Now let me ask you this. Could you love some of the people that you love if it wasn't for the love of Jesus inside of you? Do we still struggle a little bit with some people, sometimes? Of course, yes, but He said, "I'm giving you a new command. Therefore, it isn't a suggestion. He has given us a way to rise above our natural feelings. Sit in the higher place, now. What are you going to tell Jesus up there sitting on the throne with Him? They don't deserve your love? He'll just answer, "Love them like I love you."

You move into a different position of authority when you do that. You rise into a completely different place because now you are depending on His love within you to love because you are aware you don't have the ability to love like that without Him. However, when we tap into the power source, and recognize we can choose to have His love, it will shine through. You may not even "feel" like you like those people, yet you find you can have a love for them. That sets you above. That keeps your channels clear in your position of authority, for the enemy has nothing on you.

He's calling us to a higher place in Him. The same anointing that Jesus enjoyed as He obeyed the Father and died to his own feelings, will come upon us to give us that unconditional love. He gave us the authority to "Go into all the world and make disciples..." (Matt. 28:19) His love compels you beyond what is comfortable. It compels you beyond what is natural, but as we learn to yield to it, it will become more natural for us to accept our own supernatural abilities given us by God, as normal for us ... and life-changing for others.

*"Love them like I love you."*

## Significance Of Prayer

### Day 324

One night during a prayer meeting at our church I felt the prayers of the Holy Spirit being prayed through our people; each would swell within me as I wept before God for each scene the Holy Spirit would bring before me.

I thought my heart would break as I saw the hurting, the abandoned, the hungry, the abused.

It hurt so badly, I cried out to God and He said, you asked Me for My heart. This is how I feel. Then He said, "Do you hate all the sin as I hate it?" He said, "Whatever part of sin you accommodate will keep you from complete repentance. That will keep you from the blessing I have in your life."

I wanted to be pure like Him. I wanted to respond like He would. He said, "Now in the scenes you have seen, do you love them?" "Oh yes, I do, I do," I replied … then He said, "Even the perpetrators?"

I could not answer that with a yes. I was angry at those that caused the pain. I was not sure I could get past it. I asked Him for help. "Show me someone in your word as an example."

He said, "Look at Saul. He killed children in my name. And I loved him. Those are the ones that will understand love and grace and bring others into a different place. They know they don't deserve forgiveness, yet they receive it. Because of love."

"Someone must want to reach them also. But it will take my heart, it will take my love. It will only come from times like this of being with Me."

*Whatever part of sin you accommodate will keep you from complete repentance. That will keep you from the blessing I have in your life."*

# Principles of Revival

**Day 325**

One day while studying I came across "The 10 Principles of Revival" taught by Charles Finney. These were taught by him in cities across the country and brought revival wherever they were taught. As I looked at them and compared them to what God has been doing at Liberty Life Center, I realized that most of them we had already been focusing on and experiencing, and the others were "in the hopper" ready to come out.

I am excited because I know we are moving with God into a time that has never occurred before. He is directing us. He is leading us and He has more in store for us. But it will take some of your time, some of your attention, a lot of your affection and God's direction in your life. I want to talk to you today about your part in being part of the end time revival. (Or movement, or whatever.) He is requiring us to act differently than we have in the past. Let's look at what Paul exhorts us to do.

*Romans 12:1-4 Message {Place Your Life Before God} "So here's what I want you to do, God helping you: Take your everyday, ordinary life—your sleeping, eating, going-to-work, and walking-around life—and place it before God as an offering. Embracing what God does for you is the best thing you can do for him. Don't become so well-adjusted to your culture that you fit into it without even thinking. Instead, fix your attention on God. You'll be changed from the inside out. Readily recognize what he wants from you, and quickly respond to it. Unlike the culture around you, always dragging you down to its level of immaturity, God brings the best out of you, develops well-formed maturity in you."*

Paul is speaking from a heart that understands he could not change himself, but God did it as he gave God permission. He knew he must train others to do the same, and the way to do it, was allowing God to bring it to you as you lean on Him, desire Him, and be transformed by Him. *"…I'm speaking to you out of deep gratitude for all that God has given me, and especially as I have responsibilities in relation to you. Living then, as every one of you does, in pure grace, it's important that you not misinterpret yourselves as people who are bringing this goodness to God. No, God brings it all to you. The only accurate way to understand ourselves is by what God is and by what he does for us, not by what we are and what we do for him."*

**He is leading us and He has more in store for us.**

# Being The Church

**Day 326**

This Kingdom Guide series is a prophecy that the Holy Spirit gave me for the Body of Christ as His church today:

Even as you hear the languages cry out, I am raising a voice, I am raising a voice among My people. The church will arise again. Arise out of its stupor. Arise out of the places where it's been in hiding. For I have swung open the gates that no man can shut. And My church is beginning to walk through the gates and take their position.

You are out of transition and you are in position now--where I am securing you for the greatest time in history. For My finger is on the page. And the page is turning and they will look back at this time in history and they will talk about what occurred. But only you and I will know that it has been happening during the transition as you sought Me, as you prayed, as you cried out for the change and the shifting to take place for I have sent forth the angels and they are doing their work. And they have touched and they have moved amongst you even now.

And now the sons of men will begin to understand that they are also the sons of God. And they will begin to show forth that which has already been imparted to them--power, truth, effectiveness, completeness, ability, gifts--changing the hearts of men. For the change that you will begin to see is [that] they will not only just remain silent, but they will also no longer withhold their hand from helping the poor or the helpless or the needy. For I have dropped inside a compulsion, a compulsion that compels them into the streets, and into the darkness as never before.

*You are out of transition and you are in position now--where I am securing you for the greatest time in history.*

## Being The Church

**Day 327**

You can see those who are praising, you can see those who are worshiping, you can see the true believers. You can hear the prayers of the saints as they join in unity with one voice, and one heart and one purpose. And I am causing those seeds that have been sown into the air to now join forces with heaven and the glory will begin to rain down back upon the earth. It is bringing down the dew of heaven and it is bringing forth the harvest that you have longed for.

No longer will it be hard to win the lost, for now it is the season for the lost to be found. And now you will hear My voice as never before--for reason, for purpose, for souls. And all of the training and all of the inner hearing and all of the inner healing and all of the things that I have trained you with, and tools that I have given you will now be realized with the purpose that I have given them--to save those that are lost, to go into the darkness and bring the light, the hope, and the truth. And there will be a turning, there will be a radical turning. Even the church will come alive again--alive in a way that they have not been able to say before or realize. They will arise and they will proclaim Me as never before, for in the darkness, My church shines brightest. And yes, there will be darkness that is on the earth, and it will increase, as it is written. But in the increase of darkness, there is also a flood of glory. A flood that is coming out of you, a flood that is coming as you join as one, a flood that as those that are called by My name realize who they are and speak it out with majesty and might as kings and as priests, of those that have authority, who cause the seas to split, and the earth to shatter, and the skies to thunder with truth and with purity. For now My voice will be heard from those who have remained righteous, by those that have chosen truth, by those that have walked in purity, for those that have been unbendable according to My written word. Now you will begin to feel the authority mantle dropping upon your shoulder as you rise into positioning. For now you will no longer read about it, you will be it.

I have longed for this day, I have longed for the time when My church would be ready, when there would be enough cries from My people that would enable Me to pour out that which I have been longing for. For I have been waiting for this day, I have been longing for this people. I've been watching for the passion, I've been watching for those who would be relentless in their pursuit.

*You will be it.*

# Being The Church

## Day 328

I told you to look, I told you to ask, and yes, you can have all of Me now, all of Me now, all of Me will be seen, now all of My glory, now all of My power, now all of My majesty, as I walk through the streets with you as you open up your door to the poor, as you open up your wallets to the hungry, as you open up your mouth with truth. Multitudes, multitudes in the valley of decision, but they're coming, they're coming, they're coming into the truth, they're coming into the place of being able to hear, for your cries have opened deaf ears. Your intercession has taken scales off of eyes. And now you're positioned, ruling and reigning with Me on the earth, as it should be, as I've always intended it to be.

See yourself as the victorious church because that is how I see you. That is how I've built you. I have not built you for anything less than victory. So victory I declare and victory I decree. Now come into agreement with Me. You are My people--victorious, triumphant--you do not have to rely upon your ability, you never have. You only rely upon Mine. Is there anything too difficult for Me? And so I will turn things around for you. As you believe, as you come out of doubt and back into trust. You see, trust is where faith is born. When you trust Me whole-heartedly because of relationship, your faith is automatically grown; you don't have to work at it if you just know Me.

If you know Me you can trust Me, so know Me some more--you can have all of Me. You can have all of Me. I've made Myself available. You cried out, and I answered. You asked for more of Me, and I said yes.

*You are My people--victorious, triumphant--you do not have to rely upon your ability, you never have.*

# Being The Church

**Day 329**

And so the truths of the ancient pasts will be revealed to those who are hungry, to those who are willing to dig deeper yet still, to those who will look into My word and look for the treasures that have been hidden for the ages. For now is the time for the revelation to be revealed of the ancient truths that will now become present truths. And you will take them from eternity past and you will bring them into eternity present and you will speak them into eternity future making a way for the generations.

There will be those that will grab hold of those that are young. They will mentor and disciple them as never before. You will see the transition begin to occur, as the young ones begin to be as wise as the old ones. There will be an absolute that will be put upon you that you will not be able to contain what I've entrusted into your care unless you are pouring it into someone else, mentoring will come to a new level of discipleship in order.

Now is the time that you are going to see the Timothy's, now is the time that the Paul's will have to take hold, they will have to raise up, they will have to impart, and the Timothy's will rise all across the world, and they will begin to be assigned to regions. They will be assigned to cities, they will be assigned to places, and it will rock the world. Like Titus, who was sent, placed in Crete, to structure, to build, to oversee, to spread the good news. So have I sent you, for this reason I have placed you in your city, for this reason I have placed you in Africa, for this reason I have placed you in Belize, for this reason I have placed you in Asia, I have placed you in Europe, I have placed you in South America, I have placed you. There will be a sending that is mandatory--and you won't feel like you're able to, that's why you're ready.

*And you will take them from eternity past and you will bring them into eternity present and you will speak them into eternity future making a way for the generations.*

# Being The Church

## Day 330

All the seeds that have been sown will now come back, but they will come back with different purpose, they will come back with a different assignment. You've been believing Me, but you've been believing for Me to make your life easier. But I declare to you tonight that if you will believe me to make someone else's life easier, then I will give you more than enough and your life will be easier too. But the truth in giving and then receiving still stands. There will be a release now, a release, a release, a release, a release that My church will not be able to hold on to the things which come in. It will come in and it will go out, it will come in and it will go out, it will come in and go out because My church is being set now in position to do that which I have called it to do and as the church, as you touch those that have been on My heart and change the lives of those that have cried out to Me. Oh, you'll see them in the night. You'll hear their cries, you'll know exactly where to give, you'll know how much to give and you'll believe Me for it. And I'll give it to you because I can get it through you.

Earmark it, write down where you're putting it, tell Me what you'll do with it and see how fast I will answer. I've just been waiting, I've been waiting for a people who will say "give it to Me and I'll assign it there," "give it to Me and I'll send it there," "give it to Me and I'll see that this gets done, that which has been on your heart." Raise your level of faith for a particular group and I will raise the funds and release them to you. Begin to declare who I am in the situation. Go back to the declarations of faith. Go back to the place of not doubting Me any longer. Go back to simple truth. I Am Who I said I Am--Provider, Healer, More Than Enough, All Sufficient One, the One who cares for you, the Great Shepherd, your Husband, your Friend, your Guide, the Friend that sticks closer than a brother, the Mighty Judge, the One who will defend you, your Rock, your Fortress, your Hiding Place. I still Am Who I said I Am.

*Go back to the place of not doubting Me any longer.*

# Being The Church

**Day 331**

All the things that Satan is planning, keep being thwarted, but it is prayer that has raised up the shield. It is prayer that has kept America intact. There are many that say prayer has ceased, but I have heard the prayers of many over this nation. Even as the cries continue, I will protect, I will shine the light of where you are to go. I will show you the path that is safe. And I will open up the doors in other places for you to walk through.

There is a shift that has taken place in the heavenly realm, there is a pathway that has opened up into the realm of the spirit that is an ancient pathway for you to walk through. I am calling you to go up higher and to see the truths of what takes place, to grab hold of those truths and to bring them down and proclaim them out. It won't be your imagination, it won't be things you've heard from somewhere else. It will be walking up into the heavenly realm and seeing what you are seeing, and hearing what you can hear, and then bringing forth those truths, and bringing it out with revelation and with power. They will be accompanied by signs and wonders and miracles, but do not look for signs and wonders and miracles, look for Me. It is in My face, it is in My countenance, it is in the fierceness of My eyes, it is in My presence that you get filled up and those things will just happen. Don't be looking for a name, don't be looking for a title, don't be looking for fame, and don't be looking to be free of things where I have placed you for now.

*I am calling you to go up higher and to see the truths of what takes place, to grab hold of those truths and to bring them down and proclaim them out.*

# Being The Church

## Day 332

Some of you have said so many times to Me, "if only, if only, if only." Do not box Me into an "if only" moment. For I have strategies for your life that you need to walk out. In the strategy of where you are rejoice, rejoice, and again I say rejoice, because in the midst of the circumstance that you don't understand, there is a rumble going on. There are those that need to hear the truth and see that somebody in the midst of where you are still praises the One and only true God. And then the release comes. And then the release comes. And then the release comes. You're trying to get free before there is a release. Look around, who are you there for, what are you there for? The hold up is not Me, it's you. There's a soul, there's a soul right in front of you. See it. Become the church. Disciple.

There's an awareness of who you are in Me. It's the answer to My prayer to the Father in John 17. I have made you one like the Father and I are one. There will be one in agreement, singly and successively. There will be a oneness that will come to the body of Christ like never before, an awareness, a oneness, a one voice, a community. I am creating a community, a linking of arms. I am causing the army to come together. It will cross enemy lines, it will cross denominations. I am making you one. There can no longer be fortresses, there can be no fences, no judgment, I am forcing you out of your hiding places into interaction because that is My heart. Uncomfortable as it is, you will grow to see the power in it; you will grow to love it because I love it. I love seeing walls come down, I love changing minds. I love melting people into one. And then you will see the oneness in 2010 that will come to the community as you reach out one to one. I'm sending you one to one to win them.

That's why discipleship is important, for there is no other way but to befriend them and be there for them. Reach out. Somebody's been waiting for you. Somebody's waiting for your gift, someone's waiting for your voice, for your touch, for your hug, for the truth that I've placed on the inside.

*You will grow to love it because I love it.*

# Being The Church

Day 333

Someone's waiting for the power that I've invested on the inside of you. Someone's going to pull it out of you. There will be a day where the sickness and disease cries out in front of you and the Me inside replies, "Be free!" The glory is already there, the power is already there, now walk in it.

Be the sizeable church. Huge—billions--one heart, one voice, and then that day, that day, that day when all the languages come up before My throne, as one voice saying, "Come, Lord Jesus, come! Come, Lord Jesus, come! Come, Lord Jesus, come!" And I will hear from My heaven, and I will come! And I will set up that which I have planned. I will put things in proper order and you will begin to see exactly why I structured things the way I have as you rule and reign with Me for a thousand years.

Are you ready to be My church? Are you ready to face whatever is necessary? Are you ready to praise Me? Are you ready to take that which the enemy has used against you and pull back the bow? Are you ready to shoot into your future? How far will you go? How far will you trust Me? How far will you take that which the enemy has used against you and use it as a place to thrust you forward? How far back will you pull before you let go? Release! Release! Release! The future is yours! The future is yours! The future, the future is yours! It's up to you-- My church! My church! The future, the future, it's yours! It's yours, it's yours!

*"Come, Lord Jesus, come!*
*Come, Lord Jesus, come!*
*Come, Lord Jesus, come!"*

# It is Here

## Day 334

There are those among you waiting for it, saying, "When is it going to fall like it is in the past?" I say it is here! Can't you see it? Can't you feel it?

I Am ... I Am ... I am no respecter of persons! I Am the One and only true God to all who come! Who are you to question Me how My Fire and Glory will fall here? Or what it should look like? What are you waiting for? I am here! Can't you see it? Can't you feel it? I AM who you allow Me to be in your lives. Who are you to deny My power and movement in this time in history in this place?

Let me out of the box! Come one and come all - seek My face, seek My presence, seek My heart. You will find Me. I'm not a withholder. Allow Me to transform you into My likeness.

As you continue to come before Me corporately I will be faithful to show up and demonstrate My power to you with signs, wonders, and My Glory will reside here. Continue to prepare yourselves. This is big - bigger than anything you could imagine. Nothing will stop this move of My hand. You have never seen anything like this before. You have never heard anything like this before. You will hear Me in ways that are very unusual. Yet you will know it is Me - so follow My Glory Cloud. There are those who don't join in corporate prayer - they have their own agenda. I call out to them again and say come - come to Me!

If they do not heed My voice I will pass by them, and replace them with those whose hearts are after Mine. There is a separation occurring in the Body of Christ. Those who are on their way to you are unusual, and a peculiar people not unlike those who are already here. Be ready to expand in all ways.

*Come one and come all -*
*seek My face, seek My presence, seek My heart.*

# It's All In Your Perspective

## Day 335

My love, compassion, My characteristics, and humility are being embedded in your hearts.

There are those who have My heart and are not able to be here. They will not miss Me or lose out; they too will have their reward - they will find Me! These are times of glory and victory as well as times of war and trials that you are living in.

Draw the blood line and cross over into MY territory of peace, safety, victory and My undeniable presence.

I have won. I have the victory. Victory is mine and you get to taste it! It is finished - all you have to do is walk it out. I go before you. Don't run away - No Defeat! No Defeat!

Stand in My Son Jesus - He is ALL you need.

My glory, signs, wonders and miracles will overtake you. There will be no sick among you - No not one! I am orchestrating this move like beautiful choreography. It is My beauty manifested to the masses. Keep seeking Me, keep pursuing Me. Keep focused on Me, and do what I ask you to do. I will not disappoint you - in fact you will be dancing and singing for joy!! This move is exceedingly abundantly above what you could ask or think.

I am your Daddy, and I take care of My children. Don't you know how much I love you? I love you with ALL My heart!

*...cross over into MY territory of peace, safety, victory and My undeniable presence.*

## Seed of Prayer

### Day 336

As God has been focusing on teaching us about seeds, we are coming to realize the importance of sowing and that everything we do is actually a seed sown. At the same time God is re-establishing the importance of prayer. We now must begin to recognize that intercession is not only important; it is our avenue of planting seeds with our prayers through the expectancy of reaping our harvest. We need to take solace in God's Word, that prayer changes things. It affects the things around us and causes heavenly involvement to bring about the resolution that is needed from God.

Let us remember that we must first plant the seed, then there is time before there is a harvest. Even in prayer. When you pray, there are things occurring, but it is not instant. You must understand this so you don't become discouraged while things orchestrated from heaven are being prepared to manifest on earth.

Read Daniel's experience: *Now while I was speaking, praying, and confessing my sin and the sin of my people Israel, and presenting my supplication before the Lord my God for the holy mountain of my God, yes, while I was speaking in prayer, the man Gabriel, whom I had seen in the vision at the beginning, being caused to fly swiftly, reached me about the time of the evening offering. And he informed me, and talked with me, and said, O Daniel, I have now come forth to give you skill to understand. At the beginning of your supplications the command went out, and I have come to tell you, for you are greatly beloved; therefore consider the matter, and understand the vision. Daniel 9:20-23.*

When did the command of God occur? At the beginning of his supplications; however, it didn't instantly manifest on earth. Yet when prayer is sown from us to God, when we ask according to His will, we can be sure that things are being orchestrated by God on your behalf.

Prayer is a power source that we as believers have been given! If you sow seeds of fervent, earnest, heartfelt and continued prayers you will be partakers of dynamic power!

*We need to take solace in God's Word, that prayer changes things.*

# Seed of Prayer

**Day 337**

There are many things that occur because of prayer that we will discover. Prayer is the place God provides to bring you to healing and restoration, as well as power.

*Confess to one another therefore your faults (your slips, your false steps, your offenses, your sins) and pray [also] for one another, that you may be healed and restored [to a spiritual tone of mind and heart]. The earnest (heartfelt, continued) prayer of a righteous man makes tremendous power available [dynamic in its working]. James 5:16 AMP:*

Several dynamics occur when we sow seeds of prayer.

1. Through repentance in prayer, we sow the seed of humility; and in praying for others we reap the benefit of being healed and restored.

2. Continued prayer releases seeds that will produce power that is dynamic in its working.

Where does the presence of the Lord now dwell?

 Inside of us!

Praying with HIM is a privilege. Worshipping Him is a privilege, sowing seeds of every kind to Him is a privilege that brings the harvest to us.

What do you display before Him?

Total abandonment or a resentful heart for what it takes from you? Time? Sleep? Effort? Funds?

We must constantly make sure that the seeds we are sowing to Him are being looked at not as a sacrifice, but as a privilege. Every time we pray, every time we praise, every time we offer our lives, it is not costing you, it is seed time that will produce a harvest that only He can bring.

*Prayer is the place God provides to bring you to healing and restoration, as well as power.*

# SEED OF PRAYER

## Day 338

We must not just pray, but keep praying, increasing our expectancy beyond what we have recognized in the past.

Prayer connects us to our family in heaven. We must understand that in those times we are building in the Spirit with those beside us and with those that are in heaven.
- We are building relationship with each other
- Taking territory from the enemy
- Hearing from God and obeying
- Seeding specifically for specific harvests
- We are building our faith through the Holy Spirit
- We are providing a place to train others - offer them the same opportunities God has given to us

The prayer times we share together become more powerful because it provides a way for the prayer of agreement.

*"Again I say to you that if two of you agree on earth concerning anything that they ask, it will be done for them by My Father in heaven." Matthew 18:19*

What are these two doing? Agreeing. Not only with each other, but with the prayer agreement that includes God in the midst. Prayer of agreement. What does agreement mean? This is where we get our word symphony. This is when we come into harmony with heaven and with each other. Once that is accomplished, it produces this harvest: "It shall be done for them." So the seed of prayer in agreement will bring God's power to assemble something that will be ordained to be fulfilled. And that is not all…

If you and I pray together in agreement, we have harmony, and we have created a symphony of agreement with God, His word, His will, His nature, in His name, and an amazing dynamic begins to take place!

*The prayer times we share together become more powerful because it provides a way for the prayer of agreement.*

# Seed of Prayer

Day 339

This may be a little hard to conceive, but when we pray in agreement with Him, in heaven our prayers exist where He exists, where He has already been, where He was, where He is and where He "am" meaning, also right now. The great I Am is with you, causing the harvest to be formed that He has already seen, already created for you to be partakers of. So, part of our harvest that we can expect from sowing our prayer seeds is: God's Presence and God's Attention.

*Then the priests, the Levites, arose and blessed the people, and their voice was heard; and their prayer came up to His holy dwelling place, to heaven. 2 Chronicles 30:27*

Your seed of prayer has come to Him and God is taking action to bring about the harvest to your prayer.

*But certainly God has heard me; He has attended to the voice of my prayer. Psalm 66:19*

Your prayer seed goes to heaven. It is planted. Then God begins to do something with your prayer. He waters it, He nourishes it, He attends to it. God Himself is giving heed to, marking your prayers, and giving regards to them. So is prayer important? Are prayers seeds worth sowing? YES INDEED! It also says in this scripture your prayers have a voice.

I was very happy to see the explanation of the word "voice"; for it includes proclamations, it includes lightness, and it also includes thundering, yelling and sparking. That is why prayer is different at times. Sometimes, there is a sweet gentleness to it. No volume, barely heard. Then there are the times of thundering, and yelling and God says this simply is the voice of prayer. If the Holy Spirit is in charge, let Him be in charge. You may prefer one style or the other, but we must let our preferences fade in the background as we allow the choice to be made by Him.

*The great I Am is with you, causing the harvest to be formed...*

# SEED OF PRAYER

## Day 340

We are looking at the truths of seed, time and harvest that are all throughout the Word. David demonstrates another example of what is available to us through prayer. There is a place we can reach beyond what we have reached to date. We have been promised that God is raising up the tabernacle of David again in our midst.

What does that mean and how do you think that meshes with seed time and harvest right now? Is it a physical place? No, it is a place of prayer, a place of worship, a place of honoring and serving God with all our heart where His presence is tangible and available 24/7.

Why did David experience such glory? David had an insatiable passion for God that kept bringing him back to the place of repentance and willingness to do whatever it took to have proper relationship with Him again. The seed of prayer and worship was inside of him. That seed kept producing a harvest from inside of him that would provide a way for others. It would overtake him on occasions. He became willing to be a fool for his God.

When David danced with ALL his might, it released the people to worship with him.

How do you keep your heart and mind lined up properly? Like David did. David loved God and he wanted to just celebrate their relationship. He wanted to invite others to join him. In prayer, in praise, in offerings.

We are called to prayer. We are called to praise God. We are called to offer Him the best that we have in every area of our life, but especially in our acknowledgement of His love and great grace and mercy towards us. We must desire to give Him all we have to offer in prayer and praise.

*We are called to prayer. We are called to praise God.*

# SEED OF PRAYER

**Day 341**

After the celebration, what was the next response of David? His love, his passion drove him to do something for his God. The seeds of prayer and praise had produced a love relationship that compelled David to another place. A place that made him want to build something where others would be able to meet and be with this God of the Harvest.

David was at rest in his palace, and in his time of contemplation, he considered how he might best employ his leisure and prosperity in the service of God. He must have begun to think of all God had done for him, in spite of his frailties.

David's heart hurt him from the realization that from the harvest he had received, he focused on himself and his desires, but suddenly he wanted to provide a place where God would dwell. His presence. He began to realize this as he said, "See now, I dwell in a house of cedar, but the ark of the God dwells within curtains."

He wanted to provide a place for God that would give Him the honor due His name. God had done much for him. He had provided a harvest of peace for him.

*When King David dwelt in his house and the Lord had given him rest from all his surrounding enemies...  2 Samuel 7:1*

David had fought, he had worshipped, he had danced and he consistently sowed seeds of prayer. His harvest? God had given him the victory over his enemies.

He will do the same for you. But you must fight, you must worship, you must dance, your must consistently pray. You must give God the glory due His name. You must continue seeding into the heavenly realm.

*His love, his passion drove him to do something for his God.*

# Seed of Prayer

## Day 342

When you offer up your prayers to God, He always gives back to you. God is looking for a people who will make a name for HIM. He is redeeming them, gathering them and trusting them. He chose them, you and me and His desires will last forever, no matter what the tactics of the enemy are.

David and his people were sending the seeds of prayer, praise and declaration into the heavens and God was inclining His ear, establishing the harvest for them. David knew and acknowledged that if God was the one that established the house, it would endure forever.

*And let thy name be magnified for ever, saying, The LORD of hosts is the God over Israel: and let the house of thy servant David be established before thee. 2 Samuel 7:26 KJV*

You see, where the will of God is seen, there is the ruling presence of God, and where His will and your will line up, there is harvest. Wherever the Spirit of the Lord is allowed to demonstrate the Lordship of Jesus, harvest and freedom are the result.

Another way to say it is that when the King of kings manifests His dominion to you because of the seeds you have sown, the fruit of that dominion is freedom and harvest. God, in response to our cries, brings His world into ours. His kingdom comes and establishes things that secure our hope and our future.

He is releasing vision and power and provision through His people who will proclaim truth without apology or compromise – the current trumpeters — the people who pray, who come together, who worship, dance, sing and blow trumpets in the temple of the Living God.

*He chose them, you and me and His desires will last forever, no matter what the tactics of the enemy are.*

# Seed of Prayer

## Day 343

The Word of the Lord is blowing. It is blowing through the written Word and the revelation of the Lord so that we can be involved in the harvest He has provided for us, and for the world to hear the truth.

The seeds we sow in prayer and praise cause the harvest of not only the answers to our prayers, but the harvest of a closer relationship with the Godhead. Prayer should be born first out of love, not just out of need. Like David, we must seek Him because we love Him. Not for what He will do for us, but because we appreciate what He has already done for us. We must pray because we just can't stand being without Him; prayer is the way we communicate with Him.

God never said it would be easy, but if we are going to establish a place for Him to dwell, then we must understand the importance of seed, time and harvest in our prayer and praise times. If you still wonder how important the sowing of prayer is, I want to encourage you to understand where the prayers you have already prayed, are right now.

They are in heaven in golden bowls with incense (Revelation 5:8). They continue to ascend before God again and again, even unto the last days. (Revelation 8:3-4). God has a greater harvest for you than you could ever realize in the natural (1 Kings 9:4). Your seed has gone before Him and your harvest is His heart. Oh my goodness, what more could we want?

*Let us pray: Let our seeds ascend to the heavens where they are watered and return to us with heaven's will, power and love released to our life. He gives us strength by His Spirit on the inside, the inner man. We must continue to pray. The more, the better. It is the seed of prayer that will nourish the insatiable desire to be with your God. He placed it on the inside of you and it cannot be denied for long, for you were made to be His.*

***Prayer should be born first out of love, not just out of need...***

# Prophetic Word

## Day 344

"You've come to Me with all of your needs, but today I come to you with the answer to your needs, because outside of Me there is no answer. But when you draw near to Me, I draw near to you. You can't outrun Me because I'll run to you faster ... to embrace you, to speak a word you need to hear, to touch you, to heal you, to be all that you have need of, for I chose it and I chose you from the foundation of the world. You see haven't I already proven there is nothing that I won't do, for I've already done it. And now I hold you and I speak to you and I love you right through life, into everlasting things, into eternal purpose, into the things that have substance that will last forever and ever. For this is fleeting and yet important.

This is beyond that which is natural, because I am beyond natural and I have made you beyond natural. It is spirit to spirit. We are one. It is the holy of holies, the secret place. The place where I cover you, the place where I build you, the place where I secure you, the place where I impart to you. The place where you are able to be yourself with me and be changed from the inside out. Where I can invade every room of your house, of your heart, for I come without condemning you, but I come with abiding love. I take away that which is harmful to you and I replace it with that which will glorify you in Me. You see it's from glory, to glory, to glory, to glory. So when you come to Me the glory is there. I leave a deposit in you. But it runs out if you run away.

From glory to glory, to glory, to glory, it's with Me here in this place, the place of My presence, the place of the unexpected love that you feel right now. I don't operate as a man would. I operate as God--yours. If you've chosen Me, you'll find I've already chosen you, pre planned. I have laid down milestones along your way, the pathway of life. I'll take you by the hand, I'll lead you through. I'll take you to the end result--just Me and you. Then others will see and they will know and they will realize that I am still alive because I am shining through your eyes, and touching through your touch and speaking through your lips. I'm walking through your feet. Sons, daughters, kings, priests, prophets, all the gifts, all the callings, all the talent, here in My arms. One on one. Face to face."

*...haven't I already proven there is nothing that I won't do, for I've already done it.*

# It's All In Your Perspective

## Day 345

So many are looking for love. They're looking in the wrong place. Is there any love that feels like mine? Impossible. For there is no greater love than can be found in Me. I am love--love that transforms, love that teaches you to have expectations beyond your wildest dreams. Love that gives you confidence and security, love that perfects you in Me. And as you sit and as you absorb this love, it becomes a part of you. You begin to think like Me, you begin to care like Me, and then you can begin to act like Me. There is no formula. You see I am a personal God and I care about you personally. I come to you when you come to Me. I teach you one on one—personal tutorship. Sons, daughters, set apart. I'll tell you things in a way you can receive it. I'll give you assignments that only you can do.

I'll reveal things to you that will make you explode from the inside out with peace and joy and love that cannot be contained. And then it will spread, it will spread, it will spread. Diminish the enemy's work and his tactics. Don't allow his voice to be so loud. Hear Me in a whisper drown out his loudest screams. I am all powerful. There is none like Me.

But I chose to make you in My image and in My likeness, My image. How do you see Me? Imagine My image. Just, good, pure, holy, unable to sin, for there is no sin within Me. In My likeness. The things I like will become things you like. The things I hate, you will begin to hate and be able to separate it out as sin, not people. For yes, I hate things. I hate things that destroy My people. I hate things that hurt others. I hate lying tongues. I hate sexual sin. Destructive. Destroying lives, destroying dreams, destroying destiny.

But I love to restore and to replace and to renew and to give hope again and to restructure from the inside out until they are whole, piece by piece by piece, because I've made them anew. Just be. Just be, as you are with Me. In this place, do you feel unholy? Unrighteous? Unable? No. Because in this place you are righteous, you are holy, you are able. Let My love be absorbed, let My power be transferred, let My thoughts invade your mind. Hear My voice. Obey Me. And find peace and joy and fulfillment. I am. I am. I am all that you'll ever need Me to be. And I am yours through eternity.

*I'll reveal things to you that will make you explode from the inside out with peace and joy and love that cannot be contained.*

# Fulfilling Your God-Given Dreams

## Day 346

Most of us understand that dreams are not just day dreams if they have been birthed by the heart of God.

We, as believers must maintain an attitude of faith.

A continued faith-filled attitude will attract the miraculous to our lives. God can work through those who trust Him completely. Throughout our prophetic words, "trust me, and trust me at a higher level" was reiterated many times.

Sometimes we think we trust God, but when put to the test, we often find out, we, like Peter, have something on the inside that makes us want to back up when adversity comes.

No matter what level of influence we come to, we must always first be sure we say what we say, and do what we do because we are fully persuaded by God on two things:

1. Who He is  and

2. Who we are

If you have accepted Jesus as Savior of your life, that is the first step. If you are declaring Him as Lord of your life, then you must acknowledge Him as such. A savior rescues you. A Lord is someone who is the ultimate authority of your life. You understand you live in His Kingdom, under His rulership and that He is the boss. Now, our Lord is the best Lord because He isn't just a dictator, but a savior, a savior who came with the compassion to restore. He is in LOVE with you. He wants the best for you. In fact, He paid the price for you to have a covenant with him and you are invited to co-labor with Him.

*A continued faith-filled attitude will attract the miraculous to our lives.*

## It's All In Your Perspective

**Day 347**

Many times in co-laboring we think we are equal partners. Equal partners never really exist in my opinion. People with different responsibilities co-laboring ... yes, equal ... No. Someone is delegated to have the final say. Therefore someone is the boss.

So then, the question is do we have delegated responsibility to a higher authority, or are we the higher authority?

If your answer is that God is the final authority, then you agree, He is the boss.

We are the co-laborers. But we work in His field - correct? So if the boss has given you the dream, who is in charge of the dream?

*"For the vision is yet for an appointed time, but at the end it shall speak, and not lie: though it tarry, wait for it; because it will surely come, it will not tarry."* Habakkuk 2:3

God gave the vision and it will come to pass in His time. What do you do in the meantime?

You fulfill the work you know to do right now.

You may not know everything that needs to be done, but you certainly can see something that needs to be done.

### DECLARE:

*My vision that the Lord has given me is yet for an appointed time, but at the end it shall speak, and not lie: though it may tarry, I will wait for it in faith; because it will surely come, it will not tarry!*

**God gave the vision and it will come to pass in His time.**

# It's All In Your Perspective

## Day 348

Don't wait for your destiny to be fulfilled, fulfill your destiny daily. Understand that as you begin to live a life of faith to fulfill God's dreams for your life, adversity is sure to arise.

Your faith is a threat to the devil. When trouble arises it is very easy to lose strength and back up on what you have been believing God for. When trouble arises it is very easy to change what you are standing for. When trouble arises it is very easy to make concessions and yield to the temptation of giving up or letting go…

Three necessary attributes to your victory:

1.  Be relentless
2.  Be unwavering
3.  Be uncompromising

Relentless - showing or promising no abatement of severity, intensity, strength, or pace, not only not quitting, but not letting up on the severity of your commitment.

Unwavering - Not varying, you can't overcome if you don't make a decision to stay steadfast and consistent in whom you believe in and what you believe.

Uncompromising - making no concessions: inflexible, unyielding, If Satan knows you will make no concessions, he will have to know you have a no-quit attitude

God is looking for people who will persevere and stay in love with Him when things are good, and when things are bad. To do this, you will have to stop trusting in yourself and trust God.

*Don't wait for your destiny to be fulfilled, fulfill your destiny daily.*

# It's All In Your Perspective

## Day 349

It is easy to stay positive when everything surrounding you is bliss, but to fulfill your dreams, you will have to stay dependent on God, and happy with Him. God said in prayer that there are people here who need to forgive Him. I said them forgive you? He said yes, they have decided that I have done something against them instead of for them. My intention is to get them to reconcile with Me. If they go through the process of forgiving Me, it will help them.

Now of course, this will rattle you because I said that we all know God has done nothing wrong. He is altogether ... well ... all together. But I also know that one of the biggest issues people deal with in their Christian walk is being angry at God. God wants you to be in a place where you can trust Him again. So, do whatever it takes.

Deal with it, and move forward by giving Him the proper place in your life. He will give you something that will fulfill your heart and give Him glory. If you are experiencing something hard to go through, then look at it like this:

You are in the process of a great testimony!

They didn't kill Paul. And it wasn't because of his influence, his brains, or his abilities. It was because of GOD. Have you ever been rescued in the past? God has a great track record. We need to work on ours. Don't focus on the problem, focus on God!

### DECLARE:

*I was crushed and overwhelmed beyond my ability to endure, and I thought I would never live through it. In fact, I expected to die. But as a result, I stopped relying on myself and learned to rely only on God, who raises the dead. And he did rescue me from mortal danger, and he will rescue me again. I have placed my confidence in him, and he will continue to rescue me. And now, I will help others by praying for them. Then many people will give thanks because God has graciously answered so many prayers for our safety.*

**You are in the process of a great testimony!**

# Saturation Compels You to Share

## Day 350

Have you ever had too much food on your plate and you begin to ask others around you if they would like some of what you have? Have you ever had a good thing happen to you that you just couldn't keep silent about it, you had to tell somebody? Have you ever heard something that changed your way of doing things or had a revelation that was just so good you had to share it with someone?

Saturation compels you. Overflow. The same thing happens to us as we sit with Him, as we set time aside to be with Him.

As we fast, we deny the flesh of natural food, but we sit at His banqueting table and drink in His love. As we pray, we both talk and listen. And when we do that, He will always have something profound to say, because, well, He is GOD. And when you are so full of Him, and you know how He feels and you know how He LOVES, you will be saturated, and then you are compelled to DO something.

… Which is good since we are in DO season. Even more than ever, we must be aware of the God that lives within us.

Jesus was discerning the times; He knew it was DO season. It was time for them to learn how to love, how to draw others to the Father, by love. Therefore, it was time for them to be busy.

It should always be a delight for us to engage in doing any work for God. How much more if we understand by the signs of the times that this is the proper season for that work, realizing then it will certainly prosper.

### Action Step:

*Get saturated… Get sharing!*

---

*It was time for them to learn how to love,
how to draw others to the Father, by love.*

## Saturation Compels You to Share

**Day 351**

Our Lord Jesus was intent upon finishing His work. Our Master has herein left us an example that we may learn to do the will of God as He did. The work we get to do is to preach the gospel, and to set up the Kingdom of God. Gospel time is harvest time, and gospel work is harvest work. The harvest is appointed and it is to be expected.

**Harvest time is busy time. All hands must be busy gathering. Harvest time is opportunity, a short and limited time.**

It will not last forever.

Harvest work is work that must be done then or not at all. We must understand if we miss our "do season" it cannot be recalled. Once it is gone, it is gone, forever. But God will help us to complete our work if we are willing to do His will.

*Now may the God of peace who brought up our Lord Jesus from the dead, that great Shepherd of the sheep, through the blood of the everlasting covenant, make you complete in every good work to do His will, working in you what is well pleasing in His sight, through Jesus Christ, to whom be glory forever and ever. Amen. Hebrews 13:20-21*

In this process, we must go ahead and make faith steps forward even though it is not clear. As we step forward, He will continue to clear our vision.

### Prayer:

*Lord, I thank you for the GOOD work that you have completed inside of me. I thank you for your will for my life which is good and prosperous. I ask you to help me today to see clearly, to see the harvest that you have placed all around me and to see your will clearly done through my hands.*

Amen!

*God will help us to complete our work if we are willing to do His will.*

# PROPHETIC WORD "WHOM SHALL I SEND?"

## Day 352

Who will shine for Me, in the midst of the darkness? Who will allow My glory to come in, to push out, to make right the things that are wrong? Who will trust Me? Who will obey Me? Who will care not about their life even unto the death?

Who will stand and confront the darkness that invades My earth, My world, My people? Who will be the ones who will examine themselves before Me, at My feet? Who will stay pure, who will cry for holiness, who will reach for the righteous God? Who will fall upon the altar of repentance, and who will arise clean and holy and strong and able to overcome the enemy because their light is now bright to the fullest day?

For Satan has announced himself. He has given his voice and proclaimed his works throughout the media, all over the nations, trying to prove that he is stronger, that he is the victor. But My people, who are called by My name, are humbling themselves. And they are praying and they are turning from their wicked ways. And I am healing their land. Their personal land first. And then I will arise within their territories. Their pockets, their places, their assigned spaces. And I will join those of like mind and like spirit. And there will be no weapon that Satan can think of or come up with or even try that will work because the gates of hell cannot prevail against My church. My church. My people. The ones I love, the ones I pour My oil out upon, even today. The ones that I secure as they come humbly before Me. The ones I take by the hand, the ones I reach into My arms, the ones that I hug, that I kiss away their pain. The ones I restore, the ones that I have chosen – from before the foundations of the world, with Me.

For you see, you are in Me, aren't you? Are you not one with Me? And was I not chosen? Did I not even die before the foundations of the world so that you could be restored to who you are? Your inheritance is sure. Your God is in the heavens – ruling and reigning. And I live in you. In you. Will there be anything too difficult for Me then? Can you do exploits if you come to the knowledge of who I am in you? Will there be fear in the face of the enemy if you are hidden in Christ, in God? Can you be bold? Will you open your mouth? Will you praise Me in the midst of what you do not understand, knowing that there I am with you caring for you, sorting things out, putting things in proper order. Why? Love! Why? Love! Why? Everlasting, unconditional, forever committed love for you. You see it really is, for Me, about you. That's why I gave My life.

*Who will trust Me? Who will obey Me?*
*Who will care not about their life even unto the death?*

# Prophetic Word "Whom Shall I Send?"

## Day 353

The announcements have begun. The Church is rising. The Church is rising into their place of fierceness, of peace that brings the victory. They will no longer waver wondering who they are or what they shall do. My remnant, not all, My remnant. Many say what they want others to hear. Many proclaim that they are one thing, but I am reading their hearts. That's why I pray, that's why you should too. But I have those who still trust Me, who still love Me, who still believe in Me and I still believe in them. And I will have a Church without spot and without wrinkle. It has already been declared. It has already been decreed. And Satan shakes at the thought for he knows they cannot be defeated. And victory has been won. So let the proclamation of victory come from your mouth. Humble yourselves before Me, and become a part of who I am in these last days. And understand there is nothing too difficult for Me, in you, through you. I do love you. I do love you. Let My love rescue you again today. And rise, for the glory of the Lord has risen upon you.

Have you listened to the importance of those whom I have enlisted? Have you listened and written upon your hearts the message that has gone forth? Do you understand that Abel knew the importance of the blood? Do you understand that it all begins with the shedding of blood that covers sin? Do you understand that any other sacrifice is not acceptable until the final sacrifice was made? Do you understand that the blood covers? Do you understand that it is the final outcome? Do you understand that the blood is the victory? Do you understand that you are covered in the blood by the covenant that was shed when I came into agreement with My Father, and died in your place and shed My blood for all mankind? Do you understand the blood?

The blood, the blood, the blood was the final sacrifice. Do you understand the importance of acknowledging it in your life? Do you understand that there is nothing and no one that has the power against the blood? Every sin that has ever been confessed is covered in it, unable to ever be found again. The accuser of the brethren has lost because of the blood. Because of the blood. Do you understand that I am taking people from out of where they are into faith that translates time, that translates this space, that translates them into My glory? Like Enoch, just a visual of what can happen when you walk with Me. And he was not any more like he used to be. He was not in the physical realm for he lived and dwells with Me.

*So let the proclamation of victory come from your mouth.*

## Prophetic Word "Whom Shall I Send?"

### Day 354

But I have translating faith that applies to you. I have translating faith that if you will only grab hold of, you will go to the places in glory with Me and you shall behold Me face to face and you will be changed. And then you shall become the visual on earth. Just like he returns to preach righteousness. Who will be translated into My glory today? Who will see the things that count in heaven? Who will see the important things? Who will see those things that last throughout eternity and then come and announce them and proclaim them and give opportunity for others to partake of them? Who will have translating faith? Who will be preachers of righteousness that build arks of safety? Who will not care if they've ever heard of it before? Who will proclaim what I say even if it makes no sense to the senses?

Who will spend hours and days and months proclaiming truth and building places of safety with the call of those I'm willing to give My life for? Who will follow Me into the unknown? Who will leave those things behind? Who will only go forward with nothing but a promise? Who will be like father Abraham--who steps out of the place of comfort, who continues down the place that looks like a desert, who continues on trusting in Me, and building altars to My name even though the circumstances keep coming against him over and over and over--and yet he looks to the stars and he looks to the sands. The things that I have given him, the things that I have given you, the promises that I have written before you, the things that I have told you individually, the things that I have told you corporately. Who will continue to walk forward? Who will build an altar to Me, trusting that it will come to pass? Who will be willing to come into a place of covenant with Me, where they have allowed the flesh to be severed, so that it can be joined to the spirit? Who will understand that whatever I have is yours? That I have taken that which you have offered Me in the place of circumcision covenant. I have taken your brokenness, I have taken your sin, I have taken that which is inconsequential, and I have made it great in Me. We have traded. You have My robes, you have My word. You have My blood, you have My riches. You have My promise.

*You have My promise.*

# Prophetic Word "Whom Shall I Send?"

**Day 355**

Who has faith and confidence in Me, that when it looks as though I even require you to lay it on the altar? You know--the thing I promised you. You know--the thing that makes no sense to you that I should ask you to give it up now since I was the One that gave it to you. Oh but I'm looking, I'm looking, I'm looking for those who are willing to walk up that mountain by faith, knowing I am not a withholder. Should it be burnt, it will live again. Should it be taken it will come back to you. For I am not a man that I should lie, but I am your God. I am your hope, I am your future. Everything I have promised you is still true. Who will dare to confess it in the midst of the fire?

Who will look into the future with Me? Who will look into the future and behold who is there? Who will go with Me and do what is necessary so that their faces and their lives will be joined to eternity because of your obedience? Who will look beyond that which is seen in the natural, to see that which is eternal and be motivated past the hardships? Because it's reality to you when it's reality from Me. Who will believe Me with irrevocable blessing faith? Who understands that because I simply declared it to you, I will fulfill it? Who will dare to look at the wells that are dried up and proclaim that they shall spring forth with water again? Who will look into the dry places and say they are no longer dry before they are no longer dry?

Who will give in times of famine, proclaiming that I am still your God, who will dare to have faith to seed, so that I may multiply? Who will dare to proclaim that I am still King, and I am still able, and that which I have said shall come to pass even for you? Who will continue to trust Me in giving?

*Who has faith and confidence in Me, that when it looks as though I even require you to lay it on the altar?*

## Prophetic Word "Whom Shall I Send?"

**Day 356**

Who will lean upon their staff, who will lean upon My authority, who will lean upon the truth of who I am? Who? Who will understand that I can be leaned upon every day? Who will understand that I have never left you, that I am never forsaking you? Who? Who will listen? Who will have faith today in Me, in Me? Who will lay aside the things that have so easily beset you and look once again into the Author and the Finisher of your faith? Who will trust Me, that even as the enemy has planned the plagues, that I have prepared a place in Goshen for you? Who will enjoy the lemonade as I rule and as I reign with My people? Who will rest in Me? Who will realize that they're living in a miracle because the plagues can't come near you? Who will not be like the Israelites who grumbled and complained even though I protected them? Who, who will understand that their faith can overcome every plague, that I have already prepared a place of safety, of protection, of provision? Who has faith today?

Who understands that you've been tagged by Me?

Who understands that I've given you authority?

Who understands that you resemble the King?

Who understands that you have a place in My kingdom?

Who understands that it is the kings and the priests that are arising out of the rubble, out of the place of the unknown, out of the place of their fear to proclaim once again faith – faith in Me – wins the war!

Who will wear My name? Who will represent the King? Who will work together? Who will become one in Me, who will be those who will join forces with those who trust Me, who love Me? Who will be this army? Who will be the army that I'm looking for, that I will join forces with that the princes of heaven will join in the heavenly realm to assure the victory to bring forth the victorious songs, and the dances of victory that set My people free? Who has faith? Who has faith?

*Who, who will understand that their faith can overcome every plague, that I have already prepared a place of safety, of protection, of provision?*

# Are You In Season?

**Day 357**

God is waiting for you to take a step into the spirit world, and walk by faith and not by sight. It may not look like a season of harvest to you. But it is. It may not seem like a time of reproduction but it is. Your needs are being met by faith in God and in His promises.

Liberty is growing because God said it is. We are multiplying because we are commissioned to be fruitful. It doesn't look like much is going on, but VERY much is going on. If we can get into God's way of thinking, nothing that we are looking at in the natural will affect us.

You see, Jesus still has a need. He is hungry to see a hungry people who are able to see beyond the natural, who will not live according to the dictates of the seasons of man, but will begin to operate under His system of fruitfulness in every area.

Jesus wanted the disciples and us to live by viewing things differently.

Jesus said...

If you refuse to live according to God's system that causes you to reproduce after your own kind, then you are going to live by the other system, which is death to you.

Let me say it to you this way...

If you are not going to live with Kingdom mentality then you can live below Kingdom results. Kingdom results will always include the harvest.

## Now tell yourself...

*Today and every day, I am going to live with Kingdom mentality! I will see Kingdom results in EVERYTHING that I do. Therefore, in everything that I do I am grateful for the HARVEST that will come.*

**Your needs are being met by faith in God and in His promises.**

# Are You In Season?

**Day 358**

In the Bible we read a story of Jesus looking for figs in a fig tree, the strange thing is that it is actually months before the natural harvest. That's because in His system, it is ALWAYS the season to produce.

We can't say, well I am unable to talk to anyone about Jesus; I am just in a different season of my life right now. What season would that be? The one where you don't care about souls?

I am just in a season where I can't be involved? I don't recall when Jesus was calling people that it was convenient for them to follow. They had to change. They had to embrace His truth to the place of passionately going after Him.

They would have to choose to join Him, join His thinking and be willing to be transformed into His image. Jesus is leading His disciples into something of such great importance. They would have a visual to remember. He was looking for fruit in every season. He was looking for something to be produced. Something for others to partake of.

Jesus wanted them to know what would be necessary for them to DO when He left them in charge of the earth. That includes us, His disciples who are alive right now.

Then He gave them, and us, the key.

*And Jesus answering saith unto them, Have faith in God. Remember Jesus only did what His Father told Him to do. As He spoke to the fig tree, He was being obedient to the Father. Mark 11:22 KJV*

The Father wanted them to see that when you are expecting to receive something, it doesn't matter what season it is in the natural way of doing things. It matters that you speak to the original intent of God and you speak truth and faith and life.

*They had to embrace His truth to the place of passionately going after Him.*

# Are You In Season?

**Day 359**

*Say not ye, There are yet four months, and then cometh harvest? behold, I say unto you, Lift up your eyes, and look on the fields; for they are white already to harvest. John 4:35 KJV*

What Jesus is trying to get them to understand is this. Don't delay the purposes of God. Don't say "someday I will produce fruit. Someday I will live in the harvest." No, realize, the harvest is here.

We have come up with acceptable ways to console one another with disobedience. We just encourage each other that things will change, it's just coming. We want to encourage the sower at seed-time, that it will be just four months to the harvest.

But we must change. We are the new order of priesthood for the world. The priests still are to make a way for others to come into His presence. Jesus is our high priest and we are all priests of the Most High. We must change the way we see, the things we say, the things we agree with and the things we do. We, the priests still serve as a conduit to bring down God's radiant blessing and influence into this world. We must represent Him the way He originally intended. When we do, we will bring forth fruit.

But we must move past looking at things according to the times of harvest, in the ordinary course of things. If you are looking through spiritual eyes, and you are discerning the times, you will see that this is no ordinary time. Just as Jesus was dealing with them, when He told them not to look and say in four months we will finally produce. Jesus wasn't talking about corn, or grain. He was talking about the gospel harvest.

Their reasoning was about to be impacted by a radical God with a radical plan. It was going to take radical action.

<u>Action Step:</u>

*Take intentional-radical action!*

*We must change the way we see, the things we say, the things we agree with and the things we do.*

## Are You In Season?

**Day 360**

To institute change we will have to have a purpose. The purpose now is not to just have fellowship, not to huddle amongst ourselves. The plan is to gather in the harvest of souls. That will mean we will have to pursue. The pursuit must first be after God's heart. For if we have His heart, we will win souls.

I am happy to report that many of you have come to me and said how you realized you have been blind to many things and many people. There has been much impact from those words that God dropped in our hearts. He ended the beginning, and now we're free in Him with a job to do. He put an end to death and Jesus' resurrection began a campaign of life. Jesus said, "It is finished." In that moment, He reinvented life and provided new freedom for all of us.

Your destiny is no surprise to God. THANK God! He knows what you will do and He understands you. God knows how much you are willing to give and He knows if you are holding back. It's up to you to make your destiny about Him instead of about you. We have experienced His love. That simply means, we have love to give, love to show, love to share. Embrace, display and share His love is our motto at Liberty.

We are made by Him to reproduce, so we can, we are and we will continue to do so! Jesus' love simplifies what is complicated about change. It's time to change into harvest time. That harvest is personal to us; we will receive what we need, as well as be fruitful and multiply.

It is DO season.

God showed me that as we tap into our potential, and we present Him and promote HIM to the world, that the dreams we have on the inside of us to do through Liberty will come.

*So go today and present, promote, and prevail!*

*It's up to you to make your destiny about Him instead of about you.*

# Altar of Remembrance

**Day 361**

You are rising into proper position because you are seeing Me and giving Me place as King of kings and Lord of lords. For haven't I said and haven't I made My name known in this place already? And haven't I already shown Myself strong on your behalf on many occasions? For now build yourself an altar of remembrance. Now build yourself an altar and remember that which I have already done. And build yourself a remembrance today of what I am doing right here and right now, with you and through you. For I am more than enough. I am more than able and I am taking this country. I am taking back the territory with you at My side. For I have included you in the process. I have included you in My process. For I want you to know My power. I want you to know My glory. I want you to know your authority. I want you to walk in your position. I want the world to see My church the way I've always wanted My church to behave.

The glory will be upon you and the power will be with you. And you will raise your sword of victory, and it will cause the enemy to run in defeat. And you will raise your sword, and you will strike the enemy down by your faith in Me, and by being fearless against him. For I am your God and I am working with you and I have the sword in My hand. And you are not alone and you will not see defeat. You will not see defeat. But you will see the victory that I have placed in your hands. So release the joy shout. Release the shout of the Lord! Shout with Me….

Response in Prayer:

Lord we thank You, we honor You, we praise You, Lord. We thank You that we have won a victory here today. We thank You, God that we are working along side of you, God. And that we will not forget but we will build an altar of remembrance to You. That we will remember this day. That you are our peace and that you have made us valiant warriors. You have made us victorious in this place, and in this city, and in this territory, and in this land. And we will stay in our positions. And we declare it to be so. And we declare it to be done. In the name of the Lord, Jesus Christ. And everybody said: AMEN!

*For I am your God and I am working with you and I have the sword in My hand. And you are not alone and you will not see defeat.*

# A God of Change and Transformation

## Day 362

Change is a normal way in the Kingdom of God to provide new life, new hope and new beginnings. Change means: to cause to become different, alter, transform and convert. Change is not easy, comfortable, or popular. But change is necessary.

It provides new opportunities, brings about creativity and helps us let go of the past. What season are we in? "DO Season." That means we have to recognize we are in a season for change and we must continue to have a desire to change. To do that, we must not only see things differently but we must also have a plan to actually DO things differently. We must pursue change with passion by renewing our thinking and redirecting our focus. God said that we would have to do things deliberately. That means, on purpose, for a reason, with a goal in mind.

You see, we have a life worth living and a journey worth taking. God has designed a road for us that includes success. He is the answer for our struggles and our needs. We must remember we have staked our claim. We are standing on the promises of God. We are taking new ground as we step out and up in a different place of faith.

Jesus was always imparting more to His disciples than it looks like when you initially read the stories of their interaction. They were written by the Holy Spirit with hidden truths. How exciting when we read it over again and find new truth to what Jesus is really saying, doing and imparting to them, and to us.

*It is the same with us.*

*With every revelation, there is more revelation.*

He is walking with us, and leading us to a different place in Him SO THAT there is change that will enhance our lives and utilize them to touch others' lives with IMPACT and bring lasting change to them.

*God said that we would have to do things deliberately. That means, on purpose, for a reason, with a goal in mind.*

# A God of Change and Transformation

**Day 363**

*There was a famine in the land, besides the first famine that was in the days of Abraham. And Isaac went to Abimelech king of the Philistines, in Gerar. Genesis 26:1*

*Then Isaac sowed in that land, and reaped in the same year a hundredfold; and the LORD blessed him. The man began to prosper, and continued prospering until he became very prosperous; for he had possessions of flocks and possessions of herds and a great number of servants. So the Philistines envied him. Genesis 26:12-14*

The reason that Isaac could sow in famine and reap a hundred fold was because He had faith in God, and famine had nothing to do with meeting his need.

God is changing things again. We say we are tired of many things being the same as it has always been. We say that we want things to change, but in reality, we are a people that like to have patterns. So when change comes, we are not always willing to change some things about our mindsets and what we are used to. But you see, God has included us in a very important season. A season where:

God is changing church to Kingdom. He provided Jesus to bring us back to His original intent. His original intent is that we are to reproduce after our own kind. He says it's time for fruit. But what we have been doing, is allowing "the tree" to tell us that it is not our season of harvest and fruitfulness.

*MAKE THIS DECLARATION*… BUT GOD SAYS…

- *Our season is not based upon the world's season*
- *We are in this world, but not of this world*
- *We are to live in faith and faith is not based upon what Wall Street does, what the economic advisers say, or what comes natural to us*
- *Faith in God will defy the natural in us and in our circumstances to prove His love and His power to this generation.*

**He had faith in God,
and famine had nothing to do with meeting His need.**

# My Presence is the Remedy

**Day 364**

"These are the praises that I've been waiting for. This is the Hosanna that I want you to sing – the Hosanna that opens your heart. For you see, the word hosanna means 'to be open, to be wide, to be free, to be safe.'

You're calling for Me to be willing to defend those that need to be defended; you're calling Me to come into the place for those to be avenged who need to be avenged. I've opened your eyes, ears, arms, hands, to receive what I have for you in order to be the answer to those that are crying out to Me, for My ears can hear them daily and My eyes see them. I know them. I know where they are and I know where you are. I will guide you by My life, I will guide you by My love, I will guide you by My peace, I will guide you into the places where eternity meets eternity.

They're coming. They're looking, they're seeking. They may not be saying it out-loud, but they're saying it. It may not be visible to the naked eye, but it's visible to those who can see. I'm putting My heart inside of yours. You'll wear My hands like a glove. My presence will bring them through. My presence will bring you to them. My presence is the remedy, for all humanity, everywhere, in every walk of life."

*The LORD is a God who avenges.*
  *O God who avenges, shine forth.*
*Psalm 94*

*My dear children, I write this to you so that you will not sin. But if anybody does sin, we have an advocate with the Father—Jesus Christ, the Righteous One.   1 John 2*

*I've opened your eyes, ears, arms, hands, to receive what I have for you in order to be the answer to those that are crying out to Me...*

# MY PRESENCE IS THE REMEDY

**Day 365**

"So come with Me and I'll let you see. Come with Me and I'll cause you to be the ones, the ones that show forth My praise, My freedom, My glory, My love, who carry the answers. Come out of the world's system. Don't box Me into your thinking. Allow Me to rule and reign and I will. I'll rule, I'll reign and you'll reign right with Me. I'm bringing you out to bring you in. I'm taking out things that need to be extracted anyway. I'm filling you up to overflowing ... with life, abundant life as you've never seen before, abundant life as you've never experienced before. The abundance that comes from the presence of Me.

You're about ready to be happier than you've ever been before. You are about to experience more joy, more peace and more glory, because you've opened up your hearts for Me. For the joy that was set before Me I endured the cross, and now the joy that is set before you, you'll endure a cross too, and it will seem as nothing, for I've paid the price and done the suffering. Now you'll just carry your cross, openly, unashamedly, boldly, proclaiming the truth of who I am to all to see. Your eyes are open today. Your eyes are open.

So walk forth in victory. Expect more of Me. Expect Me to walk before you as I did with My disciples. I led them right into sonship, right into kingship, right into priesthood, as they put their confidence in Me—in the Spirit where they would be really free. Freedom is yours, value it dearly. Freedom can't be taken lightly. But I've set you free to set them free."

### PRAYER:

Lord, here we are at your table, at your place of freedom.
Now Lord set us free even today. Lead us to those who have eyes to see. Fill this place with people who were in darkness who are now going to see the light, experience the love, experience the answer, because we are obedient to you.

*So walk forth in victory. Expect more of Me.*

We hope that you have enjoyed this Kingdom Guide. We pray that the investment of time and meditation that you have made into your devotions will continue to be manifest for years to come in your spiritual journey with Jesus Christ and through the Holy Spirit who lives within you. May your personal impact be on this earth as it is in Heaven from generation to generation!

Many of these devotions are printed and sent throughout the nations annually free of charge for the equipping of the saints and furthering of the Kingdom. We ask you to consider giving online and partnering with us as we support our brothers and sisters in Christ throughout the world!

Visit us at:

www.LibertyLifeCenter.org

www.ingramcontent.com/pod-product-compliance
Lightning Source LLC
Chambersburg PA
CBHW080432110426
42743CB00016B/3145